Victorian Testaments

Victorian Testaments

*The Bible, Christology, and Literary Authority
in Early-Nineteenth-Century British Culture*

Sue Zemka

STANFORD UNIVERSITY PRESS
STANFORD, CALIFORNIA

Stanford University Press
Stanford, California
© 1997 by the Board of Trustees of the
Leland Stanford Junior University
Printed in the United States of America

CIP data appear at the end of the book

*For my grandmother,
Florence Stockton Foley*

Acknowledgments

Parts of this book have been published previously in slightly different forms: Chapter 2, "Thomas Arnold and Spiritual Authority," appears in *Victorian Studies* 32 (1989): 429–62, and Chapter 6, "The Holy Books of Empire: Translations of the British and Foreign Bible Society," appeared in *The Macropolitics of Nineteenth-Century Literature*, ed. Jonathan Arac and Harriet Ritvo (Philadelphia: University of Pennsylvania Press, 1991).

Work on this project began as a doctoral dissertation at Stanford University and was assisted by a Whiting fellowship. During the process of rewriting that earlier manuscript, the University of Colorado, Boulder, provided various forms of additional assistance: a Junior Faculty Development Award, a semester of course relief, and a Weigers faculty fellowship for research travel.

But of course my greatest debt is to the teachers, colleagues, and friends who have inspired and demanded the completion of this project. At Stanford, Robert Polhemus, Regenia Gagnier, and Ian Watt oversaw the first version. Afterwards, Norris Pope at Stanford Press provided encouragement, research tips, and patience. In Boulder, David Simpson, Jeffrey Robinson, and the late Edward Nolan contributed in a multitude of ways to my efforts at revision.

Additionally, some chapters have benefited from the specific recommendations of other colleagues. For improvements to Chapter 4, I would like to thank Katherine Eggert, Charlotte Sussman, and Jane Garrity. For improvements to Chapter 2, I am greatly indebted to the anonymous readers at *Victorian Studies*. For editorial suggestions to Chapter 5, I wish to thank Alfred Lutz. And for encouraging a thorough revision to Chapter 6, I am grateful to Jonathan Arac and Harriet Ritvo.

Other acknowledgments are due friends whose influence is profound and impossible to measure: James English, Trip McCrossin, Katheryn Rios, Elizabeth Robertson, Daniel Kirkpatrick, Russell Samolsky, Robert Frodeman, Jay Fliegelman, Karen Jacobs, Jessica Neeley-Cannelakis, and Chris Byrne. And finally, acknowledgment of a different order is due my most cheerful colleague, Baseman Zemka.

I also wish to thank the British Library, the Firestone Library at Princeton University, and the Florence Nightingale Museum Trust for allowing me access to their collections.

S.Z.

Contents

Introduction: "In the Kingdom of Zion, the Lord is Here"   1

1. Of Tongues, Texts, Nerves, Opium, and Flesh: The Disappearance of the Invisible in Early Victorian Spiritual Epistemology   13

2. Thomas Arnold and Spiritual Authority   68

3. Christ and the Holy Family: Two Victorian Sites of Subject Constitution   100

4. Emasculating Christ, Mediating Authority: The Sentimental Logic of Literary Influence in Dickens's *The Life of Our Lord* and *Dombey and Son*   117

5. "But Do We See One Woman Who Looks Like a Female Christ?" The Messiahs of Florence Nightingale   148

6. The Holy Books of Empire: Translations of the British and Foreign Bible Society   188

Notes   227
Works Cited   261
Index   275

Victorian Testaments

Introduction

"In the Kingdom of Zion, the Lord is Here"

When in the winter of 1814 Joanna Southcott died, following a long illness which her followers assumed to be a sign of pregnancy, and her detractors a sign of madness, she left vacant the powerful role she had created as the prophetic leader of a sizable if eccentric millenarian following. Over the next two decades, several disciples and latter-day converts would claim to be her rightful successor. Among them was John Ward, an Irish shipwright and shoemaker who in the mid-1820s received several visitations from Joanna's effusive spirit. At the time, Ward was living in Southwark with his wife and children. His lifelong pilgrimage through a variety of religious sects—a flight, as he described it, from the fears of eternal damnation that tortured his childhood—had most recently found him among the followers of Mary Boon, herself a claimant to Joanna's title. Boon was illiterate, and Ward, who had served a minister for both the Sandemanians and the Methodists, became her advisor and amanuensis. But around 1825 Ward began to have visions of his own, visions that tormented him almost nightly for two years. During this period he was visited by Joanna, received enlightenment from her conversation, and by "divine impregnation of the Word" was born into a new name—in fact, two names: Zion and Shiloh (Holinsworth, *Memoir* 3–8).

The two names reflect the uncertain genealogy of this Messiah.[1] At times he is, like Mary Boon, a contender for Joanna's vacant ministry, and it is Joanna's spirit that enters him, revealing him to be her promised "Shiloh," the god-child with whom she was allegedly pregnant for fourteen months preceding her death.[2] At other times it is God, and not Joanna, who devastates John's soul and pronounces him—over Christ as well as Joanna—the new man, the Son of God. In either case, the visions bring with them the spiritual satisfaction that Ward has been seeking, and after 1828 the days of uncertainty which troubled his youth are gone forever. Also gone are the days of work, for soon after the visions begin Ward finds it impossible "to pursue worldly business" and quits his job as a shoemaker. The news does not sit well with his wife, who fears that she and her children will starve, and she reports her husband to the Southwark parish officers. The magistrate attending Ward's case believes he is insane and orders him sent to Bethlehem hospital, but for unspecified reasons Ward winds up in Newington workhouse instead. There he refuses to work, fights with the officers, and pleads with a local Southcottian congregation for assistance. All the while, the visions continue: Joanna comes to him "in the flesh," dictates letters to him, and "opens up" the mysteries of the Scriptures and her own writings (*Letters*, letter 1). Personages from the Bible and from his life visit him as well, not only Joanna but also Saint Paul, Ananius, and Mary Boon (*Zion's Works* 1: 65-67). Of such consequence are his visions, they require a new calendar, one that reflects the shift to a new, post-Christian dispensation whose agonizing birth has been staged in Ward's soul. Accordingly, he begins to date his correspondence "Year One."

The workhouse is a crucible for a man in a state of distress and psychological susceptibility; Ward is there for six months, and while the experience fails to reform him as a working man, it does consolidate his sense of vocation. Having "attain[ed] inward satisfaction as to his call and mission," Zion emerges from the workhouse "a new man" (Holinsworth, *Memoir* 3-4) and begins the curious ministry—a blend of political radicalism, furious anticlericism, and breathtaking egoism—that would occupy him for the remaining nine years of his life.

Here we have, then, a self-proclaimed messiah of the working class, a man whose life, although interesting in its details, is not, as such, unique. For there were several such working-class messiahs in the early nineteenth century, not only Southcott, Mary Boon, and Ward, but also Sir William Courtenay, John Wroe, and Richard Carlile.[3] But because of his unabashedly self-referential interpretation of the Bible, Ward provides the best exemplar for this book, which takes as its subject the relationship between nineteenth-century attitudes toward biblical authority and nineteenth-century constructions of cultural authority. It might be objected that the term "cultural authority" is too general a rubric under which to group the mostly religious writers and movements discussed in these chapters. The problem with the alternative "religious authority" is that it is too narrow, insofar as it implies a strict focus on theological ideas and denominational concerns. And, when we approach figures such as Ward, Coleridge, Dickens, and Nightingale, for whom the narratives and principles of Christianity are inseparable from social, political, aesthetic, and psychological formulations, such strictness is misleading. Whether they conceived of themselves as artists, social critics, or religious thinkers, the writers discussed in this book undertook cultural projects wherein art, politics, and theology were related not only to one another but also to a self-reflexive discourse on the power of literacy and print. For the medium of print enjoyed an unprecedented and unrepeatable dominance over nineteenth-century English culture, and this dominance forced the attention of writers and readers alike to the sources, motives, and reliability of literary authority. It is in this context that I wish to place John Ward.

A contemporary of Samuel Taylor Coleridge, Ward had been born on Christmas Day, 1781 (so his evangelist, Charles B. Holinsworth, records).[4] A working man, a sailor, and an autodidact, he lived in a world far removed from the literary and philosophical movements to which Coleridge was a seminal contributor. However, he was occupied with a similar concern—the nature of the inspired man, the visionary poet, the genius—and he held the similar belief that the writings of such a man evidenced in an exalted form the contingency of human and divine natures. He also shared with Coleridge the belief that human genius has a special relationship with the Bible, which Ward understood to be a supernatural text, a hermetic key to divine wisdom. Moreover, he shared with Coleridge a profound susceptibility to the power of literature, its ability to map subjectivity as an internalized repertoire of emotionally charged textual encounters. But it is here that the differences between Ward and Coleridge begin: for Coleridge, literary authority is always decentered between readers and writers in complex, sometimes hostile, but always mutually constructive ways; for Ward, no such distinction exists, because he conceives himself to be both the signified of Holy Writ and its first true and comprehensive exegete. His engagement with Scriptures results in the birth of an apocalyptic interiority: the world, its history, its sins, and its divine redemption he transforms into personal psychological events. Indeed, the religious significance of Ward's mental life was the chief tenet held by his followers, as shown by Holinsworth's summary of the Shilohite faith: "The whole language *recorded* in ancient times by the Prophets is shown to be *figurative* of [Ward's] mental experience under the power and visitation of God" (*Shilohite's Bible* 3). Even though Coleridge believed in a similarly mystical correspondence between the Bible and the subjectivity of its readers, he never fell into such megalomania; unlike Ward, he tried to sustain the surprisingly precarious difference between the spirit of the Scriptures and the spirit of its readers, between man and God. Between them, Coleridge and Ward might be said to define the parameters of the early-nineteenth-century conception of a human psychology predicated on biblical literacy, on the mental internalization of the Bible. Where they differ, Ward is arguably the more exemplary man of the nineteenth century. He substitutes the incarnation for the Bible, which is to say, he transposes a human form onto a literary landscape, making the individual (its character, its soul, its gender, its flesh) the incarnate resolution to the social anxieties and epistemological dilemmas of English print culture. And thus Ward's gospel capitalizes on the early-nineteenth-century cultural trend that Coleridge most feared; he compensates for the inadequacies of textual knowledge, its inability to provide interpretive certainty, with a hermeneutics that centers authority in the deified individual.

The ministry of John Ward begins in 1828, upon his release from the workhouse. He publishes a tract titled "The Vision of Judgment, or the return of Joanna from her trance." Still anxious to prove his affiliation with Southcott, Ward presents himself as a witness to the truth of her prophecies. But Southcott, he adds, was limited in her powers of divination—a fact that she herself, in ghostly form, confided to Ward—and hence the final revelations have been postponed until now, fourteen years after her death (*Vision* 20–22). Ward's attachment to Joanna is strong, but not quite as strong as his desire to supersede her. Perhaps this is because the cryptic power of her verse-prophecies has inspired him to imagine religious possibilities outside of traditional Christian doctrine; perhaps it is because she left behind a ready-made and sizable following eager to embrace a new leader. In either case—and I suspect the truth lies somewhere in between—the following narrative takes shape: Shiloh, the promised son, was conceived in Southcott by the spirit of God, but upon her death, rather than being born in the flesh, he was born in John Ward's soul. According to this chronology, Ward converted to Southcottianism in the year of its founder's death and, at his conversion, received the gestating spirit that left Joanna's womb. Between 1814 and 1828 he harbored in himself, for the most part unconsciously, Shiloh. But then something even more remarkable happened, and the spiritual Shiloh was supplanted by the spiritual Zion, the name God gave to Ward when he (and not Joanna) revealed to him the full and final meaning of the Scriptures.

No more explicit enactment could exist of Margaret Homans's thesis that in early modern culture literal levels of meaning are more readily identified with the feminine, or the mother, and symbolic levels of meaning with the masculine. For Homans, this substitution is also a subordination, as it relegates the feminine and literal order of language to that of the symbolic order, its interpretive key and fulfillment.[5] Surely there are exceptions to this schematic picture, but they are not to be found in the textual psychology of Zion Ward. Absorbing into his own mental history the reproductive and spiritual powers of the prophetess he calls simply "the Woman,"

Ward struggles to discredit those followers who might take literally the prophetic implications of Genesis 3.15: "[the woman's seed] shall bruise [the serpent's] head." The "man's seed," he argues, must also have a part in this victory, and thus he has, with Joanna's ambiguous assistance, spiritually conceived himself, Zion, a fusion of Scripture and manhood, of the divine word and human suffering (*Vision* 51–52). Having already overtaken Mary Boon, he now overtakes Joanna, who was fated to become a prefiguration of her own meaning by her status as a purely figurative mother. Among this community of prophets, with their rivalries buried just beneath the surface of their interdependence, spiritual ascendancy devolves on control of the written word. And neither the illiterate Mary Boon nor the barely literate Joanna Southcott possessed interpretive and inscriptive control of their prophetic effusions. Their wisdom is incomplete, a riddle needing an answer, and thus Ward has a plausible reason for conceiving himself to be the signified of their cryptic pronouncements. The meaning and the control of their prophecies come down to the same thing: Zion holds the answer to the riddle and is himself the answer to the riddle.

In his appropriation of female authority, Zion is also a figure in a larger cultural pattern. Throughout this book, and most expressly in Chapters 3 through 6, we will encounter instances where authority is meditated through alterity, where mediation works to accredit, to validate, to purify, a narrator's authoritative claims. Because the goal of such mediation is to anchor opinion in a source outside the self, and because the self of Christian culture is inherently a suspect, fallen creature, the mediators typically purchase for their narratives, through their ideological images, disinterestedness and spiritual purity. Elevated to a complex subjectivity by guilt, the individual everyman of early-nineteenth-century Christian narratives validates his spiritual knowledge by channeling his religious and ethical truth claims through certain objects, and primary among these objects is idealized femininity.

Importantly, Zion Ward does *not* participate in this cultural pattern in a typical way. For him, the purchase of innocence is unnecessary, because the parameters of his allegorically inflated selfhood already encompass all forms of alterity. Hence the women in his narratives share a similar fate with the entire cast of characters, the fate of being redefined as an aspect of Ward himself. Consequently, it is of little importance whether womanhood in his writings is the signifier of spiritual strength or weakness; they can be either, since it is Ward's spiritual state that determines the allegorical import of their characters. Thus in one tract Ward interprets marriage as the union of the sinful man and the immaculate woman within himself (*True Explanation* 9). But in another tract, womanhood becomes a metaphor for the weakness and passivity of the human condition:

Understand what God means by a Woman....God calleth all men Women, in that they are all in weakness, they have not in them the strength and power of God....Therefore he calleth all men Women, but one out of those in the end, the fullness of time, he chooseth to visit, because his time is come to finish transgression and make an end of sin; ... he chooseth to visit one Man, one of these Women, and to destroy the weakness, and overshadow him with his Cloud of Glory, his Spirit of strength, light, and holiness, changing the person from a vessel of dishonour to a vessel of honour, making the person his bride, taking the person into marriage union with himself, and this union produces the true word of truth, the child of innocence, and truth, and love; and this is the Woman that is saved in child-bearing, and this is the Son of God made of a woman; so Zion is the Woman and the Son of God, whether you believe or not. (*Complete Refutation* 21)

"Whether you believe or not": one can play along with Ward's game or not—it is all the same to him, as long as those who do come along are willing to accept the visionary new world on his terms. We are encountering here what E. P. Thompson calls Ward's "surrealist solipsism" (799), for Ward seems blithely indifferent to the fact that his hermeneutic system cannot accommodate a human subjectivity other than his own. Everything signifies Zion Ward, an event in his mind or an event in his life. In Ward, God has prepared "a vessel to sustain all the characters from Adam to St. John the Divine (so called)" ("Zion's preface"). Of Hymenaeus and Alexander, Ward comments, "these two characters are only one, i.e., Zion" (*Zion's Works* 1: 10–11). Referring to himself, Ward writes: "Here was the church, the woman (of whom Joanna Southcott was the type), striving to alter the decrees that God had made for herself; here was the serpent, the man of sin, giving the woman the forbidden fruit; and the man Shiloh is the woman, the church, the standard, the man and woman in one" (*Living Oracle* 33). Zion is church, man, woman, Christ, and Antichrist: beneath the weight of his allegorical demands, the referential structure of language implodes on this, its self-proclaimed primary speaker. Hence it is appropriate that the female mediators Ward might once have needed, the prophetic partners with whom he was formerly in collusion, are absorbed into the subjectivity that began its messianic mission by manipulating their literary remains. For Joanna and Mary Boon were, in a sense, never more than objects of his interpretation. Indeed, male or female, human or animal, animate or inanimate, the manifold objects in Ward's scriptural commentaries are leveled out on the plain of his all-consuming identity. Even the promised land is subject to the revisionary definitions of his insatiable anthropormorphism, and thus he devises a succinct and appropriate greeting for his correspondence: "In the kingdom of Zion, the Lord is here."

And yet, despite his apparent self-preoccupation, Ward's scriptural hermeneutics had a more active and radical social agenda than most. This outward turn of his inwardly directed spirituality is the most compelling paradox of Zion Ward. His anticlerical views were tied to his politicized identification with the working and non-working poor, who Ward believed suffered physically and spiritually because of a political establishment built upon the Church's illegitimate power. Ward's most conspicuous political activities occurred in 1832. In this year he traveled to Derby with his devoted follower, Charles William Twort. For several weeks the two missionaries gathered crowds to hear their inflammatory denunciations of the clergy and the established church. While they were in Derby, a national fast day was declared by the king; this unlikely and controversial action was the result of a parliamentary debate led by the

Evangelical M.P., Spencer Percival. On the evening of the fast day, Ward and Twort opened their doors to local workers returning home, inviting them to a dinner of mutton. Since the poor fasted every day, Ward and Twort explained, the national fast was wrongminded, and only a blind and abusive religious establishment could conceive such a perversion. Nothing was immediately done by the local authorities to punish this act of impertinence; it took a more direct confrontation with a representative of the Church to result in legal action against them. A minister, Rev. James Dean, encountered Twort in the street, and the two men exchanged words. (Dean was an Oxford tutor with connections to Newman's circle.) Whether in the ensuing discussion Dean attacked Twort with his umbrella (as Twort maintained) or Twort accosted Dean for demanding that he remove the placards (as Dean maintained), one thing is sure: the two men got into a fight. Afterward Dean had both Ward and Twort arrested and charged with blasphemy. Among radicals such as Richard Carlile, the case of Ward and Twort became a brief *cause célèbre*. In the House of Commons, the last unreformed Parliament debated their trial. Four thousand men in London reportedly petitioned for their release. Ward and Twort were convicted regardless. Ward endured incarceration by doing what he had done while in Newington workhouse—writing—and since his sentence stretched to eighteen months, his time in Derby jail accounts for a significant amount of his sizable literary corpus.

In this context, Ward stands as one among many working-class leaders whose political challenges were thoroughly intertwined with unconventional religious beliefs. Certainly the spiritual entanglements that expressed themselves in his messianic delusions seem, from our perspective, to compromise his integrity as a political activist and thinker. But it is also because of his messianic delusions that Ward prefigures a definitive heresy of the nineteenth century, variations of which are articulated by Blake, Schleiermacher, Feuerbach, and in more cautious terms by Carlyle, Irving, Maurice, and Nightingale: Christ is a metaphor for the incarnation of God in every individual, and sin is a metaphor for the various impediments (evil, ignorance, inculturation, institutions) that prevent the divine nature of man from developing fully.[6]

Even where this heresy was not, in so many words, endorsed, its influence could still be felt. Under the reigns of liberalism and positivism—movements populated primarily by members of the Broad Church and by intellectual skeptics—the impediments to an ongoing improvement of human nature were thought to be tractable, at times almost negligible, and it was this optimistic reliance on anthropocentric resources which, probably more than anything else, divided John Henry Newman from other influential English religious thinkers of his day. Ironically, in his war on liberalism, Newman was following more closely in the footsteps of Coleridge than the Broad Churchmen who traced their theological ancestry to the great poet. In the 1820s it was Coleridge who heard the nascent expressions of human perfectibility in his society and hoped to defuse them with a sophisticated religious hermeneutics that made human inadequacy into an inescapable, even necessary condition. Ward, in contrast, seems to have believed that he had discovered the idea of human perfectibility, of unconditional Christological imitation, solely on his own, and, finding the idea intoxicating, he extrapolated from it a mythology of himself that disarms the reader by marching unabashedly toward excess.

Excess is key to the sensibility of Ward: this Victorian messiah differs from other messiahs before and since in his condescension to his precursor. Again, this anomaly illuminates the more conventional formulations that we will explore in subsequent chapters. It illuminates them by calling attention to the complex and counterintuitive functions performed by guilt in Victorian narratives of cultural authority. In Ward's system, guilt is not so much a hindrance to authoritative claims as it is an asset; "Now Jesus is come for real, for the real Jesus must experience and overcome sin, must die unto sin, and the earlier Jesus did not experience sin. And the earlier Jesus was not flesh; now Jesus comes 'clothed with flesh incarnate'" (*Complete Refutation* 36). Or again: Zion is the one "out of the whole mass, who was predestinated for the very thing, viz., to have both the evil and the good revealed in him" ("Zion's preface"). Having experienced and overcome sin, Zion is more the Christ than Christ was, for he has enabled God to enter fully into the alien condition of his creature. At the same time, this merger enables Zion to enter fully into the no longer alien condition of God. As Holinsworth summarizes this Shilohite doctrine, "A conjunction was formed between the Divine Wisdom and the purified human mind" ("Introduction" viii). Once again, we are confronted with a statement that manages to combine orthodoxy and radical heresy. Zion does not deny his sinful nature, nor does he deny the necessity of doing battle with this nature. On the other hand, his manipulation of these orthodox positions points to a hidden premise in Christian narratives: the legitimacy of a narrator depends on an acknowledgment of guilt, the ascent to the place of a full human subject entails owning up to one's inner divisions, one's capacity to feel powerfully the allure of sin. Guilt is not only a condition requiring expiation, but by a curious twist of Christian conventions a necessary credential for the narrator of Christian truth claims.

To a greater or lesser extent, this tension is felt in many Victorian religious narratives. They create within themselves loci of disinterestedness as well as loci of sinfulness and fallibility, and such distinctions are part of the necessary structure by which these texts replicate a Christian economy of salvation, where sin is as fundamental as grace, where sin, in fact, is a prerequisite of grace. To be sure, that religious writers divide and distribute their narrative voice among these various loci does not imply that all Victorian religious narratives are solipsistic in nature, for this would deny the lively dialogism and intersubjectivity they often achieve. But whereas most Victorian narratives of social and cultural interpretation establish a network of references, quotations, and voices that connect their authority to social and historical externalities, John Ward moves in the opposite direction, encompassing all references, quotations, and voices inside the expanded boundaries of his own ego. In a sense, his narratives are also dialogic themselves, but rather than using either dialogism or intersubjectivity to imply a broad social base of contribution for his views, Ward undermines these seemingly desirable strategies by insisting that all voices, characters, and landscapes are inwardly divided elements of his imagination, voices that comprise the rich schizophrenia of his singular consciousness. His literary interiority was to an exceptional degree shaped by the Bible—indeed, it was commensurate with the Bible. If that focused intensity lessened his fear of subjectivism, it was for the wonderfully simple and dangerous reason that he experienced it as a source of grandeur and liberation. In retrospect, we might read his hermeneutic solipsism as a contestatory inversion of a larger social repression, a repression of the fear that all religious beliefs (increasingly disconnected, as they were, from either historical legitimacy or social consensus) are ultimately subjective in nature. For from within the logic of the Shilohite faith, the social landscape of mediated authority looks like a rhetorical ruse. Zion the solipsist, perhaps in spite of himself, may have spoken a disconcerting truth.

CHAPTER 1

Of Tongues, Texts, Nerves, Opium, and Flesh

The Disappearance of the Invisible in Early Victorian Spiritual Epistemology

They had come up in the evening to the sick chamber of their sister, who was laid on a sofa, and, along with one or two others of the household, they were engaged in prayer together. When, in the midst of their devotion, the Holy Ghost came with mighty power upon the sick woman as she lay in her weakness, and constrained her to speak at great length, and with superhuman strength, in an unknown tongue, to the astonishment of all who heard.... It was so also the first time that silence was broke in my church. I have put the question directly, and been answered by the person who was raised for that purpose, that she never had so strong an impulse; which, thinking to restrain, she fled out of the church into the vestry, but found it quite irresistible, and was forced to give vent to that volume of majestic sound, which passed through two closed doors, and filled the whole church. And so, according to the example of the Scriptures, it ought to be....They did not, and could not, refrain themselves, but all spake with the tongues as the Spirit gave them utterance.
              Irving, "Facts" 759–60

In the self-oblivion of these heroes of the Old Testament, their elevation above all low and individual interests,—above all, in the entire and vehement devotion of their total being to the service of their divine Master, I find a lesson of humiliation, a ground of humiliation, and a shaming, yet rousing, example of faith and fealty.... If these men are not men of like faculties and passions with myself, but rather a Divina Comedia of a superhuman—O bear with me if I say—Ventriloquist;—that the royal Harper, to whom I have so often submitted myself as a many-stringed instrument for his fire-tipt fingers to traverse ... that this sweet Psalmist of Israel was himself as mere an instrument as his harp, an automaton poet, mourner, and supplicant;—all is gone,—all sympathy, at least, and all example.
              Coleridge, *Confessions* 35

On first reading, it is difficult to say if these two descriptions of inspired moments are more alike in their emphasis on the resistance and strength of will displayed by inspired individuals in the face of divinatory torments or more alike in their emphasis on the inspired individuals' demonstrations of humility and self-oblivion. For if Rev. Edward Irving, in recounting the miraculous return of the gift of tongues to his Presbyterian congregation, emphasizes the resistance exerted by those visited by the Holy Spirit, their attempts to override its "constraints" and "refrain" from its impulses, so does Coleridge wish to differentiate the Old Testament prophets from mere "automaton" poets who record, without the interference of their own individuality, a divine dictation. And yet the resistance of individuality also appears as an impediment to be conquered, for why else would the prophets be remarkable for their "self-oblivion" and "shaming," and why else would the spirits in Irving's congregation speak in a voice so unlike the voices of those possessed by it, and in a language they do not understand?

To be accurate, there is an important temporal distinction in these two accounts of a divine intervention in the human order of communication, since the members of Irving's congregation, once possessed, are little better than the automaton poets or divine ventriloquists whom Coleridge disparages. It is really only Coleridge, still anxious about the claims of materialist psychology, who wants to preserve the operations of an autonomous ego (although, ambiguously, self-oblivious, devoted, and humiliated) in the moment of inspired testimony.[1] To Irving's mind, it is enough that the ego put up a fight before submitting—so much is necessary to demonstrate the absence of self-promoting motives or hysterical eagerness in the experiences of "the gifted." Structurally, however, the tensions between the spirit and its chosen agents in both narratives—the ways in which the agents submit, but do not *simply* submit—perform the similar functions of situating the source of revelation outside the individual. In this way, elements of the paradigm of conversion are appropriated in Irving's and Coleridge's accounts as a means of objectifying the truth claims of a spiritual epistemology: the sins of self are conquered by a higher force, the inspired self is a tamed soul and not an originary source of spiritual wisdom.

Beneath the paradoxical emphases on resistance and submission in these accounts is a fear that inspired revelation is equivalent to subjective knowledge in all its vulnerability to delusion, sin, and self-interest. As a limiting condition on truth claims, subjectivity qualifies the credibility not only of those who deliver the word but also of the readers and audiences whose important role is to interpret it. Coleridge exacerbates the problem of subjectivity in the larger schema of his biblical hermeneutics and then attempts to resolve it dialectically: *Confessions of an Inquiring Spirit* celebrates the sympathetic reader of the Bible as the most credible witness to its sacred intentions, but he later retracts this apparent surrender of interpretive authority to an individual reader by asserting that religion is a synthesis of subjective and objective, a process of dialectical growth into the exegetical harmonies of a transcendent spirit. Ultimately, the influence of the individual in Coleridge's theology is regulated by a process. The mediations of the spirit that he describes enlist the prophets, readers, exegetes, and finally the preachers of the holy word in a vast communal interpretation. As a consequence of this communal process, biblical revelation is entailed to the interests of a national church, a transpersonal agent of the invisible spirit. In this way, the individual's apprehension of God in the Bible gives emotional credence to Coleridge's theology, but in a highly regulated fashion.

Subjectivity likewise played a key role in "the manifestation of spiritual gifts" among the members of Irving's Regent Square church, insofar as the credibility of a glossolalist depended largely upon her or his description of the singular emotions and physical sensations that accompanied the presence of the Holy Spirit. As in the case of Coleridge's hermeneutics, the importance placed upon personal testimony (both of the tongues themselves and the descriptions of the feelings that accompanied them) was counterbalanced by a transpersonal process. Spiritual authority among the Irvingite glossolalists was distributed through several agents—the preacher, the gifted, and their interpreters—and this decentralization of sources helped reassure the participants that supernatural powers, and not individual charlatanism, were at work. Indeed, Irving's London congregation oversaw the unfolding drama of the divine visitations with solicitous attention to the control of this potent phenomenon for good reason, since in the end, much to Irving's shame, several of the glossolalists recanted their inspired pronouncements, confessing that pride and self-promotion had been their true motives.

Given the problems that subjectivity introduces, what is striking in these accounts is its apparent inexpendability. In spite of the difficulties they court, both Coleridge and Irving pay salient attention to the common humanity of subjects who attain, with few earthly distinctions, glimpses of divine wisdom. Their preoccupation with the implied special dignity of the individual was historically congruent with the oscillating rise of British middle-class democracy; the outbreak of tongues in Irving's church, for example, occurred soon after the First Reform Bill had made its initial failed passage through Lords. In the following pages, I will not directly examine the relevance of political events to the religious hermeneutics of Coleridge and Irving. What should be evident, however, merely from a glance at their environment, is that neither Coleridge nor Irving, in spite of their shared political conservatism, was immune to the influence of democratic social movements. Both men, although opposed to the progressive and generally more tolerant measures of Whig reform, incorporated into their theology attitudes that had distinctly democratic ramifications. By showing an interest in the phenomenological aspects of religious experience, they accorded an integrity, difficult to control, to the individual's descriptive account of the process of illumination. Coleridge bequeathed a dense but ennobling body of religious writings to a Broad Church movement that sought to elevate the working-class Christian and to relax the strictures of church doctrine. By 1848, the ideas of the poet who died a Tory had found their way into a short-lived movement called Christian Socialism.[2] For Irving, the inspired voices of his parishioners created in his own lifetime a tension between a hierarchical ecclesiastical body and subjective claims that unsettled such organization. The months that followed the first manifestation of prophetic gifts in his Regent Square church were a period of great trial, for during this period he was barred from his church for preaching the humanness of Christ, Christ "in the flesh," and a few months later the tongues were saying vexing things, claiming authority for themselves over the preacher. Banned from the ministry by his native Presbytery of Annan, Irving found himself additionally humbled by a phenomenon that his own preaching had unleashed, a unique and purportedly literal instance of *vox populi, vox dei*. Democratic movements, although disdained by Irving and other members of the breakaway "Catholic Apostolic Church," were as irresistible as the spirit in the years of William IV's reign.

Rather than focusing on the external political environment in which Coleridge and Irving articulated their models of inspiration, the following discussion will attend to a political resonance inherent in the models themselves. The psychological and exegetical aspects of these models combine to form elaborate structures of belief, structures that in part create the invisible spirit whom they claim to represent. Broadly conceived, what is at stake in these acts of creation is not so much theological or political issues per se but rather the legitimation of authorities that pronounce upon theology or politics. Consequently, in our reading of these theological narratives the emphasis will fall not on the claims they make but rather on the internal constructions of their own legitimacy. In Coleridge's and Irving's spiritual epistemologies, as we have seen, this legitimacy depends upon the preservation of an ambivalent attitude toward the individual; the challenge for these religious thinkers is not to decide whether to purge or privilege the voice of the individual, but how to do both at the same time. It is this paradox that gives their religious dilemma broader cultural and political ramifications. For insofar as interpretive hegemony can be situated within a literary culture, where the apprehension of meaning occurs within the privatized space of reading, the projected locus of authority must at once preserve and overcome the subjective conditions of its occurrence. This chapter will explore the causes and effects of this dilemma as it played out in Coleridge's and Irving's attempts to form theories of divine inspiration.

The first section will begin by discussing the influence of print culture upon representations of subjectivity, focusing primarily on Coleridge's religious writings, but also, by way of comparison, on some passages from De Quincey. My objective in this section is to argue that Coleridge's late religious writings employ images of resistance and submission in Bible reading in order to create a model of sacred history as ongoing literary interpretation. Hence his version of sacred history organizes culture around literature, establishing reading as the cornerstone of both self-creation and social structure. In this way, the religious hermeneutics which Coleridge forged in his later life are another version of the literary history and literary culture that dominated his imagination for most of his life—a more regulated version, insofar as theodicy enables him to reify and centralize the elusive and diffuse powers of literature.[3] While the *Lay Sermons* foregrounds the social aspects of this centralization, *Confessions of an Inquiring Spirit* gives priority to questions of personal literary interpretation. In the *Confessions*, Coleridge devises a reader-response criticism in which errors in biblical interpretation—themselves the result of flaws in the scriptural record no less than in the reader's soul—are worked out via the reader's receptiveness to the presence of the Spirit in this highly animated text. According to a logic that is distinctly typological, a readerly inspiration repeats and completes the writerly one, and thus Coleridge posits a hypothetical reader who becomes, in a process that is itself unfolding in history, the text's more perfect product.

The first section will conclude by returning to the topic of print culture. The thorough dependence of Coleridge's theology upon a literary epistemology, I will suggest, is congruent with his burial of the spoken word. Struggling to preserve the privilege that Protestant tradition assigns to orality and voice, Coleridge's prose produces images of an interwoven fabric of voice and text, an imbrication of media which ultimately betrays the fact that texts dominate his system. Indeed, Coleridge's religious faith is composed of psychological and philosophical patterns inherent in the deeply literary disposition of his mind, because issues of textuality—authorship, reception, interpretation, and the social repercussions of reading—are the materials with which he defines human and godly natures. In this context, one goal of my inquiry is to investigate the interplay between technologies of communication and the relationship between self and knowledge generated by this interplay. What we will find is that Coleridge's epistemology necessitates guilt and incompleteness as conditions of the reliable Christian, and thus he is an important representative of a cultural tradition wherein these states of being are the hallmarks of full subjectivity. Man is the creature who sins, and the identity-bestowing refraction of his image through the eyes of God depends upon the preservation, at some level, of his guilty nature.

The second section of the chapter will turn to the story of the outbreak of "glossolalia" (speaking in tongues) in Rev. Edward Irving's church. As in Coleridge's theology, resistance and submission play key roles in the discourse surrounding the phenomenon of the tongues. Indeed, in a striking fashion, the glossolalia in Irving's church dramatizes a definitive tension in Coleridge's ever-evolving theories of inspiration—the tension between an image of the inspired individual that embodies her in a discrete identity and one that absorbs her into oblivious transcendence. However, unlike Coleridge, the Irvingite glossolalists staged their dramas of resistance and submission in an oral theater, and in a manner consistent with the more general mystification of the spoken word in their religious tradition. Additionally, whereas the tensions between sects that so dominate English religious history of the early nineteenth century are present in Coleridge's texts as distressing realities beneath the dream of a national church, the struggles of Irving's church are visible on the surface of its history. The explicit priority assigned to the medium over the message of their inspired communications enables us to see precisely those things which the "economy of divine revelation" in their church seemed engineered to conceal: namely, the extent to which the phenomenon was driven by contests for influence and prestige, by a desire on the part of the glossolalists to celebrate their personal spiritual privileges and to reassign religious authority in their church accordingly.

To a large extent, the redistribution of authority in Irving's church was made possible by something that might at first appear irrelevant: Irving's heterodox teachings on the doctrine of the incarnation. Because these teachings have important ramifications, the debate between Irving and Coleridge concerning the nature of Christ's incarnation will be the subject of the third and final section of the chapter. Meditating on the human body of Christ, Irving gave voice to a heresy that would become doctrinaire in many Victorian intellectual and political movements. The temptations conferred on God by the inhabitation of a man's body facilitated a reversal of that formula, conferring on man the potentials enjoyed by God. Such intimations were anathema to Coleridge, whose theological system was built upon a dialectical separation of humanity from divinity. Consequently, these two theologians of late Romanticism, compelled by a similar fascination with the possibility of a sublime convergence of supernatural wisdom and individual consciousness, arrived at antithetical conclusions. And despite its enormous influence, Coleridge's nuanced model of a scriptural metaphysics required a greater negative capability than his society as a whole was capable of; indeed, the deferral of knowledge built into his hermeneutics rendered it inadequate for the hegemonic purposes that he wished it to fulfill. In contrast, the human Christ of Irving's theology more readily anticipated the faith in a perfectible humanity that was so influential in the nineteenth century, the more satisfying if more dangerous replacement of textual ambiguity with a deified human nature.

Textual Subjectivity and Coleridge's Scriptural Society

As scholars of Romanticism have observed, a distinctive feature of much of the literature of the period is the tendency to represent identity as an effect and register of reading.⁴ While this tendency exists side by side with romanticized images of experiences unvitiated by a textual mediation, both modes of representation might be understood as attempts to adjust images of human consciousness to the impact of an expanding print culture. Because of their shared penchant for autobiography and the personal mode of address, De Quincey and Coleridge fall into the prior camp: most frequently, they portray themselves as the sum of reading experiences both remembered and forgotten. This manner of representation might be referred to as textual subjectivity, since it often brackets experiences other than reading as secondary to the literary ones that are portrayed as seminal influences.

De Quincey, for example, in a rhetorical move that might be thought self-serving on the part of a paid essayist, solemnizes the relationship between personal psychology and literature as one too intertwined to succumb to analysis: "And of this let everyone be assured—that he owes to the impassioned books which he has read many a thousand more of emotions than he can consciously trace back to them. Dim by their organization, these emotions arise in him, and mould him through life, like forgotten incidents of his childhood" ("The Poetry of Pope" 59).⁵ Books are the source of a subconscious mental life; however, De Quincey has, in earlier writings, located two other sources of his vast and buried emotional life—opium, in *Confessions of an English Opium-Eater* (1821), and childhood grief, in *Suspiria De Profundis* (1845). Between the confessions of 1821 and the autobiographical essay of 1845, De Quincey's obsession with the power of dreaming passed through certain changes which rendered childhood a more acceptable and marketable topos than opium for representing the subconscious absorption and reflection of life-changing experiences. Thus in *Suspiria de Profundis* the origin of the "convulsing" faculty of "the whole dreaming economy" is moved back in time from the opiated years of his young adulthood to the childhood memory of his sister's death: as De Quincey informs us, the "nursery experience had been the ally and natural coefficient of the opium" (137). But insofar as both opium and childhood grief have become, through De Quincey's autobiographical efforts, a part of the half-forgotten reading material that organizes his own as well as his reader's mental life, literature seems to be the most powerful of the mind-altering and self-structuring experiences that De Quincey celebrates. In this regard, the image most representative of his corpus is one that conflates mind and text: the second section of *Suspiria de Profundis* begins with a discourse on the similarities between the palimpsest and consciousness. As Mary Jacobus comments on this famous passage, it is a "work not so much of exorcism as conjuration, [unleashing] the demonic hubbub of incoherence and bacchic laughter stored in the human brain" (237). Like opium and childhood memories, textuality is for De Quincey a material pathway to the sublime experience of expanded consciousness. Hence the habit of extensive reading is made remarkable less for the information it puts at one's conscious command than for the extension of subconscious memory into an infinite, inexhaustible regress.

Coleridge also thematized in the course of his career a dialectical relationship between books and subjectivity. The autobiographical possibilities of *Biographia Literaria*, to take the most obvious example, are defined in terms of the protagonist's various forms of involvement—as consumer, author, student, and critic—with literature. During his later years, however, Coleridge's faith in the cultivating influence of good literature was eclipsed by his fear of the debilitating effects of merely popular literature. In reaction, his religious writings offer images of an ideal readerly regimen wherein the Bible is the primary text that shapes and inhabits psychological spaces. The depiction of the Bible as a psychologically centralizing text, one that enlists, encompasses, and orders its reader's mental life, is everywhere evidenced in Coleridge's writings of the 1820s, such as this marginal note from that period: "O let a man afflicted with disease or with self-condemnation *pray* the Psalms on his knees—& he will find, in how narrow a circle all the deep joys & sorrows of human nature are contained" (*Marginalia* 1: 429). The act of reading or praying the Psalms circumscribes a sublime range of human feelings—from joys to sorrows—within a circle that is reassuring, even healing, in its narrowness. The ambiguity as to *what* exactly is "narrow"—the psalms, human nature, the heart of the afflicted reader?—only underscores the interdependence of reader and text: what is important is the claim that the act of reading the Psalms effects the sense of enclosure. However, it is not mental containment per se that Coleridge desires but more precisely the enclosure of a mental amplitude; the beauty of the Bible is that it provides him with both. Thus he glosses Saint Paul's exhortation to read the Scriptures continually with the following paean to the effects of the mystery of Christ on the reader's mind:

All things are but parts and forms of progressive manifestation, and every new knowledge but a new organ of sense and insight into this one all-inclusive Verity, which, still filling the vessel of the understanding, still dilates it to a capacity of yet other and yet greater Truths, and thus makes the soul feel its poverty by the very amplitude of its present, and the immensity of its revisionary wealth. (*A Lay Sermon* 179)

A central, singular truth begets inexhaustible meaning and with it inexhaustible mental growth.[6] Given the imagery of awesome expansion in this passage, the centrifugal forces ascribed to an amalgam of magical texts, it is no wonder that Coleridge proceeds to harness this sublime literary phenomenon to the insistence that the Christian faith requires the logic of a system and the guidance of doctrine.

Coleridge's images of an organized, comprehensive subjectivity enlisted by Bible reading differ sharply from De Quincey's articulations of the psychic exchange between literature and consciousness in this regard: De Quincey routinely enlists expansive modifiers that unsettle any sense of ontological totality. Indeed, the spatial restrictions imposed by the literary journals to which he contributed supply a necessary nemesis to the illusion of psychological infinity, as in his characteristic lament that "the accidents of the press" preclude his ability to launch the readers of *Suspiria de Profundis* "upwards through the whole arch of ascending visions" (137). This point of contrast between Coleridge and De Quincey holds up, even when

De Quincey enters his most Coleridgean mode, as in the following passage, where he describes the national church as the best cultivator of children's souls:

> Wheresoever there is a national church established, to which a child sees his friends resorting; wheresoever he beholds all whom he honours periodically prostrate before those illimitable heavens which fill to overflowing his young adoring heart; wheresoever he sees the sleep of death falling at intervals upon men and women whom he knows, depth as confounding to the plummet of his mind as those heavens ascend beyond his power to pursue—there take you no thought for the religion of a child. (*Suspiria* 114)

De Quincey's homage to the nurturing qualities of a national church might signify the distance he has traveled in the twenty years since he ironically introduced his first confessions as "the doctrine of the true church on the subject of opium: the church of which I acknowledge myself to be the only member" (*Confessions of an English Opium-Eater* 42). But his true interest has always been in the apprehension of infinity, in the mind's transcendence of quotidian boundaries. This interest is betrayed in the direction the above passage takes toward inscribing an awareness which has at once depth and height. That his remarkable interior life indeed benefits from the guidance and patronage of an established church is a point De Quincey asks his readers to take on faith. Coleridge, less casual in this matter, attempted a systematic defense of the established church that was based in large part on the assumption of a predictable affective response to Scriptures.

The fundamental precept of this defense turns on Coleridge's spiritual psychology, wherein each Christian comes to recognize in church doctrine a reflection of his or her own consummate soul. In this regard, Tilottama Rajan's observation that early-nineteenth-century hermeneutics is shadowed by an "increasing sense that signs may not adequately convey interiority," although a persuasive description of Coleridge's secular criticism needs to be altered slightly to describe his religious writings (36). The ideological basis of these texts is the assumption that the signifiers of the Bible not only adequately convey interiority but indeed largely create it. According to

Coleridge's unabashedly circular logic on this score, the proof of the Bible's sacred status lies in its ability to perfect and complete the soul of its reader, even as the only credible reader of the Bible is the one whose occult experiences of spiritual completion are a consequence of Bible reading. It is an important feature of this argument that spiritual wholeness or completion is articulated as a goal that is never fully achieved, even though it is glimpsed in oracular moments. As an imaginary and always unfulfilled projection, the whole and unified psyche of the Coleridgean reader is analogically mirrored at several levels: in the unified spirit of the Bible, which is potentially perceptible to the devout and persistent reader; in the church, whose potential for unity is one thread of the narrative of sacred history; in the conscience of the nation, which is, or should be, univocally articulated by the church; and ultimately, in the unity of God's consciousness, which is Coleridge's unmistakably Hegelian version of the Christian telos.[7] Unity is the essence of Bible, reader, church, and God, but essences are revealed gradually, over time. In this way, Coleridge's model of sacred history simultaneously acknowledges and defuses certain real conditions—the struggles, errors, and divisions that were the undeniable hallmarks of Bible reading in his society.

The emphasis on totality and inclusion in Coleridge's religious hermeneutics is striking, especially when we recall how for De Quincey a similarly text-based notion of subjectivity emphasized the openness and non-inclusiveness of the mind-as-text, its ultimate attenuation into a consciousness without boundaries. Coleridge, in contrast, values an ontology of wholeness that is encircled by boundaries; such inclusiveness, within the parameters of the Bible, the soul, and the church, testifies to the spirit's ability to contain, circumscribe, and encompass an invisible body of authorizations. Both of these images of consciousness—the limitless one of De Quincey, and the vast but circumscribed one of Coleridge—reflect Clifford Siskin's observation that the "self-made mind" of the Romantic period is "full of newly constructed depths," depths which might suggest imaginative and erotic liberty, but not without encouraging "specialized intervention" and "surveillance" on the part of the individual who makes himself or herself an object of study (13). From this perspective, it is a fitting irony that the trope of the spirit in Coleridge's writing, while evocative at times of the sensations that connect his consciousness to timeless forces both natural and supernatural, is also evocative of the power and the necessity of taming his consciousness, of bending it to the will of an abstract necessity. In his later life Coleridge discovered in Christian theology a suitable narrative for the process of expanding and disciplining consciousness. The creation and the interrogation of interior spaces were projects shared by British Romantic and Protestant thinkers; Coleridge was a master in both movements because the creative discomfort he experienced in the former was allayed by the structure, logic, and purpose he found in the latter.

For the spirit at work in Coleridge's religious writings is a reformed vision of the powers of literary genius that were the objects of his secular devotion. In his religious writings, Coleridge restructures Romantic idealism around a reified invisibility—around God, construed as a centrifugal topos of Genius, Imagination, Love, and Reason. Religion is a compelling and useful substitute for the effects of literature: it enables Coleridge to concentrate its elusive powers in a benevolent agent and a rational design; moreover, it extends the subjective pleasures of the literary life into a grand historical scheme. Because of the importance of this latter effect, the challenges that Coleridge confronts in the religious writings are at once psychological and sociological in nature. Having consolidated a recalcitrant expanse of literary sensibility into a theological system, he must legitimate that system as a viable ideology, in spite of the rampant religious sectarianism and (to his mind) cultural chaos associated with it.

Popular literature was an adversary that Coleridge battled all his life, but when he assumes a theological perspective, his condemnations are reinforced by the powerful canon that he wields as its antithesis. Outside the boundaries of religiously sound literature and learning, popular literature existed for Coleridge as a mimetic monstrosity—idle reading, he asserts repeatedly, is the most dangerous irritant to the harmonious organization of English Christian society.[8] Changes in the publishing industry were largely to blame for Coleridge's anxiety, insofar as the propagation of cheap print unsettled a literary social order that had arisen around the expensive particularity of books. Given the premium he placed on reading in spiritual life, the expansion of the reading public and the cheapness of print have mixed ramifications for Coleridge, on the one hand spreading biblical literacy and on the other hand depreciating the value of literature in general. Thus he laments the print industry's success in placing books "in every hovel," even as he is bound to rejoice when he finds the Gospel "open in the market-place, and on every window seat, so that (*virtually*, at least) the deaf may hear the words of the Book!" (*Statesman's Manual* 39, 6). But in the end the costs of these changes to Coleridge's envisioned society outweigh the benefits. Not only is the Bible's value depreciated by association with scurrilous printed matter, but more importantly, the coherence of a society avowedly based on Christianity is destabilized by the increased visibility of religious debates and rationalist critiques.

And yet, as Coleridge realized, there was a fundamental problem that preceded any of these consequences, for the propagation of inexpensive Bibles and New Testaments called attention to the fact that—despite the power wielded by the *idea* of the Bible—there was in fact no agreement on what properly constituted a complete scriptural text. What defined a canonical Bible? Which books was it necessary to include, and which, for the purposes of mass publication, was it better to exclude? Moreover, could the working poor be trusted to interpret scriptures without guidance, or should supplementary texts in the form of doctrinal commentary and glosses be provided to guide their reading? In short, how could the Bible be the mainstay of British theology and culture, given the plasticity of its canon and the multiplicities of readings that it allowed?

It was this issue, forced to Coleridge's attention by the operations of the British and Foreign Bible Society, that formed the occasion for the *Lay Sermons* (1816–17). In the first "sermon," published under the title *The Statesman's Manual*, Coleridge stands in line with the religious conservatives of his day by envisioning the Bible as a privileged text that provides guidelines for all learning and anticipates in its own wisdom all worthwhile study. Hence *The Statesman's Manual* seeks to maximize and to control the Bible's status as the anchoring text of an expanding print culture. It does so by establishing an interdependent hierarchy of readers and interpretive methods. Indeed, although Coleridge begins *The Statesman's Manual* by claiming that the Bible provides guidelines for political policy, the only example of political policy given in the essay is the one inherent in its hermeneutics, where modes of reading are organized analogously with the class system.

In brief, the argument of *The Statesman's Manual* calls for the upper classes to return to Scriptures for guidance in public policy, a return that would presumably take the form of revivified "clerisy," Coleridge's famous term for an upper- and upper-middle-class intelligentsia. From the upper classes, Coleridge explains, we should expect a more "sober and meditative accommodation to [our] own times and country of those important truths declared in the inspired writings" (7). But the Bible's apartness from other books can only be conceptualized in terms of its universal appeal, its power to override distinctions of class, culture, and educational preparation by absorbing its best or chosen readers into the body of the faithful. Consequently, Coleridge draws distinctions between modes of Bible reading, making political and historical interpretations the sole province of the upper classes, and spiritual and emotional responses a universally available and similar form of biblical reception. Thus he outlines a twofold process—on the one hand, to encourage Bible reading among "all my countrymen and fellow-Christians without distinction of class," and secondly, to urge "THE LEARNED ... to apply their powers and attainments to an especial study of the Old Testament as teaching the elements of Political Science" (48–49). In this way, Coleridge's scriptural hermeneutics of the 1810s entails a psychology as well as a sociology of reading, one that universalizes a spiritual mode of Bible reading, but also defends a specialized mode of scholarly, literary, and political analysis of the Bible as the exclusive capacity of an intellectual minority.

The mode of reception which all men must practice, and which the working classes should only practice, emphasizes humility, docility, and subordination of the will. As he writes, the proper spiritual approach to Scriptures presupposes

> a humble and docile state of mind, and above all the practice of prayer, as the necessary condition of such a state, and the best if not the only means of becoming sincere to our own hearts.... Each person must be herein querist and respondent to himself.... Am I at one with God, and is my will concentric with that holy power, which is at once the constitutive will and supreme reason of the universe? (*Statesman's Manual* 55)

Elsewhere, Coleridge elaborates on this "state of mind" as one "which looks forward to 'the fellowship of the mystery of the faith' as a spirit of wisdom and revelation in the KNOWLEDGE of God" (46). The individual's evolution toward this summit of acceptance is, as Steven Knapp argues, another version of the consummate Coleridgean gesture of self-abnegation, wherein conversion is figured as a submissive act to collective belief.[9] Submission, in *The Statesman's Manual*, is figured as a socially generalized response to the Bible, a mental posture that unites the lay reader with the clerisy via the definition of "spiritual" as an apolitical and nonmethodical response to the text.

Faced with the threat of politicized working-class appropriations of Scriptures, of men who claim the "*imprescriptible and inalienable* RIGHT to judge and decide for themselves on all important questions of Government and Religion" (37n), Coleridge thus tries to preserve both the Bible and the status quo by segregating the Bible's appeal to the classless human soul from its message for the upper-class policy maker. The goal of analyzing modes of Bible reading, it seems, leads seamlessly into the goal of organizing society along the axes of class and hermeneutic distinctions.[10] But the difficulty inherent in this dream of a regulated society of readers haunts Coleridge even as he composes the *Lay Sermons*, each of which he targets for a specific readership. *The Statesman's Manual*, he stipulates, is addressed specifically to the "higher and learned classes"; the second *Lay Sermon* is addressed to "the higher and middle classes"; and a third sermon, which was never written, was projected for "the Lower and Labouring Classes." Arguably, it was the difficulty of conceiving that third readership—of imaginatively entering their projected state of emotional receptivity detached from political and intellectual consciousness—that precluded Coleridge's completing the essay.

The social and cultural objectives of Coleridge's biblical hermeneutics rely heavily on the belief that there is a difference of kind, not just degree, between the Bible and other books. Intratextually, this difference could be defended by instancing, with judicious selectivity, the historical effects of Scriptures on the course of Western civilization. Intertextually, however, the sanctity of the Bible was a concept besieged on several fronts—by philological and manuscript studies, by rationalist critiques, and even, indirectly, by those among the pious who retrenched behind the doctrine of plenary inspiration. Advocates of plenary inspiration provided the rationalists with an object of ridicule and the fundamentalists with an apparent vindication of all theological ideas that could find even a fragmentary precedent in Scriptures. When Coleridge resolved, as part of *Aids to Reflection*, to relieve his mind on the "momentous Question" of plenary inspiration, the ancillary manuscript grew to such a length that it was refused by the publisher. Eventually, in 1840, six years after Coleridge's death, the manuscript was published under the title *Confessions of an Inquiring Spirit*. An epistolary essay, the *Confessions* is the response of an Englishman well read in the Higher Criticism to a fundamentalist interpretation of the Scriptures. But it is also a reaction against both the Higher Criticism and Protestant fundamentalism, as it resorts to subjective rather than scholarly criteria for evaluating the sacred merit of biblical passages. In this way, the *Confessions* instances the tendency by which, as Elinor S. Shaffer notes, historically informed biblical critics embraced a "more tenuous, non-literal, and a-historical" approach to the word of God, the upshot of which, in Shaffer's account, is Coleridge's attempt to recreate the Evangelist John by making "historical inauthenticity the essence of his character" (82). The refuge of historicism was a new and more sophisticated Pietism; in *Confessions of an Inquiring Spirit*, this Pietism takes the form of a phenomenological account of Coleridge's own experiences of reading the Bible.[11]

Granting this claim, it might seem that the *Confessions* would offer an extreme instance of a tendency that is ascribed to much literary criticism of the period—namely, a shift toward assigning readers a greater importance in the creation of textual meaning. However, the hermeneutic logic of the *Confessions* is ultimately a better example of Tilottama Rajan's modification of this thesis, according to which the power that Romantic hermeneutics appears to give the reader requires "a fidelity to its spirit that takes away the very liberty conferred on the reader" (23). The narrator of the *Confessions* achieves this double movement by crafting a descriptive prose wherein both objective standards and interpretive autonomy come into play: "Whatever *finds* me [in the Old and New Testament] bears witness for itself that it has proceeded from a Holy Spirit, even from the same Spirit, 'which remaineth in itself, yet regenerateth all other powers, and in all ages entering into holy souls maketh them friends of God, and prophets' (Wis. 7)" (10). Any schism between biblical logocentrism and individual conscience is settled in advance by appealing to an abstract concept of the spirit of the text—a spirit that can be known only through an enlivening of the reader's most essential self, which is, in truly sacred moments of communication, incapable of misapprehending divine truths.

At several points in the *Confessions*, Coleridge offers images of biblical communication, each time opposing the flawed and imperfect subjectivity of the reader to the challenging and taming Spirit in the text:

(1) What you find [in the Bible] coincident with your pre-established convictions, you will of course recognize as the Revealed Word, while, as you read the recorded workings of the Word and the Spirit in the minds, lives, and hearts of spiritual men, the influence of the same Spirit on your own being, and the conflicts of grace and infirmity in your own soul, will

enable you to discern and to know in and by what they spake and acted,—as far at least as shall be needful for you, and in the times of your need. (61)

(2) "[The Bible is] the organ and instrument of all the gifts, powers, and tendencies, by which the individual is privileged to rise above himself—to leave behind, and lose his divided phantom self, in order to find his true Self in that Distinctness where no division can be,—in the Eternal I Am, the Ever-living Word, of whom all the elect from the archangel before the throne to the poor wrestler with the Spirit *until the breaking of day* are but fainter and still fainter echoes." (72)

(3) No Christian probationer can recognize his own inward experiences in such Writings, and not find an objectiveness, a confirming and assuring outwardness ... working in himself and in his own thoughts, emotions, and aspirations—warring against sin, and the motions of sin. The unsubstantial, insulated Self passes away as a stream. (93)

Disparate in their quality and proximity to a divine source of inspiration, the assimilated texts of Holy Scriptures are nonetheless the agents of a greater unity that is unfolding over time. The totality and unity of the Bible are thus evidenced by its ability to elicit an anticipatory experience of ontological totality in its readers—the prefigurement of a Christian telos—in spite of the fact that it lacks authorial, qualitative, textual, or historical coherence itself. In this way, Coleridge deflects resistant, rebellious, and insurgent or merely self-serving interpretations: deflects, but does not eliminate, because a place for them in his evolutionary hermeneutics is preserved. Proper interpretation is an ongoing process of outgrowing "self," of vanquishing, via encounters with the spirit of the text, an inner self that is false and divided, a self plagued by infirmities, a self that is the source of discrepancies in interpretation—also, and most interestingly, a self that is (but only from the retrospective standpoint of enlightenment) "phantom" and "unsubstantial." Importantly, this process is ongoing but never fully accomplished, until supposedly the end of time, until that Coleridgean apocalypse wherein the "I AM" of God stands face to face with the perfected alterities of the human saved. Sacred history is thus construed as agonistic textual interpretation, comprising ongoing but on the whole ameliorative exchanges between sin and redemption, error and correction, ego and transcendence.

This felicitous merger of subjective and objective energies is made possible, indeed inevitable, by the new form of autobiography that the *Confessions* provides, an autobiography limited to Coleridge's formative experiences of the Bible. As we have already seen, Coleridge reserves for the Bible a distinct role as an architect of character. In the *Confessions*, this idea is resounded by the narrator's claim that the Bible has half-created, through the dialectical process of reading, the "light and life" of his own judgment. Unlike other books, the Bible has so thoroughly shaped his character as to make him "unable to determine what [he does] not owe to its influence.... A large part of the light and life, by which I see, love, and embrace the truths and strengths coorganized into a living body of faith and knowledge ... has been directly or indirectly derived to me from this sacred living volume" (8–9). Coleridge's method for determining the inspired verses of Scriptures thus relies on the subjective judgment of the reader, the affective authority of "whatever *finds* me," and yet he sets the Bible above other books precisely because it has been instrumental in creating its reader, the textual subjectivity who is now to be its judge.

Far from being simply a fault in the logic of the *Confessions*, this particular tautology is its indispensable basis. For the cycles of scriptural inquiry and response that constitute Coleridge's life as a Bible reader are the only possible means of apprehending the spirit of the text, not only because they provide a way of knowing that spirit, but also because they provide a way of creating it—or them, since there are actually two spirits at issue here, that of the reader and that of the text. The narrator of the *Confessions*, the "inquiring spirit" who relates this phenomenological narrative, generates with his textual meditations an invisible spirit, a reified alterity within the Scriptures, and this sacred textual alterity in turn produces him.[12] Consequently, the question of God's existence is irrelevant to the discussion, because the literary phenomenon at hand has a life of its own, whether or not its alleged author exists. In a sense, this alleged author of the Bible, the spirit in and of the text, is a fulfillment of the ideal author who, as Rajan suggests, is anticipated toward the end of *Biographia Literaria*, the author who would embody Coleridge's own displaced interpretive intentions.[13] Once an author anxious about his readers' receptions of his work, Coleridge becomes a reader confident in his ability to respond adequately to the divine intentions that purportedly consolidate his Bible. At the same time, spiritual existence—both of Coleridge's readers and of his God—has evolved into a thoroughly text-based phenomenon, one which is inseparable from the heuristic process of struggle and change that transpires between himself and his Bible.

As we have seen throughout this discussion, Christian life and history are for Coleridge imbricated with models of reading and interpretation. Indeed, this imbrication is so thorough, Coleridge's theology seems to imply that literacy is a precondition of full human subjectivity and spiritual existence. This is not to say that Coleridge excludes the illiterate or semiliterate from salvation; rather, his theology is composed of images and discussions of textual communication in a way that translates even the possibility of a nonliterate apprehension of divine truths into a rhetorical counterpoint to a textually mediated existence. Generally speaking, this is the case throughout his writings, and thus we find him in *Biographia Literaria* deferring to the semiliterate but emotionally eloquent writings of Jacob Behmen and George Fox, albeit in a fashion that puts their insights in the custody of their more sophisticated readers (1: 149–52). Working with these passages, one is tempted to say that the idea of knowledge that comes from the voice or is received by hearing supplies Coleridge with images of a reality outside literacy, a reality that generates the causes and origins of the series of mediations that comprise history-as-literacy. Such valorization of a pristine orality would place him in a familiar tradition shared by English Romanticism and Protestantism, one that has become quite visible to readers from Derrida's analysis of the logocentric premises within the Western philosophical tradition.[14] Coleridge's engagement with this tradition unsettles its dichotomy of voice and text, since he tends to project voices behind texts and texts behind voices in an ongoing series of superimpositions. Consider, for instance, the complex interdependence of word and text in the following passage, where he defends the necessity of oral catechism:

> To make the Bible, apart from the truths, doctrines, and spiritual experiences contained therein, the subject of a special article of faith, I hold an unnecessary and useless abstraction, which in too many instances has the effect of substituting a barren acquiescence in the letter, for the lively *faith that cometh by hearing* (Rom. 10. 8-17).... And here I mean the written word preserved in the armoury of the Church to be the sword of faith *out of the mouth* of the preacher (*Confessions* 63-64).

The oratory of the preacher resuscitates the lessons ossified in the scriptural text. At the same time, any priority thus garnered by the voice is undermined by the fact that what is spoken is also a substitute for what is written.

While the intricately woven rhetoric of these quotations blurs the distinction between word and text, they also convey the impression that Coleridge wishes to identify the spoken word with Reason, with a presentation of truth that precludes the interpretive and self-reflexive activity of the Understanding. This possibility is more apparent in a passage from *The Statesman's Manual*. Defending his thesis that Christian principles correspond to beliefs that are innate to the human mind, Coleridge invokes an image of spoken language:

> [The] great PRINCIPLES of our religion, the sublime IDEAS spoken out everywhere in the Old and New Testament, resemble the fixed stars, which appear of the same size to the naked as to the armed eye; the magnitude of which the telescope may rather seem to diminish than to increase. At the annunciation of *principles, of ideas*, the soul of man awakes, and starts up, as an exile to a far distant land at the unexpected sounds of his native language, when after long years of absence, and almost of oblivion, he is suddenly addressed in his own mother-tongue. (24)

Hearing, in this passage, is identical with knowing, with an inner experience of comprehension and certitude that is as fundamental to the believer as his or her unaided sight and native tongue. So forcefully does this image of visual and auditory conviction impose itself, we might momentarily forget that what is at issue is an act of reading. Thus, more accurately, hearing, in this passage, is a metaphor for reading, specifically for a kind of reading that is unlike reading because it leaves no space for ambiguity or uncertainty, for the gaps that are filled by interpretive mediation. And yet, as we have seen, the lifelong process of interpreting Scriptures, with all the errors, struggles, and capitulations that it entails, is the crux of Coleridge's theology. Indeed, agonistic interpretation—even in this scheme where the text always wins—is so fundamental to his experience of existence that his existence is arguably jeopardized without it. If Coleridge has difficulty reiterating the Protestant image of spiritual wisdom breaking in upon the soul with the clarity and immediacy of a voice being heard, it is perhaps for the significant reason that he eschews a wisdom that comes with such self-annihilating force.

The suggestion that Coleridge's sense of identity was fundamentally rooted in his reflections on literary experiences runs slightly counter to the emphasis in recent scholarship on Coleridge's anxieties about the psychological consequences of the literary life. Jerome Christensen and Susan Eilenberg portray *Biographia Literaria* as a narrative driven by Coleridge's fear that his biography is letters, that he owns no identity apart from the textual fragments which inhabit his memory. Hence Christensen argues that "Coleridge's injunction, 'be not *merely* a man of letters', should be taken literally in the *Biographia* as Coleridge's statement of his most literal fear" (31). This fear Christensen connects to Coleridge's ruminations on the problem of the will, which can be rearticulated as the problem of Coleridge's life; that is, whether or not "he can be the author of a life or must remain the writer in a biographia literaria, existing to himself and his reader only by records in himself not found" (120–21).[15] I wish to suggest that by the time of the *Confessions* Coleridge has transformed this anxiety into the grounds of a new ontological security, albeit one that is only as certain as the transcendental reality of his Bible. Based on the preceding readings of *The Statesman's Manual* and *Confessions of an Inquiring Spirit*, it seems that Coleridge's search for ontological security led him away from such internal interrogations and toward a reliance on the textual dialogue between his own "phantom" self and the displaced ontological immanence of God.[16] The deluge of letters that once threatened the self is organized into a canon and a method which elicit the constitutive resistances and affirmations by which the soul knows itself and is assured of its existence.

Scholars of Coleridge's prose works frequently claim that reason is the definitive capacity of the human psychology implied by his religious thought. Thus J. Robert Barth describes the Coleridgean man-God relationship as "the encounter between the Supreme Reason manifested in Scriptures and the human reason of the reader.... As the human imagination receives its power from participation in the divine eternal creative act, so does human reason receive power from the Supreme Reason" ("Coleridge's Scriptural Imagination" 139). In a similar vein, Anthony Harding observes that Coleridge wished to counter Protestant tendencies to make the Bible "the all-sufficient *ground* of Christian belief" by marrying the Bible to the reasoning Christian; the foundation of faith was thus "to be looked for in Reason, experienced first in the individual mind as the awakening of conscience, or the knowledge of a responsible individual will" (86-87). Without denying the significant importance that Coleridge allots to reason as a feature of human nature, we should note the recurrence of words which suggest the accompanying necessity of character flaws—the soul invoked in the *Confessions*, as we saw earlier, is marked by "infirmities," "sins," and "divisions." Because these flaws contribute to his soul's struggles with the spirit of Scriptures, and because such struggles are constitutive of identity, it seems that guilt as well as reason is a criterion of subjectivity and of the subject's credibility as an interpreter. After all, guilt and imperfection, as manifestations of the will, are those traits which, as Coleridge clarifies in the *Confessions*, unite the prophetic human authors with the modern human reader of the Bible. Moreover, they are, as we saw at the opening of this chapter, the traits which preserve the discrete identities of inspired authors, saving them from the ignominious status of passive and mechanical instruments—ventriloquists, instruments, or automatons.

The implication that guilt is a criterion of full subjectivity is certainly not alien to Christianity. By making the guilt of the human subject a fundamental aspect of his or her structural function in salvation history, the Christian tradition has always assigned a paradoxical importance to precisely that aspect of the human condition which it ostensibly seeks to eradicate. In Coleridge's narrative of Christian theology, the structural function of human imperfection becomes both psychological and historical. It ensures that the reading subject has a will (even as the destiny of that will is annihilation), and it ensures that the reading subjects of England, divided though they be in their sectarian interpretations, are in truth proceeding toward the teleological goal of revealing their essential unity, the unity presaged in this still imperfect dispensation by the ideals of the national church. Finally, the necessity of human imperfection in Coleridge's biblical hermeneutics calls into question the ontological status of the voice, not because orality eliminates imperfect interpretations, but because in Coleridge's inherited Christian discourse it often provides an imagery of perfect understanding. As we have seen, Coleridge's hermeneutics unsettles the premises of that imagery by equating the struggle of textual interpretation with salvation itself. We now turn to another event in 1820s London, one in which the epistemological priority assigned to the voice is accepted uncritically and transposed into melodrama. The privilege accorded to spoken illumination, as well as the impossibility of maintaining a separate sphere of oral communication within a highly literate culture, is powerfully evidenced by the glossolalia that overtook Edward Irving's London Presbyterian church.

The Return of Apostolic Gifts in 1831

Edward Irving has gone down in history as a promising Scottish preacher who was led into eccentric excesses by the millenarian furor of the early nineteenth century. In 1822, having procured the highly visible ministry of the Caledonian church in Cross Street,

London, Irving left Glasgow and the mentorship of the esteemed Dr. Chalmers for the city whose iniquities he abhorred, only to become, within a matter of months, the darling of what his friend and fellow Annandale native Thomas Carlyle acrimoniously called "fashion." Irving and Carlyle had become acquainted in Kircaldy, on the northern shore of the Firth of Forth, when between 1816 and 1818 they served as masters of competing schools. Their friendship and mutual respect survived several tests: Jane Welsh's marriage to Thomas after a failed romance with Irving; Irving's marriage to Isabella Martin, for whose intelligence Carlyle had little respect and Jane even less; finally, Irving's self-destructive fidelity to the glossolalists who emerged in his congregation, spurred on in their charismatic practices by his apocalyptic interpretations of the Bible. After Irving's death in 1834, Carlyle composed a brief memorial titled the "Death of Edward Irving," commemorating, amid acknowledgments of Irving's flaws, his voice.

The "Son of Thunder" Carlyle called him; as Chalmers's assistant, Irving had only modest success in the pulpit, but upon gaining the London appointment he began to nurture the idea that he would serve God best by developing a new mode of preaching (Carlyle, "Death of Irving" 319). Among the several hundred individuals who would come to the Caledonian church on Sunday mornings in 1823 to hear Irving's oratorical innovations were Coleridge, Godwin, Hazlitt, and occasionally the young Macaulay. For his sudden popularity Irving owed a large debt to George Canning, who in a Parliamentary discussion of church revenues mentioned Irving as an example of a poorly educated Scottish minister capable of remarkably eloquent sermons. A. L. Drummond, the most thorough historian of the Irvingite movement, quotes at length from witnesses who later praised the remarkable features of Irving's oral delivery; one attendant, for instance, described it as a "demoniac force" (49–51). George Pilkington, a former Deist, reported that he initially avoided Irving's sermons because he did not feel himself "sufficiently established in doctrine to resist the power of his eloquence" (13). In the spirit of prophetic chastisement, Irving was not easy on his London audiences, sometimes taxing their attention for several hours at a stretch. Perhaps this was one reason why his season as a pulpit sensation was short-lived. P. E. Shaw relates that Irving's popularity began to wane toward the end of 1823; but enough of his following remained, so in 1827 he moved to a new and larger church in Regent Square (16). Even during the height of his popularity, however, Irving had his critics. James Mulvihill has traced the debates in the London periodical press over the relative virtues and flaws of Irving's attention-grabbing style, quoting from a variety of reviews that took Irving to task for his theatricality, his artifice, his subordination of content to style, and his anachronisms (182–87). Mulvihill's argument, in conclusion, is that Irving became addicted to the public notoriety which he hoped to manipulate in God's cause. From this perspective, the later phenomenon of glossolalia in his church was "merely a grotesque reflection of the earlier celebrity" which he had enjoyed and, if only to his secret disappointment, quickly lost (190). More than this, the glossolalia was a grotesque exaggeration of the faith in the voice that Irving's oratorical practice reflected. The beginning of his London ministry was, in this regard, entirely in keeping with its conclusion, for the story of the Irvingite glossolalists exemplifies the convictions and conflicts of a spiritual epistemology that sought to prioritize the authority of the spoken word and, relatedly, of the gifted orator.

Charismatic oratory was a chief component of the Evangelical revival which swept Britain and the northeastern United States in the late eighteenth and early nineteenth centuries. However, conceptions of oratorical purpose and method were important not only to religious activities in this period but to literary and political activities as well. In Drummond's estimate, Irving was "the Romantic in the pulpit," well suited in his histrionics to counterbalance the prosaic tendencies that Evangelicalism had developed (53). The association of Irving with a movement primarily conceived as a literary one is surprising, given the political conservatism and biblical fundamentalism of his views, but it is borne out by one contemporary reviewer's observation that in Irving's sermons "St. Paul and Jeremy

Bentham, the Evangelists and the Sorrows of Werther, Seneca, Shakespear, the author of Caleb Williams and the Political Justice are mingled together in the same passage" ("Dr. Chalmers" 307). Possibly the appropriation of popular culture was what Irving had in mind as a new mode of preaching; if so, it is a surprising decision in two regards. One, after his drift toward the millenarianism of Henry Drummond's Albury Circle, Irving adopted a more rigid stance on the distinction between sacred and secular literature, espousing in at least one essay the classically Evangelical position that "the only book worth reading is the Bible" ("Facts" 761).[17] Two, the deliberate use of artifice—of carefully orchestrated rhetorical tropes and oratorical histrionics—is at best a problematic companion to the emphasis on divine inspiration in religious oratory. Drummond notes that Coleridge imparted to Irving his belief that the Preacher was equivalent to "the sensible voice of the Holy Spirit" (68). A beneficiary—perhaps a victim—of the aging Coleridge's loquacious company, Irving would no doubt have been privy to such idealistic paeans to his vocation as we have already observed in *Confessions of an Inquiring Spirit*, where "the written word preserved in the armoury of the Church" is "the sword of faith" that comes "*out of the mouth of the preacher.*"

But Coleridge himself was at times skeptical of Irving's ability to live up to this ideal. He wrote to his son Edward in 1823 that Irving was "certainly the greatest *orator* I ever heard," but then suggested that oratory proceeded from "mouth + windpipe," in contrast to eloquence, which came from "the brain + heart" (*Letters* 2: 726). Such a distinction is built upon the belief that good oratory proceeds from the reliable character of the orator in a way that is not distorted by the use of rhetorical artifice. One fact we must remember as we analyze the role of the voice in the Irvingite movement is that this dilemma did not obtain only in religious communities. Analyzing the importance of oratory to leaders of the American Revolution, Jay Fliegelman argues that public speaking was "reconceptualized in the mid-eighteenth century as an occasion for the public revelation of a private self. Such a private self would then be judged by private rather than public virtues: prudence, temperance, self-control, honesty, and, most problematically, sincerity" (24). Whether the reified source of knowledge was God or Reason, the ramifications for the orator were the same: the purity of his message was dependent upon a dissection of his conscience into sincere and self-serving urges. To what extent this issue concerned Irving is unknown; it certainly concerned, as Hair and Mulvihill document, the critics of his pulpit style. And the issue became accentuated in the phenomenon of the tongues, where Irving's congregation spontaneously created a social hermeneutic system for controlling the function of the self in their unique speech acts. This hermeneutic system evolved rapidly over a brief period of time; in order to understand it fully, we need to take up our narration from the first outbreak of tongues, which occurred not in London but in some Scottish villages—Port Glasgow, Fernicarry, and Helensburgh—all on the Clyde, northwest of Glasgow.

The primary account of what transpired in these villages in the spring and summer of 1832 is Robert Norton's compilation of the memoirs of James and George Macdonald. According to the Macdonalds' testimony, the spirit first paid a brief visit to Margaret Macdonald, then entered more forcefully into the body of her brother James, a shipbuilder who lived with Margaret and a second brother in Port Glasgow.[18] It is unclear whether the Macdonalds were acquainted with prophetic or charismatic theology. Drummond's records claim that prior to their charismatic experiences the Macdonalds were unfamiliar with Irving and were, moreover, oblivious to the subject of spiritual gifts (140). Rev. Robert Story, in contrast, claims that the Macdonalds had imbibed the ideas of Alexander J. Scott, Irving's assistant and a missionary to their region who had led some of the locals to pray for and expect the restoration of spiritual gifts to the church. Certainly Scott had sermonized in the region on the outbreak of "charismata" among the early Christians at Corinth (Story, *Memoir* 205). Significantly, both Margaret and James Macdonald spoke not glossolalia per se but some inspired and supernaturally powerful form of English. They also believed themselves to be experiencing a return of the charismatic gift of healing. These remarkable events occurred in their home; Margaret, from her sickbed, broke into a discourse of two or three hours "as if her own weakness had been altogether lost in the strength of the Holy Ghost." Upon hearing Margaret's heartfelt prayer, James Macdonald "*calmly* said, 'I have got it,'" and in this altered state commanded the immediate cure of his sister (Norton 58–59). The following day James wrote a letter to Mary Campbell, a friend and resident of nearby Fernicarry, who, like Margaret, was bedridden. Reading his letter, Mary felt certain sensations which she later described in a letter to her minister:

As I read, every word came home with power; and when I came to the command to arise, it came home with a power which no words can describe; it was felt to be indeed the voice of Christ; it was such a voice as could not be resisted. A mighty power was instantaneously exerted upon me: I felt as if I had been lifted from off the earth, and all my disease taken from off me at the voice of Christ. (Story, *Memoir* 207)

Not long after, Mary Campbell began to speak in tongues. Among her neighbors, she soon overtook the humble and retiring Macdonalds as the more popular religious sensation, receiving visitors from near and far into her home.

She believed her glossolalia to be language of the Pelew Islanders. Such divine expediency was necessary if Campbell, who knew none of their language, was to convert the Pelew Islanders before Christ's return. Rev. Story later called Campbell to account for never assuming a mission to the Pelew Islanders to put her gift to use (*Memoir* 213–5). Instead, she married a law clerk named W. R. Caird and became a member of Henry Drummond's millenarian social circle at Albury, Surrey. Surrey was a more appropriate destiny for Campbell than the South Pacific, since the participants in Drummond's Albury Circle, the school of apocalyptic prophecy that disseminated "The Morning Watch," were probably more impressed with her powers of speech than the Pelew Islanders would have been. Mary Campbell's link to Irving is more definite than Margaret or James Macdonald's. Prior to her encounters with the Paraclete, she had received pastoral visits in her home from Alexander Scott. He had encouraged her to read over the Acts of the Apostles with an eye toward the meaning of baptism "with the Holy Ghost." Campbell did, and as Irving later related, "by this young woman it was that God, not many months after, did restore the gift of speaking with tongues and prophesying to the Church" ("Facts" 756). It was also a fulfillment of Irving's own prophecy. Irving had, some time previously, imbibed the belief of his protégé Scott, and he had begun to encourage his London parishioners to pray for and expect the return of apostolic gifts.

Five features emerge from these accounts of the first glossolalists that became increasingly important in accounts of the later outbreaks in Irving's London parish. One, the tongues are highly contagious. Two, they are more likely to spoken by women than men and for the most part originate with women. Three, they are associated with a power stronger than the individual's will or body. Hence for both Margaret Macdonald and Mary Campbell, the spirit occasions a cure, and in Campbell's case it additionally overrides her initial effort to resist it. Four, the manner in which the tongues are transmitted and described suggests that the medium of the communication is more important than the message itself. It is an observation that should be obvious when discussing glossolalia that the power of speech is mystified to a point where comprehensibility is not only of secondary importance but even to a certain extent undesirable, since no legible message could be as momentous as the medium itself. This leads us to the fifth feature: in their accounts of the glossolalia and surrounding events, the participants dramatize the special prerogatives allotted to the spoken word in their religious tradition, frequently obscuring the role that literacy plays in their experiences. In Mary Campbell's account of reading the letter, for instance, the power of James Macdonald's written words increases to a point that can no longer be described in words, to an alinguistic pitch of intensity that Mary identifies as the voice of Christ. By the implication of her imagery, the voice is identified with presence, power, and noncommunicative language, and yet it is an inescapable fact that this voice is only imagistically present, that it is contingent upon the written words which, in Mary's mind, it overtakes. Hence the invocation of the superior status of voice to text is impeded by certain irrepressible evidence that speech and text are too commingled to separate.

Of relevance to these observations is the story of Mary Campbell's sister Isabella. Two years before Mary underwent her transformation, Rev. Robert Story published *Peace in Believing*, his account of the spiritual life of Isabella Campbell, who had died in 1829 after a prolonged illness. Between the two sisters there appears to have been something of a rivalry, and in part Mary's gift of glossolalia might have been an attempt to supersede her dead sister's reputation for spiritual wisdom and piety. According to Story, Isabella's local fame hinged on her inspired discourse. Blessed in her final illness with a rapturous power of speech, Isabella Campbell's conversations with private visitors to her sickroom gave them a "foretaste of heaven," the experience of "manifestations of the power and reality of divine grace" (Story, *Peace* 188). A striking feature of Story's descriptions of Isabella is his attention to the manner in which her speech registers on her body. Her powers of conversation, he reminisces, "tested her body, dissolving, relaxed, distracted through all its fibres—without some strong energy sustaining and preserving the coherence of its parts, it must have crumbled to its original dust" (180). While not, to Story's mind, an augury of the Second Coming, the transformed speech and countenance of his devout parishioner do strike him as a prefigurement of heaven, a foreshadowing, as he puts it, of "the transformation of us all" (188). The descriptions of Isabella's speech are quite similar to the brief account that Robert Norton relates of Margaret Macdonald's first encounter with the spirit. Both represent an extension into domestic spaces and female channels of the emphasis placed on preaching, one result of the religious revival of the period. Both accounts describe the stimulating effects of inspired speech and exclude the contents of such speech. But the descriptions of Isabella Campbell, juxtaposed to the experiences of her sister Mary, add a new dimension to our inquiry. They suggest that a driving force in the emergence of Scottish glossolalia was an escalating mimetic rivalry between claimants to the power of a holy word. If Irving preached a sermon that brought even unbelievers to his church, and Isabella Campbell carried out conversations that gave her interlocutors a foretaste of heaven, Mary Campbell outdid both by uttering the mediated voice of God, the audible and incomprehensible manifestation of his reentrance into the world.

That rivalry was at work in the manifestations is further evidenced in the way Irving attempted to impose order on the phenomenon once it spread to London. Careful to maintain a role for himself as the vehicle who had brought the people, through "the act of hearing," to a state of spiritual receptivity, Irving also acknowledged the "place in the divine economy" given to those chosen from the "faithful members of [God's] truth" to speak in tongues ("Facts" 760). A divine economy it was: after the reports of the Macdonalds' and Mary Campbell's experiences reached London, a coterie of similarly gifted individuals formed within Irving's congregation. In this group there were those who received the gift of tongues (glossolalia) and those who received the gift of interpretation (ermeneglossia). As is sometimes the case in communities that practice glossolalia, the two were distinct gifts, only on rare occasions enjoyed by the same individual. For Irving's congregation, the division of gifts among the participants ensured that, at least for a while, no one person could manipulate their importance. However, by Robert Baxter's account, the coterie of the gifted—a group of four women (Miss Hall, a governess to the M.P. Spencer Percival; Emily Cardale; Mrs. Mary Caird; and Lady Olivia Sparrow) and two men (Edward Taplin, a schoolmaster, and Baxter himself, a successful lawyer)—was, from the beginning, really possessed by the spirit of competition. In private gatherings, they uttered condemnations of each other "in the spirit" and staged dramatic manifestations of the favor showed them by the Paraclete (88–97). Initially the gifted only spoke in tongues outside church services, during morning prayer meetings, beginning with an utterance by Emily Cardale in the spring of 1831. Irving assumed the role of an investigator, interviewing those who experienced the gifts in an attempt to ascertain whether they originated in God, the devil, or the speaker's desire for personal glory. But the divine economy of power in the Regent Street congregation was slipping out of his control; in November 1831, Miss Hall interrupted Irving's Sunday morning sermon by running into the vestry in a vain attempt to "restrain" the spirit, but being in her soul no match for God's power she soon gave way to the strange sounds. Irving's subsequent interview with Miss Hall provides the source for the passage that appears at the head of this chapter. The *Times* reported the incident on November 19; after this, the tongues became a London spectacle, and Irving's fall from public grace was inevitable. Caught between the pressures of the charismatics and the church's trustees, most of whom found the tongues to be an embarrassing interruption of their Sunday worship, Irving had no choice but to disappoint one group or the other. In the end, it was the trustees he alienated. He decided that he could not in good conscience silence those members of his flock who declared themselves subject to divine visitations, and as a consequence the trustees brought him to trial before the Presbytery of London, which declared Irving "unfit to remain the minister of the National Scotch Church" (Hair 121). Along with his surviving core of followers, he arrived at Regent Street on Sunday, May 6, 1832, only to find the gates locked against them. Some months later, led now by the affluent politician Henry Drummond, the charismatic members of Irving's congregation secured a new place of worship in Newman Street. Irving's downward spiral in the unfolding power struggle of his church continued; summoned to appear before the bar in his home Presbytery of Annan, he was removed from the ministry of the Church of Scotland. He returned to Newman Street, now formally a Dissenting congregation that would eventually call itself the Catholic Apostolic Church. Even here, the upheaval in the divine economy of Irving's congregation continued, for soon the inspired voices were requiring the former minister's relegation to a less important status in the new church. Irving became a deacon, a subordinate to the church's apostles, and for the brief remainder of his life his importance to the congregation was shadowed by Drummond and the other glossolalists. After all, Irving himself, for all the powers of his speech, never spoke in tongues.

It is a remarkable story: a preacher who rises to success as an orator inspires in his listeners a more powerful form of oratory that eventually deposes him. The cultural work performed in these events is complex and various, and at this point I wish to review the several interpretive possibilities that we have touched upon thus far.

(1) *The tongues are a symbolic communication, almost to the exclusion of any literal communication.* Beginning with Irving's sensational sermonizing in the early 1820s, the mediation of God's word in his church is moving toward nonrepresentational language. In this regard, one objective of the various speech acts that contribute to the story of Scottish glossolalia is enchantment, and the degree of enchantment experienced by the various audiences is in roughly inverse proportion to the clarity and content of the messages conveyed. This is true, in increasing order, of Irving's sermons, which were frequently derided for subordinating substance to sensational delivery; of Isabella Campbell's dying discourses, which were described by Story in terms of their effects but not of their subject matter: and of Mary Campbell's alleged Pelew dialect, which was incomprehensible to those around her. Initially, the tongues are thought to be a gift intended to expedite the conversion of non-Christian populations by imparting to potential missionaries immediate fluency in foreign languages. By the time the tongues reach London, however, the gift of foreign fluency had been exchanged for the gift of a holy, private, and decidedly asemiotic dialect. Thus the Regent Street glossolalists abandon any pretense of speaking a human language in favor of the belief that "it is of the essence of the tongue that it should be unknown" (Irving, "Facts" 761). Of such importance was this belief to the glossolalists that when George Pilkington, a sympathetic listener, set out to prove that the tongues were in fact a pidgin of Latin, Spanish, and Greek—a fact no less miraculous, to his mind—the animosity from the congregation led

Irving to request his silence in the church (Pilkington 29). But human or divine, the tongues have surprisingly little to say. Both the messages rendered in English and those untranslatable to human ears convey little more than the idea that the end of the world is near, and this information had been circulating among the parishioners at least since the time of their minister's first involvement with the prophetic school at Albury. Hence it is not so much the content of the tongues that is important, but the simple fact of them. As speech acts, their existence is thought to instance the imminent apocalypse that they portend. They bring their hearers and their speakers alike into a state of altered consciousness that is itself a proof of the thing anticipated, and this symbolic aspect of the tongues eclipses their denotative elements.

(2) *The discourse of Irvingite glossolalia privileges the spoken word, but in order to do so it must obscure and supersede its dependence upon the written word, most significantly, that of the Bible.* In one of his letters to *Fraser's*, Irving defended the glossolalists' supernatural orality by positing an essential bond between the powers of speech and reason:

Speech is the manifestation of my reason; and by our capacity of uttering, and of understanding the words uttered, is proved the commonness, the oneness of that reason, in which many persons have their being. Now when Christ does occupy the place of my reasonable spirit, and with my tongue does express whatever I am capable of expressing, he is proved to be in me as truly as I am in myself. (*The Nature* 6)

Irving stands in line with his religious tradition's association of ontological immanence and intentional transparency with the spoken word. Words spoken obviate the need for interpretation, this passage suggests, since they immediately manifest meaning to a translucent and transpersonal human understanding. At the same time, the commingling of man and God is believed to occur in and by Christ's occupation of the speaker's two most essential traits, her voice and her reason.

The assigning of these qualities to the voice requires that the voice is perceived to have autonomy from texts; it also requires that the qualities of texts are, by comparison, belittled. We noticed in Mary Campbell's account of reading the letter of James Macdonald that Macdonald's written words were replaced by the miraculous apparition of Christ's voice, commanding Mary to be healed. In similar ways, the Irvingite faith that voices are more supremely divine than texts is everywhere evident in their self-representations: the tongues, as one speaker soon instructed, were never to be transcribed, since their meaning could only be distorted by any attempt at phonic representation. And yet, the glossolalia is wholly text-dependent, since the belief in a return of apostolic gifts depends upon interpretations of the Bible and on a reader's reception of divine election through the Bible. Thus most of the speeches given "in the power" are prompted by the recitation or reading of scriptural passages, particularly from Revelation. The dependence of the tongues upon the Bible is at odds with the desire for an oral transcendence of the text, a desire perceptible in the belief that the return of apostolic gifts marks the fulfillment of the Bible, the apocalyptic completion of its sacred narrative. By laboring to sustain this illusion, Irving and the glossolalists in effect reveal precisely what the logic of their religious discourse wishes to conceal—that the mediums of voice and text are, in their religious experiences, inextricably interwoven, and not distinct in any fashion that bequeaths greater ontological immanence, either of the self or of truth, to speech acts.

(3) *The power struggles within the community of glossolalists are to a significant degree driven by gender.* Thus far, I have primarily focused on the theoretical aspect of the glossolalia, its embeddedness within a philosophical and theological discussion of the relationship between truth claims and the medium of their transmission. But the glossolalia was also embedded in sociological conditions, and these, too, contributed to the tensions that were acted on in Irving's church in 1831–32. As I noted earlier, women dominated the movement from the beginning; the first London glossolalists were two women, Cardale and the governess Hall, and before the separation of the Catholic Apostolic Church, the female glossolalists con-

sistently outnumbered the males. The anticipated return of apostolic gifts in Irving's millenarian circle thus presented the women in the congregation with an opportunity to appropriate a religious authority refused them in most other aspects of church life. However, soon after the gifts first appeared in London, one of Irving's missionaries in the church forbade all tongues except those spoken in English. Since only a "brother" was, at the time, speaking English "in the spirit," this was tantamount to silencing the several sisters who were experiencing the gifts. That the gender of the glossolalists was at issue in the missionary's mandate became more evident when Irving intervened—not on behalf of non-English glossolalia, but on behalf of glossolalia by women. As Pilkington recounts, Irving cited 1 Corinthians 14, one of the critical Scriptures for the movement, which stipulates that women were required to keep silent in church. Arguing in rebuttal that it was permitted in other parts of Scriptures that women "should pray or speak under the influence of the Spirit," he declared that he "would not be guilty of quenching the Spirit by any authority vested in him." No sooner had he made this announcement to the gathering than "a Sister commenced in Tongue, and concluded with a beautiful exhortation in English" (Pilkington 8).[19]

It is a striking fact that the women glossolalists were unusually loquacious in incomprehensible inspired speech but less gifted in English inspired speech than their male counterparts and translators. This paradox provides a particularly succinct example of a pattern that we will encounter at several points in subsequent chapters: the Victorian ideology of gender dictates that women possess a greater degree of spiritual sensibility, but in ways that often disempower them despite the privilege. As the scholarship of Barbara Taylor and Deborah Valenze demonstrates, the history of women's contributions to radical and Dissenting branches of English Christianity during the late eighteenth and early nineteenth centuries is a mixture of seized ideological opportunities and patriarchal backlash. Taylor documents, as part of her account of nineteenth-century feminist socialism, the preponderance of women in chiliastic movements; Valenze chronicles the emergence of women preachers in the Wesleyan movement and the subsequent decline of female preaching.[20] In both instances, the emergence of women in roles of power within religious movements is assisted by certain ideological premises about gender—that women possess spiritual insights, that they are susceptible to strong emotions, that they are naturally inclined to be caretakers and nurturers, and that one of their appointed duties is the cultivation of moral sentiments in the family. And in both instances—in Taylor's history of female chiliasts such as Joanna Southcott and in Valenze's account of Methodist women preachers—the places that women carve out for themselves within religious communities are eventually reclaimed by male competitors. This is also true of Irvingite glossolalia, a movement that resembles the others in its socially marginal status no less than its extreme religious zeal. The power that the female glossolalists usurped from their oratorically gifted minister was eventually reclaimed not by the minister, who was strikingly humble in the face of his singly gifted female parishioners, but by various male claimants to the power: initially, by the vociferous glossolalist Robert Baxter; later, and more effectively, by Henry Drummond and the several male "apostles" who assumed leadership roles in the breakaway Catholic Apostolic Church. If glossolalia opened a space for female participation among the power elite of Irving's church, it was a space that was contested almost as soon as it appeared.

(4) *The discourse that surrounds Irvingite glossolalia is organized so as to protect the integrity of the phenomenon.* This fact is discernible throughout the textual record; in their account of the origins of the tongues, in their description of the experience of speaking in tongues, and in the divine logic they impute to the manner in which the tongues occur, the Irvingite glossolalists seem acutely aware of the need to deflect any possible notion that their glossolalia partakes of human influence and manipulation. Hence Irving, in a letter published in *Fraser's*, is careful to describe Mary Campbell's first experience as unmediated and unmanipulated by human agents. Mary had been under the religious guidance of a missionary, Irving reports,

but her illumination came while she was privately reading the Scriptures. And thus, Irving concludes, by taking "from our missionary the honour of convincing her, and from [Mary] the honour of having readily opened her ear to instruction," God devised that "man might have no hand in such a work" and reserved to himself "both the work of teaching her and inclining her heart to be taught" ("Facts" 756). Equally striking is the manner in which Irving posits a schism in the glossolalist's consciousness that prevents her or him from any subjective interference in the mediation of the divine word. The glossolalist, Irving insists, does not understand what she or he says in the power; even their interpreters, when possessed of the spirit, are not "edified" while they speak. Both those who speak glossolalia and those who speak ermeneglossia must be protected from their own understandings, so great is the temptation to intrude human upon divine manipulations of the voice possessed.

However, Irving is full of contradictions on this score. One moment he asserts that the tongues must conclude with "words intelligible ... in order that the end of all signs, which is edification, may be accomplished." But in the next paragraph he repeats his earlier claim that "the tongue would in no way serve the purpose of proving the Holy Ghost to be the speaker, unless it were unknown alike to the speakers and the hearers of it" ("Facts" 761). Devising a psychological model of the inspired that fills all the requisite needs is not an easy task, since these needs dictate that the speakers' identities are simultaneously overwhelmed by the spirit and left consciously intact.

Thus we return to the predicament observed at the opening of the chapter; for Irving as for Coleridge, inspiration must be at once grounded in the self and external to the self. In a sense, this predicament constitutes nothing less than the problem of faith, as articulated from a Protestant perspective: the source of spiritual illumination must come from outside the individual, but the proof and the purpose of spiritual illumination are a devastating transformation experienced solely inside the individual. As we saw previously,

Coleridge upholds the ego in moments of inspiration because of his desire that the inspired individual retain the attributes that constitute his individuality—his will, his reason, and his guilt. Likewise, while dissecting the psychologies of his divinely possessed parishioners, Irving insists that they preserve their egos even as they are seized by the Holy Spirit. In part, he does so for the strategic reason that such an interpretation shows both the overwhelming power of the spirit and the irreproachable character of the inspired—they did not wish for this honor: it was simply thrust upon them. But Irving is also motivated to make this insistence by principle, specifically by the principle that God respects the integrity of his creation. Thus he stipulates that the glossolalist "is not used as a trumpet merely for speaking through, but is an intelligent conscious creature, to be possessed in these his inwards parts and used by the Lord of all" ("Facts" 761). Irving reveals himself to be as solicitous as Coleridge toward the sacred necessity of "true agency"; at the same time, he is as embedded as Coleridge is in a religious discourse that recognizes such agency as a source of error, deception, and perversion. It is for this reason that he equivocates, as Coleridge did, on the question of whether the will is maintained in moments of great inspiration.

With this concern in mind, we might turn to a passage from *Biographia Literaria* that is particularly relevant to the subject of glossolalia. Chapter 6 is Coleridge's famous attempt to refute Hartley's materialist psychology, which understands the will to be an effect of the nerves, to be a phantom extension of the nervous system's complex activity. In the course of his refutation, Coleridge recounts the story of a German woman who suffers mental debility after a fever. Her symptoms are particularly intriguing to the pious members of her village, as her primary symptom is a spontaneous recitation of Latin, Hebrew, and Greek religious writings. Through the efforts of a young physician, however, her mysterious utterances are eventually traced to a natural source, a period in her childhood when she lived with a Protestant minister, a man given to reciting aloud passages from rabbinical texts and from the early church fathers (1: 112–13). The physician's discovery occasions not a cure but only an explanation; the point for Coleridge seems to be that the German woman has lost her will, her capacity to repress and organize her memories. Hence she exemplifies the perfect Hartleyian psychology, and hence, alas, she is mad.

Rather than ending with this indirect refutation of Hartley, however, Coleridge is moved to meditate on a tangential concern, an image of mystically retentive human memory. The German woman's case provides evidence, he concludes that "all thoughts are in themselves imperishable; and that if the intelligent faculty should be rendered more comprehensive, it would require only a different and apportioned organization, the body celestial instead of the body terrestrial, to bring before every human soul the collective experience of its whole past existence. And this, this, perchance, is the dread book of judgement in whose mysterious hieroglyphics every idle word is recorded!" (1: 114). Coleridge's German woman is, of course, a modified glossolalist in that her utterances are initially understood to be gifts from God, not words she has learned from a conscious application of her reason. Moreover, her strangely altered memory, even after it is revealed to have origins in natural sources, suggests to Coleridge the possibility of a "celestial organization" of mind which would, in the sheer power of its infinite recall, bring one to the brink of apocalyptic vision, a vision not unlike that of God.

In a similar vein, Irving's gifted parishioners were inspired by their minister's heretical teachings on the incarnation; the unconditional merger of God and man, so Irving came to believe, also worked in reverse, imparting to men and women the capacities of God—for example, the capacity to speak in the language of God, to speak in tongues. Irving's vacillations on the question of free will in his parishioners stem from a ramification of this heresy, for the collapsed boundaries between Christ and man made it possible, although still difficult, to imagine an individual who simultaneously possessed an individual will and a divine consciousness. Indeed, the wavering in Irving's discourse between imagining the glossolalists as possessing two separate identities, divine and human, or one divine consciousness that silences the human will, is a way of both approaching and backing off from the other possibility, which is that in glossolalia the human will can be transfigured into one divine. Coleridge, in his contemplation of the German woman, makes similar passes around and through these conclusions. The German woman of his narration acquires, in the absence of a will, a permanently altered consciousness that is a distorted prefigurement of the resurrected and perfected consciousnesses of the saved. Like the glossolalists, she anticipates, if only fleetingly, a celestial organization of mind that sees things before and after.

While the Coleridge of *Biographia Literaria* might be interpreted as a sympathizer, maybe a unwitting sympathizer, with the Irvingite faith that women and men in this world might partake of the "mind of Christ," might incarnate, if only in erratic seizures or neurological disorders, a godlike consciousness, Coleridge had by the 1820s tamed this inclination in his religious imagination. Possessed by a heterodox enthusiasm for the body, Irving began to dwell on the full embodiedness of Christ. Coleridge, possessed by a no less deterministic discomfort with mere bodily existence, shunned such ideas, not least because the difference between Christ and man—the latter embodied in his guilt; the former saved from guilt by a merely nominal embodiedness—sustained the dialectical structure of his system. In this way, as I suggested earlier, the flaws and sinfulness of Coleridge's Bible reader became an improbable criterion for his interpretive authority. For the Bible reader's awareness of his flaws and imperfections ensured that he occupied his designated role in salvation history, the role of an imperfect subject worked upon by the powers and persons of God.

Improbable, perhaps, but neither heretical nor without precedent: as Coleridge saw, it was necessary to preserve a qualitative distinction between the human subject and the perfecting alterity of Jesus, if only because (and this much he may not have acknowledged) Christ's projected alterity provided a displacement that purged and legitimated human interpretive authority. Similar perspectives could be found among Irving's parishioners: Robert Baxter, who both in and out the spirit was among the most outspoken of the Irvingite glossolalists, began to question his powers as he became suspicious of Irving's doctrine of the incarnation. After his final separation from the Irvingite glossolalists, Baxter wrote an exposé of the movement. Recounting his gradual disillusionment, he writes that his early doubts were only articulated while he was "in the spirit," at which time the spirit in him affirmed of Irving "he has erred, he has erred" (101). But soon thereafter, Baxter parted openly with his minister's teaching, and he returned to the belief that only man is sinful, not Christ. "What greater provocation can we offer to our Lord," Baxter opined, "than to debase him to the experience of indwelling corruption, and lift up ourselves to an equality with his purity, and the exercise of greater powers than himself?" At this point in his narrative, the grounds of his authority shift from his potential to share in the perfections of Christ to his condition as a debased man: "Nothing can show us our utter uncleanness but the glass of Christ, wherein by contrast we see our own deformity" (141). Significantly, there is also a change in Baxter's gifts of speech, which shift from displays of glossolalia to quite articulate denunciations of Irving. It is thus in his authority as a sinner, as a dependent upon Christ rather than a potential equal, that Baxter, now divested of any apostolic gifts, exposes the Irvingite phenomenon as a hoax, a work not of God but, as Baxter would have it, of the devil.

Thus the subject of the incarnation opens up another way of understanding Coleridge's and Irving's late Romantic, late millenarian encounters with problems of inspiration. Irving's anthropomorphic Christology worked, in the end, to collapse divine into human authority; Coleridge's more doctrinal formulation impeded this collapse by erecting a hermeneutic structure that depended on the Trinity as an escape from subjectivism. Because their differing conceptions of the incarnation require some further explanation, I will devote the concluding section to this line of investigation.

Coleridge, Irving, and Problems of the Word as Flesh

Years before the outbreak of tongues in Irving's church, Irving and Coleridge had been friends. Irving sought out Coleridge upon arriving in London; a few years later, he dedicated his book *For Missionaries after the Apostolical School* (1825) to Coleridge; and in the same year, Coleridge acknowledged his friendship with Irving in *On the Constitution of Church and State* (1830), favoring him with a comparison to Martin Luther (143n). But soon thereafter Coleridge began to distance himself from the younger man's growing millenarian concerns and, more emphatically, his teachings on the incarnation. In fact, what was true for Coleridge was also true for many members of the British religious establishments: their problems with Irving had more to do with the incarnation than the tongues. Despite the scandal occasioned by the glossolalia in his church, it was his teachings on Christ's nature, and not his endorsement of apostolic gifts, that brought about Irving's dismissal from his native Presbytery of Annan.

Although his opinions on the topic of Christ's body were no secret, forming the topic of many a sermon and essay in the late 1820s, it was Irving's 1830 book *The Orthodox and Catholic Doctrine of Our Lord's Human Nature* that won him the most attention on this score. As he had been arguing for several years, Irving here claims that Christ's flesh was not different from man's, that Christ during his mortal lifetime felt the full force of carnal temptations. Which is not to say, as Irving had previously tried to clarify, that Christ sinned, but only that he participated as fully as a sinless God could in the depravity of the human condition. Hence Irving exclaims that "Christ took his humanity...from the substance, from the sinful substance, of the fallen creature which he came to redeem," and the contrary thesis that "Christ's flesh was immortal and incorruptible, or in any way diverse from this flesh of mine ... is a pestilent heresy" (*Sermons* 1: vi–vii). To Irving's mind, it is the drama of the confrontation between "the will of the Father" and "fallen human nature"—a confrontation staged within Christ's body—that bestows meaning upon the incarnation.[21] The drama began in the womb of the Virgin, whose flesh provided the "substance" of her child's humanity even as the Holy Ghost abided there as well, inseminating the fetus with the invulnerable will that prevented Christ throughout his life from surrendering to temptations. As an account of Mary's pregnancy, it is a quite striking example of what Margaret Homans calls "the flight from the literal" that results in a denigration of the mother's body as a source of matter before it is dignified with figurative significance (20).

Coleridge dismissed his protégé's incarnational theories some time before the publication of *The Orthodox and Catholic Doctrine of Our Lord's Human Nature*. That he would take issue with Irving on this score is predictable, not only because of the heterodox resonance of Irving's ideas, but also because, as critics generally seem to agree, "Coleridge edged away from the human nature of Christ" (Boulger 181).[22] The marginalia in Coleridge's copy of a volume of Irving's sermons shows him attempting to correct the flaws in Irving's model by conceptualizing the incarnation along Aristotelian lines. Unlike ordinary human flesh, "the Organismus" of Christ, as Coleridge terms it, is the "representative Sign of that Body which [was] cleansed from Sin by him who [therein] had conquered Death & Sin" (*Marginalia* 3: 14). Christ's body is a formal cause, a signifier of the generic human shape animated by the divine spirit. This nascent thesis Coleridge returns to some pages later, where he suggests that Irving's errors could have been prevented if he had begun with "a cool analysis of the term Body ... not in its universal sense as matter filling space; but as the visible Organismus of living Creatures." The "Organismus," Coleridge goes on to say, is "a unity of positive and negative poles, of abstract form and constitutive elements....The real Object in instances of this class, is neither A nor B, nor both of them together; but it exists as *a unity*." Once "the copula or unitive act" leaves this body, as a body it ceases to be, leaving behind the somewhat different because disconnected matter of its "stuff or constitutive parts" (*Marginalia* 3: 42–43). Thus Christ's body, vacated by his divine spirit, is no longer properly speaking a body but a "carcass," because the body indicated in the idea of the incarnation is by definition a unity of flesh and spirit. No before or after exists for this body—no conjoining in the womb or posthumous separation of its matter and animating principle—but only its timeless manifestation as the form of the human divine. In this way, Coleridge dismisses Irving's image of Christ's body as an aggregate of human flesh and Holy Ghost with the counterimage of a body that cannot be dissected, either physically or mentally, into physical and spiritual aspects. For the spiritual aspect is itself a principle of unity that conjoins the two.

What is gained by Coleridge's correction of Irving's incarnational teachings is a little obscure; perhaps more to the point is what is at stake. For Irving, there is no difference in kind between Christ and humanity. Anything less than a full experience of carnal existence, so Irving feels, reduces Christ's body to a nominal status, which is precisely what Coleridge seems to have in mind in his many allusions to Christ's body as word and form. To Irving's way of thinking, such abstractions deflect attention away from the astonishing truth of the incarnation: just as the divine savior felt the yearnings of destitute man, so does destitute man possess the divine capacities of the savior: "The whole mystery of the incarnation is to shew to mortal man what every one of them, through faith in His name, will be able to perform" ("Facts" 757). In fact, the goal of creation necessitates Christ's participation in the fall, for if he was "a creature unfallen," how could he behold God's grace, insofar as "grace, and mercy, and forgiveness, do necessarily presuppose guilt, and offense, and hatefulness?" (*Sermons* 1: 11). One can hear in these words how Irving's audience might understand him to say that Christ carried the taint of sin, so fully does he conflate the spiritual path taken by Christ with that taken by the Christian pilgrim. Sin is lamentable but also necessary to the narrative of the encounter between God and man; the manifestation of God's love depends upon it. By pushing the idea of the incarnation in this direction—a direction so far Calvinist as to be anti-Calvinist, for it presupposes the essential degeneracy of the flesh even as it makes Christ a partner in the experience—Irving defined man as sinful but not abject in his sinfulness.

Moreover, he freed mankind of the need for a savior of a fundamentally different nature. Christ was demoted to a character who, in a strikingly Carlylean image, did "toil and sweat, and travail, in that mass of temptation with which I and every sinful man are oppressed" (*The Orthodox and Catholic Doctrine* 2).[23] From the orthodox perspective, there is a dangerous hubris in such an approach, and indeed Irving's sermons frequently turn from meditations on the humanness of Christ to expositions which, to varying degrees but with remarkable consistency, contemplate the deification of man.[24]

Whether or not it succeeds, Coleridge's countermodel of the incarnation is motivated by the desire to sustain the essentially different because divine nature of Christ's identity. But clearly that essential difference is under siege—as it would be throughout the century—and in his attempts to reinforce a distinction between God and man, Coleridge has to complicate his understanding of symbolism in such a way as to make the principle of the incarnation ascendant over its empirical occurrence. As a result, he compromises his usual preference for symbolism over allegory. That he would do so recalls the argument famously offered by Paul de Man, who demonstrates that despite Coleridge's attempt to enforce a distinction between symbols and allegory, the manner in which he relates both tropes to transcendental sources makes the distinctions between them less significant than their resemblances.[25] As Steven Knapp notes, echoing de Man's thesis, Coleridge's debate with empiricism stems from "the deeper and more persistent danger [that] lies in identity....The symbol must be saved by allegory from its innate gravitation toward the literal" (22). Likewise, Coleridge seemed intent on saving Christ from a gravitation toward the literal. He speculates, for example, that the idea of Christ's "flesh" served the purpose of distracting the apostles from the "visible Organs" of the Lord and drawing their attention to his true spiritual Body (*Marginalia* 3: 27–28). Such a notion reverberates with his earlier description of Christ's body as the "representative Sign" of a Body cleansed from sin. In both instances, the body of Christ is the sign of a sign—

not so much a body per se as a body that symbolizes the idea a body, specifically of a body that could be imbued with divinity. Thus Coleridge dispossessed his Christ of personality, flesh, and temporality so as to make him the reified figure of an impersonal and sacred perfection. A symbol personifying the excellence of symbolization, Coleridge's Christ signifies embodiedness to the exclusion of the traits that define a body, and in this regard he is another manifestation of what de Man identifies as the repressed allegory illuminating Coleridge's attempt to distinguish and valorize the symbolic.

While Coleridge shied away from the carnal body of Christ, he frequently explores metonymic figurations of the body and the book, of Christ and the word. Christ's body is figured as a textual physicality, a body that is best understood as the counterpart of a literary revelation. But here as well, the figural logic is unsettled by the body's contingency with sin. Thus, on the one hand, Coleridge identifies the word or logos with Christ, and as we know, this is an entity that he conceives as perfect throughout, uniformly imbued with the spirit of God. On the other hand, Coleridge often imagines the Bible as an all-too-human supernatural text. Returning to *Confessions of an Inquiring Spirit*, we find images of the body occurring in this text as emblems of the hermeneutics that Coleridge wishes to establish. A living but composite unity, the body is an image of the uneven way in which Coleridge imagines divine inspiration permeating the Bible. Not universally and uniformly divine, but rather a mediation of the divine through the languages of human authors who are moved by the spirit sometimes grandly, sometimes imperfectly, and sometimes not at all: this is Coleridge's Bible, a text as heterogeneous in inspiration as the human body is in composition. An important passage for this concern occurs in the third letter of the *Confessions*, where Coleridge details his metaphor of the book as a body:

Because the Doctrine in question "petrifies" at once the whole body of the Holy Writ with all its harmonies and symmetrical gradations,—the flexible and the rigid,—the supporting hard and the clothing soft,—the blood *which is the life,*—the intelligencing nerves, and the rudely woven, but soft and springy, cellular substance, in which all are embedded and lightly bound together. This breathing organism, this glorious *panharmonicon*, which I have seen stand on its feet as a man, and with a man's voice given to it, the Doctrine in question turns at once into a colossal Memnon's head. (31-32)

In effect, Coleridge here does to the Bible what Irving does to Christ, embodying it in the flesh, as a heterogeneous living entity.

Coleridge's preference for an organic Bible over an organic God is a choice in keeping with what we have seen of his growing faith in the hegemonic potentials of scriptural interpretation, his belated confidence that the Bible provided the necessary knowledge and authority for doctrinal and social organization. And yet, in this regard, as in so many others—the rise of popular fiction, the plausibility of a national church, the expansion of the reading public and of the electorate—Coleridge was a conservative battling the defining tendencies of the nineteenth century. If Christ could have a psychology—if his life could be described in phenomenological terms as an experience of temptation and an awareness of his own Godhead—once this avenue of speculation was opened to religious thinkers, the mystery of the incarnation was revitalized, and Christ became, in a newly importunate way, the unthinkable center of Christian theology. Certainly the Christ found in Strauss's work, as in Renan's and later Farrar's, was each a uniquely psychological portrait, uniquely interested in the phenomenological process by which a man comes to identify himself as God. Along these lines, Shaffer makes the following observations of an earlier generation:

As dogma was psychologized, the personal experience of religious feeling became increasingly important; and this personal experience had to centre on Christ. Yet historical and psychological rationalism made the primary matter of Christianity—the Crucifixion and Resurrection—repugnant to the young men of the 1790s. Their nascent mythological understanding told them inescapably that the vision of Christ was the fundamental experience of Christianity, and that their age was incapable of it.... Coleridge's own religious writings to the very end circle round and round the image of

Christ but never face it, and the "personeity" of God he could justify only by a tortuous and indirect argument. (59–60)

Indeed, the "personeity" of Christ was so charged an issue for Coleridge that he seems to have circumnavigated it altogether. As Jerome McGann argues of the older Coleridge's model of the genius, so with his model of Christ; he retreated from the vision of Christ as an individual, psychologically construed, and resorted instead to an image of Christ veiled by an institutional framework, an individual Christ constituted not by his psychic particularity but by his embeddedness in the transhistorical source of agency which is logos.[26] Thus Coleridge writes in the margins of his Bible: "Do we not fix our imagination too much on Christ, personally or individually, in the interpretation of these prophecies?—Is it not more often Christ in his *Church*? rather than Christ in his divinity?" (*Marginalia* 1: 434). It was an observation consistent with his disparagement in *The Friend* of "the age of personality."

Edward Irving was no sympathizer with progressive causes, either those of a political or a theological nature, but his very human Christ, his Christ who knew personally the power of sin and guilt, is a representative man of the anthropomorphic orientation of nineteenth-century thought. One might say of the debate between Coleridge and Irving that in a sense, Feuerbach cast the deciding vote, insofar as what was at issue in theological approaches to the incarnation was not so much the nature of God as it was the nature of man. Projections of the divine—as Father, Son, or Spirit—fueled in some sense by desires to conceive an other to mankind, to escape the insularity of nineteenth-century humanism, inevitably displaced the dilemmas of humanism onto these Gods.

Conclusion

Repeatedly in this investigation, we have encountered a tension between images of oral and literary communications of sacred knowledge. The manner in which this tension unfolds in Coleridge and Irving's conceptions of divine inspiration suggests that what is at stake is not the integrity of these modes of communication in themselves but rather the different models of agency which they imply. Coleridge privileges a literate mode of divine communication because the human ontology implied by his conception of the literary life is one of unfolding deferral. The dialectical exchanges that transpire between the spirit that writes and the spirit that reads the Scriptures displace hermeneutic authority from the reader's consciousness to his or her textually dependent process of becoming. Truth, in this model, is not immanent in speech or identity but is divided between a reader's engagement with the scriptural text and the correcting, ultimately annihilating, and always imperfectly known author within and behind the text. Irving, in contrast, attempted to sustain the privilege of speech as an unmediated manifestation of one's self and one's meaning. Truth and identity are inextricable in his model because the character of the speaker, presumably revealed in all the reality of his nature, is the proof of the integrity of the message, of its origins in a holy will that animates this visibly elect agent. While this conception of religious authority glorified the function of the pulpit in a manner that aroused some concern, once displaced onto the phenomenon of the tongues, the dependence of the integrity of the message upon the character and psychological experience of the messengers resulted in a crisis. For here the speakers (inspired by Irving's own teaching) erased the distance between their identities and that of Christ; they collapsed the divine message, its divine origin, and its chosen mediator into a single grandiose act of mystical utterance, a performance, in effect, of the irreducible authority of a glorified individual.

This chapter began by observing the paradoxical necessity both to preserve and annihilate the subjective consciousness of the individual inspired (as prophet, as reader, or as a glossolalist) by God. This necessity obtains both for Coleridge's images of literary inspiration and for Irving's descriptions of the state of inspiration suffered by those who speak in tongues. The reason for this paradoxical necessity is inherent in Christian epistemology, where the self is a battleground between a will vitiated by sin (a locus of consciousness that must be vanquished) and a soul that provides the only witness to God's mercy that matters (and this locus of consciousness must be preserved). It is in this regard that the changing landscape of early Victorian theology begins to take on an increasingly anthropocentric character, a tendency to contain religious and spiritual concerns within an expanded discourse of humanism.[27] Within this expansive humanism, guilt and godliness emerge as two salient and interactive conditions. While it is partly correct to say that guilt problematizes any claim to religious belief or knowledge, some of the late permutations of this Christian tenet in nineteenth-century religious culture actually press toward an inversion, necessitating guilt as a criterion of full human subjectivity, and spiritual perfection as its equally necessary alterity.

The need to regulate the powers of guilt and godliness results in interwoven models of interpretive agency as a social and as an individual construct. Coleridge's social map of Bible readers is complemented by a personal phenomenology of Bible reading that divides scriptural reception into acts of intellectual and psychological labor that at times corroborate and at times ignore social distinctions. Likewise, the seemingly individualistic claims to a special revelation made by the glossolalists in Irving's church were inspired, even in the opinion of some participants, not only by the Paraclete but also by a gendered and socially elaborate competition for religious privilege. But in both cases, the tension between an individualistic and a social model of interpretation is regulated by assignments of guilt. Coleridge's ideal Bible reader is certified by the inadequacy that he owns in the face of the perfecting spirit; at the same time, the perfecting spirit is arguably only a projected alterity created by and dependent upon his textual subjectivity. Irving's incarnational theories allowed his parishioners to relinquish their guilt, and, believing in their suitability for divine gifts, they produced a mimetic rivalry of revelations. Robert Baxter reclaimed his guilt and lost his gift of tongues, but the renewed abjection of his personality certified his denunciation of Irving.

Another and related thesis that has emerged in this study concerns the relationship between Christology and scriptural hermeneutics. Even as British Christians maintained the belief that the Bible should provide a source of social harmony, they utilized the incarnation in such a way as to acknowledge the Bible's inadequacy for this task. That this was a distinctly Victorian tendency is borne out by the fact Coleridge did not share it; he was the only nineteenth-century religious thinker to devise a scriptural hermeneutics which paid negligible attention to Christology. Indeed, the hard-won balance between the depth of his philosophical engagement with literature and his ability to endure a fairly high level of hermeneutic uncertainty demonstrates just how difficult it was to inhabit the parameters of a textual epistemology. For many Victorians, that difficulty was alleviated by Christology, a Christology that took several forms—debates over incarnational doctrine, interest in the imitation of Christ, the search for a historical Jesus, and representations of Christ in art and literature. Certainly, in the case of Irving, incarnational doctrines eclipsed the importance of other theological doctrines; in other instances (Ward, Arnold, Nightingale), this emphasis worked in such a way that Christ became a respite for the hermeneutic inadequacy of the Scriptures. In the next chapter, we will follow this dilemma as it develops in the life and legacy of one of Coleridge's most influential disciples, Thomas Arnold.

CHAPTER 2

Thomas Arnold and Spiritual Authority

On June 7, 1815, less than two weeks before British and Prussian troops defeated Napoleon at Waterloo, Thomas Arnold, then a recent graduate of Oxford, read the essay that had won him an English Prize to an audience in the Sheldonian Theatre. Looking ahead to the period of peace that would commence as soon as French imperial expansion was overpowered, Arnold envisioned the colonists of his own nation as men motivated by a benign wish to extend globally the influence of European culture and religion: "The Colonist shall appear, not bearing in one hand the sword, and in the other the Bible disfigured and polluted with the blood he has so plentifully shed: the sword shall be turned into a ploughshare, and the sacred volume shall light his path with its mild and unclouded radiance" ("Effects of distant Colonization" 29–30). At the time, Arnold's own future looked promising. He had just won, through the intervention of his mentor Whately, a fellowship to Oriel College, and his chances for a successful ecclesiastical career seemed favorable. There was little to suggest the less dignified employment as headmaster at a boys' school, but when events dealt him that fate he accepted it with the same ambitious idealism he had once imparted to Bible-bearing colonists. That idealism, with its emphasis on earnestness, honesty, and a balanced harmony of intellectual and physical pursuits, was the hallmark of the legend of "Dr. Arnold," the great reformer of English pedagogy, the Victorian savior of public schools.

In his own lifetime, Arnold was known not only as an educator but also as a preacher, a Liberal Anglican polemicist, and a historian who cautiously borrowed from German scholarship. The controversial nature of Arnold's beliefs and activities is reflected in Arthur Penrhyn Stanley's biography, *The Life and Correspondence of Thomas Arnold*, which was written two years after Arnold's premature death in 1842 at the age of 47. Stanley's biography is a tribute to a beloved friend written in a spirit of controlled grief. He elevates Arnold to the stature of a Christian hero, a principled individualist whose motives were threefold: to save the church by mollifying sectarian dispute, to save the Bible by providing it with a historical basis, and to save the intellectual dignity of Christianity by emphasizing God's moral principles over his alleged intrusions into the natural order. Such motives identify Arnold, as well as his biographer, as members of the Broad Church movement. While Arnold's legacy to the Broad Church movement included a biblical exegesis compatible with modern belief and an ethical code that placed Christian practice above Christian doctrine, his most important gift was that he provided it with a dead hero. For in the years after his death, Arnold was memorialized as a uniquely Victorian *imitatio Christi*, an example of faith translated into masculine Christian behavior. One generation after Arnold's death, many of the social reformers and colonial agents of Victoria's reign might still envision themselves—as Arnold had envisioned them in his prize essay—as foot soldiers in a forward-moving history, but the book under their arms could as well be secular literature as the Bible. It could in fact be Stanley's best-selling biography, which passed through six editions in the first three years of its publication history. The popularity of Arnold's biography reflects the paradox of his life's work; his efforts to reinforce the Bible's centrality contributed more forcefully to its diminishing importance.

In the following pages, I will offer an account of this particular instance of Victorian secularization, the Arnoldian trajectory from Bible to biography. The chapter will begin with a description of the intellectual environment in which Arnold carried out his studies of history and Scriptures. I will discuss how Arnold's use of German historical criticism worked to dehistoricize Scripture by condensing its narrative content into synchronic, divinely ordained principles of behavior. This ethical condensation of the Bible was alien to English Christian traditions on two counts: it disqualified the importance of biblical narrative, and it employed methods that often led to religious heresy and skepticism. Both for himself and his audiences, Arnold sought to overcome these resistances by deploying national stereotypes. He conceived of Germans as racial kin of the English, superior in intellectual achievements, but lacking the inclination toward social and practical activity that protected the English from heresy and skepticism. Consequently, Arnold's approach to the Scriptures—foreign as they might have been to the majority of early-nineteenth-century English Christians—became an important force in Victorian culture precisely to the extent that they were filtered into an image of the English national character. Within this image, moral acumen and piety, traits purportedly strengthened by the study of biblical principles, were sustained by a healthy love of pragmatism and social intercourse.

In part, Arnold's concern with national stereotypes was an externalization of his ambivalence toward the internal effects of reading, his simultaneous faith in the critical spirit and his disdain for the psychological effects it may have. To his mind, devotion to the scholarly life entailed a careful negotiation among malevolent influences, not only of German rationalism but also of Newmanism, the chief domestic nemesis. In the pedagogical philosophy of the new Rugby School, Arnold modeled a regimen for living that might control these threats; early exposure to modern critical methods was tamed by bracing physical activity, and the introspective excesses of theological inquiry were tempered by the higher claims of team spirit.

However, the communal coherence that worked so well at Rugby was more difficult to initiate at the national level, where conflicting religious, political, and social identifications created a more heterogeneous society. The second section of the chapter will recount Arnold's attempts to find sources of religious harmony for a nation separated by sectarian alliances. In the years following the First Reform Bill, he argued that the Established Church should take a more flexible approach to the 39 Articles of Faith. But the 39 Articles were a particularly disastrous place to test a nonprescriptive approach to religious language because their very importance hinged upon the doctrinal implications of their syntax and diction. One way in which Arnold hoped to correct this problem was by increasing the number of scriptural words and passages used to articulate church doctrine. Such hope only served to underscore the problem, which was that texts, biblical and otherwise, were inherently insufficient to the interpretive demands—for doctrinal, ethical, and political truth claims—placed upon them. Faced with growing evidence of this insufficiency, Arnold began to advocate, in his subsequent sermons and lectures, the belief that right interpretation depends less upon a spirit in the text than upon the spirit in the reader. In this regard, his lifelong efforts to incorporate history and theology into a mutually corrective hermeneutics led him to the uncomfortable and only obliquely acknowledged conclusion that the ultimate source of interpretive authority is the moral integrity of the interpreter.

Thus, although he wished to reinforce the Bible's role as a cornerstone in English society, Arnold's experiences pointed him toward other conclusions. What the Bible could not provide in the way of ideological coherence was sought elsewhere, and for Arnold the desire to allay sectarianism led to the image of Christ. Increasingly in his last years, his hope for a source of religious solidarity moved from sacred literature to the incarnation, from biblical exegesis to the worship of Christ. The conclusion of the chapter will discuss this emphasis in Arnold's beliefs. The irony in this case, I will argue, is that in the years after his death the proponent of Christ worship became himself the object of a more secularized worship. The readers and reviewers of Arnold's biography elevated him to the status of a revered character, an earnest reader of the Bible who courageously put his interpretations into practice. As a biographical embodiment of the moral revelation that he gleaned from the Bible, Thomas Arnold enacted for Victorian readers the validation of his own interpretive claims.

Much of the information and some of the ideas presented in this chapter will be familiar to Victorian scholars. My rationale for repeating a familiar story here is to bring that story to an argumentative conclusion, which is that the case of Dr. Arnold exemplifies a larger nineteenth-century tendency to locate cultural authority in individual character. Hence this chapter is both a review of the intellectual history of one man's life and an inquiry into the cultural functions performed by that man's biography. For Arnold's textual remains are accessible only through the mediating history of what Victorian society did with those remains, which was to pose the manly Christian hero as a social remedy. The concerns of the previous chapter were also situated in this context, insofar as Coleridge's scriptural hermeneutics was fueled by a desire to shore up a cultural and social organization threatened by the divisive and democratizing forces of heretical biblical interpretations and cheap literature. As in the case of Coleridge, the case of Dr. Arnold instances a pattern wherein religious sectarianism is resolved initially by an appeal to communal scriptural reception. Faced with the absence of any sound objective locus of scriptural interpretation, Arnold resorted, as Coleridge had done before him, to the testimony of the reader's virtuous subjectivity. In *Confessions of an Inquiring Spirit*, Coleridge's search for a means of separating inspired from human scriptures led him to conclude that a Bible reader is qualified to judge the sanctity of a given passage insofar as he or she is the psychological product of Bible reading. Dr. Arnold's reputation exemplifies the extent to which many Victorians were willing to accept a similar remedy by judging theological authority on the basis of personal character. Thus while Arnold sought to displace the source of religious unity from the Bible to Christ, from the text to its incarnate supplement, those who revered his memory moved in a more quintessentially Victorian direction. They supplemented Christ with Arnold, the consummate manly Christian whose image became one source of social unity within a discourse of religious nationalism.

Selective Philology: Arnold's English Adaptation of German Influences

By the mid-1830s, the Higher Criticism in Germany had produced investigations of both Testaments that cumulatively dismantled the supernatural framework of traditional biblical interpretation. By comparison, biblical studies in England were undeveloped, and in fact had regressed since Robert Lowth's work in the eighteenth century. The work that was done in England, although vast in quantity, was usually constrained by theological premises. There were exceptions, however, both inside and outside the Established Church, most notably Coleridge, but also Herbert Marsh, Edward Pusey, Connop Thirlwall, Julius Hare, and Samuel Davidson, all of whom at various times in their lives undertook a rigorous study of German biblical scholarship, both rationalist and pious.[1] In addition, British lay and clerical readers alike might gain some familiarity with the Higher Criticism by perusing the essays on comparative philology, historiography, and biblical studies that appeared in the *Quarterly Review*, *Fraser's*, and the *Edinburgh Review*. German intellectual superiority in these fields was something of a stereotype; as an article in *Fraser's* proclaimed in 1849, "the Germans are the civil engineers of the intellectual world" (Conington 200). But German obscurity was also a stereotype; writing in the *Edinburgh Review*, Henry Rogers called Strauss's work an "allegorico-metaphysico-logico-transcendental 'formulae' of the most obscure and contentious philosophy ever devised by man" (372). Rogers's deriding Strauss exemplifies a widespread tendency to avoid the influence of German scholarship by retrenching behind the claims of English linguistic and theological purity. For several decades, conservative English commentators had tried to demonize Continental philosophy by associating it with the demise of English political, sexual, and religious norms.[2] The actual political affiliations which accompanied the stereotyping of the intellectual character of nations are complex and mobile, but within the England of Thomas Arnold's early career, the German Higher Criticism was associated with the theoretical underpinnings of a heretical and socially threatening variety.

It was thus for a partially xenophobic reading public that Arnold sought to increase the traffic in literary commodities between England and Germany, primarily by popularizing the ideas of the man widely recognized as his chief intellectual mentor, Barthold Georg Niebuhr, often called the "father of modern ancient history." It was through Niebuhr's *Römische Geschichte* that Arnold familiarized himself with comparative philology. Central to Niebuhr's approach was a modified Vichian or "developmental" model of parallel historical and linguistic epochs, according to which poetry belongs to the childhood of a civilization, drama or noble language to its young manhood, and prose, the medium of critical analysis, marks its maturation into national adulthood.[3] The pervasiveness of the developmental model, even apart from any immediate connection with Vico or Niebuhr, is evidenced by the frequency with which British writers—Peacock, Macaulay, Blake, and Carlyle among them—alluded to it as an explanation for the perceived shortcomings in their contemporary poetry. Niebuhr gave this paradigm a nationalistic flavor by arguing that unique national idioms and linguistic characters develop within the larger cycles of historical epochs and literary periods. And Arnold, having fully imbibed Niebuhr's maxim that a nation expresses its epistemological stage of development in its dominant literary genre and linguistic idiom, modified the developmental model of history for English readers in his own *History of Rome* (1838): "It appeared to me that [Niebuhr's] discoveries and remarkable wisdom might best be made known to English readers," Arnold explained in the Preface, "by putting them into a form more adapted to our common English taste" (vi). Niebuhr's theses encouraged the construction of nationalistic models, and consequently Arnold's employment of his work, even in the beginning, tended towards the reification of English cultural habits and modes of thought.

In writing his adaptation of *Römische Geschichte*, Arnold drew upon the nine-year-old English translation by Connop Thirlwall and Julius Hare, two men whose knowledge of German thought outstripped Arnold's.[4] Possibly the need to adjust Niebuhr to "common English tastes" was suggested to Arnold by the critical reception of Thirlwall and Hare's translation, which was chastised in the *Edinburgh Review* for advocating the notion that classical texts could be better understood by modern critics than they had been by their ancient authors (Hogg 393). As the reviewer quite accurately intuited, Niebuhr's critical method subtracted something from the notion that ancient texts were hallowed depositories of knowledge. From a philological standpoint, the truth within them was highly dependent upon the historian's interpretive analysis. For Niebuhr and his followers, Hare and Thirlwall among them, this shift in emphasis was not a pedantic issue; it led them to embrace philology as a symbol of the new historiography. Philological analysis forced the classical scholar's attention to the internal structures of words and the empirical nature of texts; more important, it invited a heightened self-consciousness about these methods, about the various ways in which scholars mediated between historical records and their representations of historical reality. Thus presented, comparative philology signaled an epistemological alteration wherein history had become the master discipline, the organizational frame of reference for literary, linguistic, and ethical constructions of knowledge. As Julius Hare suggested, "Philology, in its highest sense, ought to be only another name for Philosophy" (*Guesses at Truth* 430). For the contributor to the *Edinburgh Review*, this suggestion might have corroborated his fear that the modern critics were less solicitous of a wisdom identified with ancient authors than they were of a wisdom identified with their own methods.

If Niebuhr was perceived by traditionalists in England as a challenge to the dignity of the classics, he had a slight advantage over German critics such as Schleiermacher in that he did not directly challenge the dignity of the Bible. This may have been one reason why Thirlwall, Hare, and Arnold devoted so much of their energies to studying, translating, and publicizing Niebuhr's work. They were English scholars who had educational and professional affiliations with the Established Church, and Niebuhr's status as a classical historian buffered public suspicions and private doubts that attended the philological analysis of sacred history. Arnold tried to keep a cautious distance from the German "Rationalists" even as he argued that the lessons of scientific history were crucial to modern Christian faith. By ignoring the Higher Criticism and focusing instead on a German treatment of Roman history, Arnold perhaps thought that he could engage German scholarship while avoiding its disconcerting ramifications for his faith. In effect, he resorted to the safety of an ancient distinction between sacred and secular literature. But in the nineteenth century such distinctions were tenuous at best. Indeed, the notion of separate realms for sacred and secular traditions was untenable from any position in German scholarship, where the collapse of sacred into secular literature, as in the case of Herder, had been a fundamental tendency of the modern criticism from early on.[5] Arnold's discussions of the Bible make clear that he, too, was uncertain about the feasibility of this distinction. The fragility of the Bible's sacred status haunted him as he was writing the *History of Rome*, and, while translating Roman legends, Arnold became concerned that he was echoing the diction and rhythms of the King James Bible. Seeking advice, he wrote to his friend John Taylor Coleridge: "In trying to write in an antiquated and simple language, that model with which we are most familiar will sometimes be followed too closely; and no one can deprecate more than I do anything like a trivial use of that language which should be confined to one subject only" (Stanley 318). When Coleridge returned the first chapter with the judgment that the legends did indeed resonate with the Authorized Version's English, Arnold acknowledged that Herodotus and the Bible sounded alike because both belonged "to a particular state of cultivation, which all people pass through at a certain stage of their progress." But rather than pursue the relationship this implied between Scriptures and ancient legends, Arnold decided to take Chapman's Homer as his model for translating the Roman legends. As he responded to Coleridge, "That would be the best and liveliest way of giving them, and liable to no possible charge of parodying the Bible" (Stanley 320). Against the historical method that associated the books of the Bible with primitive stages in the march of civilization, Arnold could pose no better barrier than a willed aporia. Confining biblical language "to one subject only" was a difficult order to obey, given the blurred distinctions between sacred and secular literature that historical analysis produced. And Arnold himself, despite the piety of his motives, helped discredit these distinctions.

Arnold's inadvertent desacralization of the Bible was a consequence of his advocacy of "accommodation," a form of biblical exegesis practiced in some circles of British theology for a long time, but which found in Arnold a new and impassioned spokesman. Seen from the perspective of accommodation, both scriptural revelation and its interpretations evolved with the passage of time. God did not elevate the human authors of Scriptures to a flawless divine vision; instead, he worked through their epistemological limitations, "accommodating" revelation to what could be assimilated at any point in history into the prevailing climate of belief. Revelation, seen in this context, refers not to a mystical presence in the natural order but rather to the distribution of a Christian moral economy through humanity's evolving thought forms. The sacred content of the Bible is equivalent to the timeless moral principles that a modern historical exegete can discern beneath narratives composed by morally and intellectually less mature societies. In this light, the Bible becomes "the history of God educating and edifying mankind" ("Essay" 476), and the violent temperament displayed by God in the story of Abraham and Isaac, or of the extermination of the Canaanites, is explained by "the principles on which these commands were given, and their reference to the moral state of those to whom they were addressed" (Stanley 121).[6]

The Bible, like all epochal works of literature, is thus construed to obey the developmental rule of history. And consequently, although accommodation prescribed a resolutely historical interpretation of Scripture, in the end it worked to dehistoricize revelation, transforming the Bible into a collection of historically determined documents. The Bible's typological fabric and narrative continuity were at once unraveled and reconstituted as moral laws. What English men and women might thus gain in the way of a scientifically credible text was somewhat offset by the loss of a good story.

As is well known, the challenges to traditional scriptural hermeneutics posed by historicism and philology were compounded in the early nineteenth century by the geological treatises of Werner, Hutton, and Lyell. Had these forms of knowledge been the only forces at work in early Victorian reconsiderations of biblical authority, the Christian ascendancy in Britain might have disintegrated long before the impact of Darwin was felt. But what the Bible lacked in historical and textual credibility was compensated for by the sentimental devotion of its readers. Thus the Authorized Version (A.V.) survived several calls for revision in the nineteenth century because of the widespread feeling that the diction and syntax of the King James verses had through the generations become an organic component of the English people.[7] With some reservations, Arnold shared this feeling. His own plan for a cheap Bible proposed only modest corrections of the A.V.'s faults and obscurities, since he considered it necessary to replicate, if only for sentimental reasons, "as closely as possible the style of the old translation." At the same time, however, he intended to forgo the canonical arrangement of books so as to publish first "the more important parts of the New Testament," along with the Psalms and some of the Prophets. Some of the historical books, in contrast, he wanted "to publish last of all, as being the least important" (Stanley 185). Syntax and diction appealed to a lingering Protestant sense of readerly divination, but the Bible's traditional narrative order was dispensable. This separation of language from chronological order represents a second paradox in Arnold's search for a new locus of scriptural authority: the attempt to place the Bible "on a firm historical basis" resulted not only in its reduction to a set of behavioral principles but also, and more surprisingly, in a concentration of the Bible's sacred power into smaller units of signification, the language itself. As we shall see later, Arnold's faith in the power of the King James's English instilled in him a short-lived hope that religious sectarianism could be allayed by a doctrinal deference to the words of Scriptures, construed as the interpretively indivisible elements of God's truth.

If Arnold followed popular tradition in ascribing a sentimental privilege to the language of the A.V., he did so with a complex set of attitudes toward the ramifications of such textual piety for the ministry. His notion of clerical privilege was built on the belief that the historical and scholarly aspects of the Scriptures did not intrude upon their universal affective appeal. In this way, Arnold implicitly delineated levels of Bible reading along class lines in a manner consonant with the social hermeneutics laid out by Coleridge in *The Statesman's Manual*. Both Coleridge and Arnold maintained that the important work of gleaning historical understanding from Scriptures was an activity best suited to the Anglican intelligentsia. In contrast, the basic sentiments of Christianity, so they believed, were available to all readers who approached the Bible with a pious and earnest heart. Arnold, however, seems to have anticipated more strongly than Coleridge did that the new methods of biblical exegesis would remove the Bible from its traditionally central role among all classes of British society. As if to counteract this tendency (which his own scholarly approach so obviously encouraged), Arnold broke from Coleridge by suggesting that piety and religious sentiments alone could qualify a man for the ministry. This belief was consistent with the paradoxical confluence of intellectual elitism and religious liberalism in his Broad Church beliefs. Although the methodology of Arnoldian "accommodation" seems to concentrate authority in the hands of a well-educated minority, Arnold in fact respected not only the need for a more inclusive Anglican ministry but also the claims of most Protestant sects to a relative degree of autonomy within their own ministries.

The safeguards that underwrote this embrace of an expanded ministry were the same ones that underwrote Arnold's embrace of rationally inclined German scholarship. They included a belief in the superior virtue of "well-roundedness" over academic excellence and a belief that the national English male character was a paragon of balanced physical and mental skills. Thus in Arnold's outline of preparation for the ministry, the new kinds of knowledge were elicited along predictable lines, recommending the study of philology and antiquities rather than theology as aids to the Scriptures (Stanley 229). Even with less reading, however, he was willing to concede the potential for a beneficial ministry: "A man may do immense good with nothing more than an unlearned familiarity with the Scriptures, with sound practical sense and activity, taking part in all the business of the parish, and devoting himself to intercourse with men rather than books" (Stanley 361). Modest scholarship was the lesser of two evils, since the other—presumably rigorous scholarship—could lead to forbidden intellectual pleasures that were akin to "forbidden animal pleasures." This source of danger linked, in Arnold's estimate, the demographic catastrophes foreseen by Malthus with a potential epidemic of depression, or "mental infirmity" ("The Bible" 153–54).

For this reason, in the pedagogy he developed at Rugby School, Arnold maintained that "well-roundedness" was a necessary antidote to the potential excesses of reading and scholarship. As Ruth apRoberts observes, Arnold feared the notion of excessive or "imbalanced" intellectualism; the powers of contemplation, he believed, became "impaired or perverted" when made the main employment of life (60). Likewise, Bruce Haley suggests that Arnold's relegation of academic skills to a tertiary level of importance (behind both moral excellence and gentlemanly conduct) betokens ambivalence rather than outright anti-intellectualism, since Arnold insisted on the necessity of an informed and maturing mind for the attainment of good character (145) Consequently, Haley assigns Arnold a central role in the Victorian tradition of conceiving mental health as a register of both physical and moral attributes. Such alignments of physical with religious well-being became a common trope in the writings of the religiously angst-ridden 1840s generation. James Anthony Froude observed the absence of "vigorous employment" in the habits of the quasi-autobiographical protagonist of his novel, *The Nemesis of Faith*, concluding that "it is as idle for the mind to hope to speculate clear of doubt in the closet, as for the body to be physicked out of sickness kept lying on a sofa" (vi). Haley determines that such assumptions stemmed from the relative clarity of physical as opposed to psychological self-knowledge, and that for the obscure condition known as spiritual backsliding, the language of physical health provided a tangible means of description and measurement (256). In addition, the ideological inflection of this alignment of physical and spiritual health coded as masculine a communal ethic (to sports, games, physical activity, business, and public duty) that was perceived to operate as an antidote to the self-absorption and asocial interiority supposedly fostered by the scholarly life.[8]

Arnold extended the characteristics associated with the Rugby ethos into a national or "racial" basis of defense against the heretical tendencies of German scholarship. In his belief that national characters carry distinct intellectual propensities, Arnold was again following in the footsteps of Niebuhr, for whom the study of race (as a national or cultural ethos rather than in its late-nineteenth-century quasi-biological sense) was a crucial component of historical understanding. Martin Bernal, in his study of the ideological underpinnings of classical studies, suggests that Niebuhr's study of antiquity was a way of providing national *bildung*, of corroborating Germanic essentialism "and so promoting the fatherland" (302). The integrity of the nation was grounded in the integrity of race, and the concept of race, with its significant Romantic genealogy, was the guiding premise and "first principle" behind Niebuhr's scientific historicism (Bernal 305). Arnold, who emphasized in his Oxford lectures on modern history the importance of "national personalities," determined that the national personality of the English made them naturally disinclined to the religious skepticism that elsewhere accompanied modern criticism. For the English people, with their predilection for outdoor activity and healthy physical exertion, would find in such activity a faith-preserving balance of mind and body. Thus although the English and the Germans belong to the same race—one that is not Greek, Roman, or Jewish—the English national character was immune to the theological "infections" that beleaguered German theologians (*Introductory Lectures* 44). Or, as he elsewhere puts the case, German literature and theology are pervaded by "a spirit of restless inquiry," while in England "critical and metaphysical questions have but small attractions," and thus "we have little to fear from the evil of indulging in them to excess" (*Principles* 116-17). In a passage in "Early Roman History," one which exemplifies the assumption that certain types of intellectual behavior are pathological, Arnold states that "we cannot be surprised that the energies of the Germans have been turned more towards thinking than acting; and that their understandings are tinged with that fanciful idealism for which a practical acquaintance with mankind, and with the concerns of real life, are the only remedy" (399). By contrast, as he goes on to explain, the conditions of life in Great Britain—geographical mobility, social intercourse between the classes—are more advantageous to the development of "intellectual and moral excellence" (399-400).

However, Arnold's concluding point in this essay is to chastise his countrymen for failing to fulfill their great potential, a failure that has resulted in the comparatively abysmal state of letters in England. In the competitve market of European ideas, the English lag far behind the Germans, Arnold laments, but not because of any "external disadvantages ... or want of natural intelligence" (400). A gentle and on the whole optimistic reproach, the essay reflects Arnold's discomfort with the anti-intellectualism of his countrymen, a discomfort that he dwelt upon more emphatically in his private correspondence. The advantages which, in the above essays, he attributes to the English character are here counterpointed by his perception of its disadvantages. Among the "characteristic faults of the English mind" he lists "narrowness of view, and a want of learning and a sound critical spirit" (Stanley 373). The ambivalence toward scholarly activity that Haley observes in Arnold's pedagogy is thus one version of an ambivalence toward intellectualism that Arnold also expressed in his conception of national characters. In both cases, the rubric of divided human traits—divided in the several proposed and amended curriculums for Rugby, divided in the comparison of behaviors, skills, and faults among European nationalities—fuels Arnold's faith in an ideal combination of traits, a perfect admixture that will form a society of great men.

In this discourse the celebrated sports tradition of Rugby found a higher level of validation, for the development of habits that countered reading with activity and social responsibility was the cornerstone of an ideal and as yet unachieved national character that could preserve religiosity while accommodating it to modern systems of belief and social mission. The scholars J. R. de S. Honey and C. L. R. James argue that the priority assigned to sports in the newly emergent public-school system was unfaithful to Arnold's belief that athleticism should complement but not replace academic study.[9] But the schoolmasters who made this transformation were faithful to the nationalistic if not the pedagogical side of Arnold's thought. By elevating team sports to the status of a master discipline in the school curriculum, they demonstrated themselves to be astute readers of Arnold's anxieties and his remedies for those anxieties. They put into practice the Arnoldian definition of the ideal English temperament, wherein religious, intellectual, and emotional health all hinged on daily physical and communally oriented activities.

Thus, for Arnold, what marked the proper English Christian man was neither his doctrinal conviction nor his scholarly acumen so much as his team spirit. The diffuse religiosity of Rugby graduates—"Arnold's youths," as Newman ruefully called them—was protected by the comfort of social and ideological cohesion. And indeed, Arnold's vision of a society united by a biblically based moral code, a national self-consciousness, and a millennial social goal worked at Rugby in large part because the social group was small and fairly homogeneous. The intellectual fragility of the Arnoldian brand of Christian faith is perhaps attested to by the religious destiny of Arthur Hugh Clough, who no sooner found himself at Oxford than he found himself thrown into an agonizing struggle with the 39 Articles. But then Clough might also serve as an example of the resilience of Arnold's emphasis on the practice of one's faith, no matter how tenuous and indistinct. For, as we shall see in Chapter 5, Clough died, by some reports, a willing victim of Florence Nightingale's exhaustion of him in the cause of medical reform.

In the early 1840s, Arnold conceived of his pedagogy (and its products) as the antithesis to the theologically "perverted" concerns and habits fostered among Newman's circle. Where Newman inspired a male esprit de corps built on devotional practices and the scholarly resurrection of patristic teachings as a means of defending the High Church from hostile Whig legislation, Arnold inspired a similar male fellowship united by a practice that would defend its members against heretical evils such as Newmanism. What must be remarked, however, is that the Arnoldian remedy for spiritual malaise resembled the Tractarian remedy for political disaffection in that both assumed the form of a community of men connected by strong emotional bonds. This was true in spite of the ideologically charged differences of religious and gender traits associated with the two antagonistic groups, and indeed, although Liberal Anglican perceptions of the Tractarian "perverts" cast them as antithetically other, a conflation of religious morbidity and male effeminacy, the instability of the divide between Tractarian and Rugby men is attested to by the similar instances of spiritual psychodrama and homosocial to homosexual relationships within the subsequent generations of both movements.[10] In every aspect of the discursive history of Arnold and many of his followers, what we perceive is a perplexing slipperiness of national and sexual terms of identity: Arnoldian nationalism is at times a defense against German agnosticism, and at other times, and increasingly, a defense against an internal Catholic threat; a male community organized around sports codes itself as masculine and calls the one which fosters spiritual introspection feminine, although neither femininity nor masculinity precludes the development of same-sex love relationships in each group, in spite of the growing homophobia directed most publicly at Newman over the course of the next three decades. The one stable axis of this discursive network is the perception, sometimes implicit, sometimes explicit, of spiritual introspection as a bad habit, one that is fostered by excessive or ill-advised reading, aggravated by social and physical inactivity, and results in dangerously anti-English behavior—the embrace of either European indifference to religious authority or of the authoritarian structure of the Catholic Church.

For a culture avowedly based on the belief that liberty was fostered by literacy, and most significantly by biblical literacy, this attitude carried the curious ramification that the behavioral effects which Liberal Anglicans symbolically associated with Bible reading—stable gender traits, honesty, patriotism, fraternal and familial devotion—were of more consequence than the meanings divined in close personal reading. More precisely, the meanings that could legitimately be divined in close personal reading were contained and predetermined by the behavioral effects that Liberal Anglicanism symbolically aligned with the scriptural text.

The Latitudes of Diction in Christ's Kingdom: Arnold and the Social Crisis of Biblical Interpretation

In the mid-1830s, Arnold became a polemical participant in the debate over church reform. The successful passage of the Reform Bill in the spring of 1832 ushered in a period of contentious reevaluation of the Church of England. Pluralities, nonresidencies, "heaped" endowments, and church tithes lent momentum to Dissenters' complaints and also crippled the church's efforts to hold its own against the considerable conversions that had been won in recent years by Methodists, Baptists, and Congregationalists. When Lord Henley, Peel's brother-in-law, presented a daringly extensive proposal for church reform in 1833, Arnold responded with his own more daring proposal in a pamphlet titled *Principles of Church Reform*. Arnold directly broached the larger issues which the other proposals (of which Henley's was only one) were gingerly trying to sidestep. He argued that unless the government initiated a comprehensive revamping of the Articles of Faith, the looming alliance of godless radicals and religious dissent would tear asunder the beleaguered Established Church.

Despite the sense of emergency under which he wrote, Arnold expressed hope that the Established Church could be saved if it broadened the terms of its inclusion by relaxing its rituals and ecclesiastical constitution (*Principles* 129). To a certain extent, the problems of sectarianism turned on the Articles of Faith and the interpretive constraints that they placed on certain scriptural passages. Thus Arnold observed that "although all Christians allow the Scriptures to be of decisive authority," a multitude of problems rendered the Scriptures inadequate to such demands. The inherent ambiguities and corruptions in the biblical text "prevent the Scriptures from being in practice decisive on controversial points," and consequently "the contending parties, while alike acknowledging the judge's authority, persist in putting a different construction on the words of his sentence" (82). One solution, Arnold suggested, would be to articulate the main principles of faith in a manner at once concise and conciliatory. At critical junctures in the 39 Articles, where schismatic opinions might undermine the catholicity of statement, a controlled indeterminacy would ensure compliance: "It is most important, both for the sake of truth and charity ... [that] the statement should be general and should adopt no technical terms whatever in declaring doctrines, beyond such as may be used in Scriptures themselves" (*Principles* 114). Since the words of the Bible have an incontestable authority, while at the same time harboring meanings that cannot be clearly adjudicated, it is best to quote them without gloss, in the perfect opacity of their being.

The privilege accorded biblical diction in *Principles of Church Reform* might be seen as an extension into the political realm of the privilege accorded words by philology in its archaeological approach to texts. However, Arnold's retrenchment behind a sacralized and indeterminate biblical language recalls his deference not only to the scientific methods of Niebuhr but also to the English sentimental attachment to the language of the King James translation. Hence, the hopeful solution posed by *Principles* instances a confluence of scientific and sentimental faith in an imminent truth of the written word. But the essay also marks the end of Arnold's faith that any such truth could be translated into a political consensus. Inured by the sectarian conflicts of the 1830s and 1840s, he was forced to acknowledge that even the most informed analysis of biblical language could not decisively arbitrate between conflictual interpretations. In 1841, Arnold admitted to John Taylor Coleridge that based on his twenty years of biblical study, he did not think the Bible could meet the doctrinal demands made of it, for "there are passages in the Scriptures, which no man can interpret ... others of which the interpretation is doubtful; others again, where it is probable, but far from certain" (Stanley 420). And yet, he lamented, "Newmanites like Unitarians are desperate to get more authority out of Scripture than it will furnish, and to do so by elevating Church and Tradition to the same level of authority as Scripture" (Stanley 563). Elsewhere, in the same vein, he commented that "there is no infallible authority in points of grammar and criticism, and yet men do speak confidently, notwithstanding, as to learning and ignorance." On the basis of this confidence, men deprived each other of property and called each other insane, Arnold observed, even though the appeal to an authority for doing so always led to earlier authorities, a process that threatened to "run on forever" (*Tracts for the Times* 278). In short, the search for an infallible textual authority was an infinite regress; it could never arrive at a point of origin.

In the later years of his career, Arnold subjected not only scriptural but also historical texts to more exacting questions. The answers he found for these questions had troubling ramifications for the possibility of basing truth claims on any form of literary representation. For instance, in his 1838 sermons on prophecy, Arnold sketched out an approach to prophetic Scriptures which devolved unwittingly into a hermeneutics of character. The first sermon begins by suggesting that there are two levels of meaning in prophetic Scriptures—one conveyed in "the language of history" and the other in "the language of prophecy." Whereas the language of history provides empirical detail and literal clarity, it is fraught with moral confusion; the language of prophecy, on the other hand, makes clear God's moral intentions, but by doing so it distorts the historical record. To resolve this dilemma, Arnold suggests that the prophetic passages must be read in light of their historical counterparts, and historical passages must be morally illuminated by prophetic ones. In this way, the exegete might fix his attention on "principles, on good and evil," rather than the vast particularities of the historical record ("Two Sermons" 93).[11] However, it is unclear if Arnold considers history or the Bible more trustworthy; moreover, it is unclear how the reader following Arnold's advice is to know when to treat prophecy as a text that illuminates history and vice versa.[12] Implicitly, it is the interpreter's wisdom and character that qualify him to oversee the mutually corrective process of the dialogue between the languages of history and prophecy.

The emphasis which Arnold was willing to place upon the authority of character increases in his 1842 lectures on history, delivered after he was appointed Regius Professor of Modern History at Oxford. Arnold informed the audience of his Oxford lectures that history is not "sufficient to the right understanding of itself," a situation that would lead to despair if it were not for the fact that the necessary "laws are deducible from the Bible" (*Introductory Lectures* 385–86). And yet, as we saw above, Arnold believed that exegetes can only deduce such laws from the Bible if they employ history as a corrective. Apparently aware of this dilemma, Arnold develops the resolution that was implicit in the sermons on prophecy. He supplants the authority of both Scriptures and history with an *ad hominem* appeal; religious and historical meaning are to be validated by reference to the character of the interpreter.

I would like to focus more carefully on this moment in the *Introductory Lectures on Modern History*. The lectures begin and conclude with discussions of how the astute student can infer a dead writer's character from his text. This concern echoes a premise of Romantic hermeneutics—namely, that an author's character is the key to both his literary intentions and his credibility. But even in the most cautiously executed study he can imagine, Arnold admits that the relationship between written texts and the events they record is "infinitely disputable," for no two readers will reach identical conclusions about either the events recorded or the author who recorded them. At this point Arnold turns, once again, to the stable reference point of biblical principles, but now with a new distinction: subjective differences of scriptural interpretation are dismissed on the grounds that the Scriptures "do not so much teach [plain moral notions] as suppose [them] to exist in us" (385–86). Hence the crisis of uncertainty that resulted from Arnold's descriptions of prophetic exegesis and historical study is resolved with the pronouncement that biblical principles are a matter not of communication or readerly acquisition but of a priori psychological fact; the Scriptures cannot teach God's principles but can only confirm them in hearts where they already exist. The locus of religious truth is in this moment displaced from the imperfect language of the Bible to the perfect heart of the reader.

By situating the ultimate arbiter of scriptural meaning in the phenomenological process of reading, Arnold repeats a movement which Coleridge made in his later religious writings, specifically in *Confessions of an Inquiring Spirit* and *The Statesman's Manual*. Like Coleridge, Arnold avoids subjectivist conclusions by identifying the beliefs inspired by "right" reading with an infallible linguistic transmission. Where Coleridge aligns the annunciation of principles with the soul of man responding to his "mother-tongue" (*Statesman's Manual* 24), Arnold claims that the "Holy Ghost, author of all good desires, speaks in a language no honest mind can mistake" ("The Bible" 157). A difficulty for both Arnold and Coleridge was to reconcile this highly personalized approach to the reception of biblical truth with a political ideology that posited (as a goal or an ideal, if not a reality) a seamless identity among the nation, the national character, and the religious principles espoused by the state church. Paradoxically, both Coleridge and Arnold employed this problem as its own remedy, rhetorically substituting an ideal reader for the truly contentious and divided Bible-readers of British society. In effect, they expunged the individual whose fictional presence they simultaneously invoked as the anchor of transpersonal truth claims.

One way to understand this paradox is through the importance that both Coleridge and Arnold attached to the metaphorical organization of visible and invisible realms. For Arnold, allegiance to Niebuhr's scheme mandated the construction of a "national personality" out of the analogical elements of "race, language, institutions, and religion" (*Introductory Lectures* 43). Arnold's historical method thus relied on the logic of analogical structures, but the continuum stopped short of admitting the individual as a significant link in the structure. Singular personalities played a negligible, even a detrimental role in his historiography. As Rosemary Jann observes, Arnold assumed that a historian's proper articulation of a country or a civilization's "racial identity" was most readily reached through the study of national history and not of historical individuals (63). Attention to "personal character" was a relativist pitfall in the quest to "shore up permanent principles" (29).

The similarities with the later Coleridge are as important as the differences. While both Arnold and Coleridge espoused principles as the unflagging goal of an enlightened theology, Coleridge pushed the relationship between permanent principles and their particular manifestations beyond a simply analogical level. Instead, he posed the symbolic as an instance of metaphorical reality that mystically preserves particularity even as it "enunciates" a universal unity which exists both beyond and within particular manifestations. Here there is no space for misunderstanding, either as a result of textual flaws or linguistic imprecision, for the symbol is both "consubstantial" with the truth and the vehicle of its transmission. In twentieth-century literary theory, Coleridge's definition of the symbol is often divorced from the context of biblical hermeneutics in which it occurs. But in its original formulation, Coleridge proposed the symbolic as a description of a specifically biblical mode of representation, one which supported his argument that the representation of events in Scriptures is superior to that in secular histories such as Locke's and Hume's.[13] His imagined antagonists, however, were not only secularists but also British Christians, whose disputes over scriptural intentionality undermined the Bible's credibility as a source of social cohesion. Against religious sectarians who insisted on the allegorical significances of the Bible at the expense of literal meaning, and against those who insisted on literalism at the expense of allegory, Coleridge posed his definition of biblical symbolism as a third possibility which reconciled and transcended—if only imaginatively—those antagonistic camps.

Within the chain of signifiers that comprised Arnold's analogical history and Coleridge's symbolic history, individualism was recognizable only insofar as it corresponded to general and theologically allowable principles. While this point pertains primarily to the human individuals represented in historical or scriptural texts, any glance toward the early-nineteenth-century social environment and its politically volatile British reading public suggests the desirability of extending the same logic to the human individuals who interpret historical and scriptural texts. Both the interpretive act of signifying with a book and the representational act of signifying within a book are transformed by the metaphorical organization of Coleridge's and Arnold's theories into acts of individuation that are only recognizable as such insofar as they are consistent with preconceived truth claims.[14]

By a different route, we have reached a conclusion similar to that of the previous section: within the Broad Church philosophies outlined here, the category of the Christian individual is constrained by the criterion that healthy individualism is representative of certain general rules of thought and conduct ascribed to the Bible. And yet, at the same time, the importance of Christian individualism within these philosophies is dramatically increased. For character becomes a form of religious proof; in the absence of indisputable certainties within the scriptural text, the Christian character fills the need, paradoxically reflecting back a coherent set of principles on the Bible, the church, and the nation. A uniquely Victorian twist on the doctrine of the incarnation, the Christian character who manifests biblical principles is the incarnation of a word that is itself inadequate to the task.

Conclusion: The Worship of Christ and the Worship of Arnold

As we have seen, the combined thrust of Arnold's scholarly and political opinions pushed him in two directions: on the one hand, toward an indeterminate hermeneutics that accommodated a variety of doctrinal opinions, and on the other hand, toward a hermeneutics of character that reflected his growing dissatisfaction with the limited kinds of certainty that were possible in matters of textual interpretation. And yet neither a hermeneutics of indeterminacy nor of Christian character provided the ideological coherence that Arnold and fellow churchmen wished to derive from the Bible. Consequently, given the problems that attended his work on behalf of religious harmony, it is not surprising that in Arnold's later years the source of his religious hopes shifted from textual matters to the worship of Christ. As a communal ritual, a revivified Christology became in Arnold's mind the last chance for religiously harmonious British society. Thus he proposed attention to "the person of Christ" as a proper cure for the "idolatries of [Newman's] Oxford Judaizers" (Empson 27), and he wrote with fervor of the necessity to make "human society one living body, closely joined in communion with Christ, its head" ("The Church" 12). In the worship of Christ, Arnold hoped to popularize a cultural practice that could happily circumvent the divisive issues of the church's doctrines, priesthood, and legal prerogatives.

However, a community defined in its unity by Christ worship created some obvious social limitations. The extended boundaries of Arnold's imagined Kingdom of Christ became all the more intransigent at the borders, which included only those who acknowledged Christ's divinity. Thus Arnold maintained a lifelong antipathy for Unitarianism, which did not acknowledge the incarnation, just as his political liberalism stopped short of removing Jewish disabilities. Worship of Christ was for Arnold the one licensed act of unrestrained Protestant adulation, the one form of worship free from the Catholic and "heathen" evils brought about by idolatry: "[Christ] alone cannot be made an idol, and cannot inspire fanaticism, because

He combines all ideas of perfection, and exhibits them in their just harmony and combination" (Stanley 279). In the absence of an articulation of faith free from ideologically divisive ramifications, Arnold resorted to a more pragmatic approach, proposing a kingdom of God composed of male worshipers and emulators of a Christian God's son.

As we have seen, apart from Christ, Arnold did not concern himself with the agency of exemplary individuals, either in his historiography or in his pedagogy. Of greater importance to him were the forces of society—of networks of interdependence and of communal personalities, whether those of races or the Rugbeian tradition, which he fondly called "our great self" (Stanley 62). The various turns in his thought are always based on the precept that the purpose and inclination of such a self are to develop toward perfection. If there is a tension in the philosophy that he bequeathed to Victorian England, it lies in a discordance between the two models of "the self" which he invoked. For while the Rugby model distributes character traits across a social spectrum, the Christological model concentrates them in a replete but singular individual. Two points should be made on this issue. First, any evidence of inconsistency in Arnold's ideas comes as no surprise: he was not known as a methodical thinker, and even a commentator as biased as Clough describes him as "too intensely, fervidly practical to be literally, accurately, consistently theoretical" (Woodward 3). Second, Arnold's Christology was informed by centuries of theological tradition that cannot accurately be reduced to a simple diagnosis. Thus in his own sermons, his frequent and entirely traditional invocation of the church as Christ's mystical body diminishes the tension between an individualist and a communitarian Christian practice; the symbolism of Christ's humanity is presumably coextensive with the symbol of Christ's body as an aggregate of his human followers. However, once disseminated into the larger climate of Victorian ideas, Arnold's Christology was forced into a more characteristically Victorian rubric. In the works of his followers and descendants, the dual emphases on Christic imitation and Christian community became an occasion for negotiating the conflict between an individually and a socially construed identity—between, in Carlylean terms, the goal of heroism and the practice of hero worship.

One follower who makes such negotiations is Thomas Hughes. The extent to which Arnold's notion of a socially aggregate personality permeated the attitudes of second-generation Arnoldians is attested to by *Tom Brown's Schooldays* (1857), where no one schoolboy is complete without the complement of the entire group. Tom Brown contributes boyish enthusiasm and physical skill, while George Arthur contributes gentleness and academic responsibility—together with the characteristics supplied by other schoolboys they create the Rugby team, a communal embodiment of the well-rounded and victorious male character. *Tom Brown's Schooldays* memorializes a harmonious community of young men; as fiction, the plot is driven by the various vignettes of boys' life that inculcate the obedience upon which such communal life depends. Some years later, Hughes published a devotional handbook, *The Manliness of Christ* (1879), part of his attempt to extend the nostalgic male community of his memory to the working classes, this time in the recently formed Young Men Christian's Association. Here he presents Christ as an object of emulation for working-class men and a paragon of divine virtues which no devout person can properly aspire to equal. The irony of such conflicting advice was not lost on Richard Carlile, who a generation before had invited his working-class readers to consider the senselessness of a theology which simultaneously exhorted them to imitate "the perfect man" and to accept themselves as subordinate and inherently inadequate creatures (434). Hughes certainly avoids any like-minded audacity in *The Manliness of Christ*. In a sense, he had already come to his own resolution with the conflictual impulses of worship and emulation in his earlier work, *Tom Brown's Schooldays*. Or, rather, he had come to accept the dilemma by extending it to one of Christ's superhuman emulators, Arnold himself. The headmaster in *Tom Brown* is an unseen, felt force, seldom actually present in the scenes of the novel. He is, like the Christ of Arnold's Gospel, the mystified center of the schoolboys' socially cohesive worship and a consummate authority who is, paradoxically, both a role model and an inimitable paragon of individual virtue. To the extent that both *Tom Brown's Schooldays* and *The Manliness of Christ* yearn for a male community bonded by a code of behavior that is enforced by the absent center of an idealized leader, the two are parallel texts. But the earlier text is the more heretical: *Tom Brown's Schooldays* blasphemes the Arnoldian Gospel by abandoning its Christological emphasis; instead, it appeases Victorian desires for salvific human heroes by heroizing Arnold.

Hughes was not the only second-generation Arnoldian to work with the three topoi of Thomas Arnold, schooldays, and Jesus.[15] A more successful attempt is the elegiac "Rugby Chapel" (1867). Here Matthew Arnold presents his father as a type of Christ, the member of a special legion of humanity whose work it is to renew hope among the flagging lines of a race that has been marshaled, willingly or not, into a positivistically conceived March of Time. The poem embellishes Thomas with some distinctly Christological epithets—Arnold as a Good Shepherd, Arnold as a son of God—but his sole salvific power is that he reminds the members of the quasi-mythic band of their responsibility for one another. Thus Matthew preserves his father's belief in a communal ethos, but bastardizes it by incorporating a paean to the exemplary Christic individual. Thomas Arnold exists in historical memory as a figure who tried to steer Victorian society away from individuation, from the attachment to personal beliefs which fuel sectarian conflicts. For unless all are saved, none are saved: "Factions divide them, their host/Threatens to break, to dissolve./—Ah, keep, keep them combined!" (lines 180–82). Ironically, the hero who insists on the peremptory importance of communal ties is also the only figure in the poem who appears to have a self-sufficient strength of character and resolve: it is Arnold's band of followers who suffer from a sense of incompleteness. This incompleteness is indicated by the poet's extension of his personal experience of loss and decay to society as a whole: "Sadly we answer: We bring/Only ourselves! we lost/Sight of the others in the storm" (lines 117–19). In this way, the unity of the poem's visionary army—which at once signifies Rugby, England, and humanity—is predicated on its shared awareness of inadequacy, and its shared dependence upon the chastisement and encouragement of a superman. While Arnold himself had resisted the Carlylean tendency to make exemplary individuals the driving forces of history, Arnold's followers, his son included, were not faithful to that particular cause.

"Rugby Chapel" and *Tom Brown's Schooldays* share with many of the other nineteenth-century texts that commemorated Arnold this significant feature: the cultural functions which, in his lifetime, Thomas assigned exclusively to Christ are, after his death, displaced onto his own public memory. For example, one reviewer of Stanley's *Life*, William Empson, performed a more or less direct apostasy of Arnold's beliefs by suggesting that Victorian society needed "the spectacle which [Arnold] has obtained for us—that of men of a hundred different opinions bowing down in reverence before his Christian life and noble nature" (190–91). Likewise, an essay in the *Quarterly Review* concludes its comments on Stanley's biography by noting that the inspirational effect of Arnold is only understandable to those who possess "something of the spirit of an apostle" (Lake 508). Rather than the socially cohesive symbol of Christ, these essayists celebrate the socially cohesive symbol of Arnold, the manly Christian individual par excellence. In a similar vein, a review of one of Arnold's works published in the *British and Foreign Review* soon after his death ascribes to him the functions of a role model. "We should regret the flaws in our own workmanship," the essayist concludes, "if we could hope that we have inflamed any one to reverence and emulate the excellencies of [Arnold]" (Blackett 397). The reviewer for the *Gentleman's Magazine* also details the commendable features and effects of Arnold's "single-hearted, upright, and conscientious" character, all of which goes to explain "the attachment and veneration which attended the mention of Arnold's name among his pupils and friends" ("Life" 339–40). Continuing the celebration of Arnold's biography as a cultural memorial, an essay in the *North British Review* lauds Stanley's work for revealing the dignity and uprightness of Arnold's "inner life." For it is in Arnold's private habits, the essayist states, that we see "the purifying and healing influence of his character" (Maitland 404).

The popularity of Stanley's biography was great enough to inspire a spin-off biography, condensed to one volume, by Emma Jane Worboise. With Worboise's biography, based as it is on another biography largely composed of letters and diary entries, the layers of textual mediation between readers and Arnold have become quite dense. But in the case of Arnold, as often in the case of Christ, the very inaccessibility of the object of representation works to the advantage of its mystical aura. Hence Worboise hopes that her "little book" will inspire its readers to turn to Stanley's more demanding biography and thus come to "imbibe" Arnold, "the bright example, whose lustre was all derived from the Master whom he so loved to serve" (vi). The mimetic moral of the book is repeated in its conclusion: "Thomas Arnold has passed away ... who will be his successor? ... Perhaps, nay probably, it will be long ere such another rise in God's Israel: all cannot be Arnolds, but all may be true and earnest workers in God's cause" (226). The Victorian enthusiasm for the healing and inspiring effects of Arnold's personality might have been relatively short-lived, but it exemplifies a striking example of secular hagiography. And as in all hagiography, the worship of Arnold replaces a supernaturalism grounded in the New Testament with the supernaturalism of fetishes preserved from the saint—in this case, the preservation of the fetish of Arnold's character. Years later, in an address at the Johns Hopkins University, the significance of this early Victorian cultural phenomenon was recalled by the man who had done the most to initiate it, A. P. Stanley. Recalling the influence of Arnold, Stanley observed to his audience that "the lapse of years has only served to deepen in me the conviction that no gift can be more valuable than the recollection and the inspiration of a great character working upon your own" (*Addresses* 17).

Of course, some of the enthusiasm expressed by the early reviews of Stanley's *Life of Arnold* must be dismissed as conventions of the obituary, which is what many of these essays really are. However, they exemplify the final outcome of the circuitous life-course of Arnold's scriptural hermenuetics: in its despair of grounding authority in the objective realms of text, church, or history, Arnold's hermeneutics—and strangely enough, Arnold's public memory—located religious authority in a deified image of the pious, active, and communally minded male individual. Thus the desire for a credible source of religious authority is satisfied not by the testimony of God or his book or of scientific study, but rather by the testimony of the psychic product of these influences, a valorized character. As an inspiring and eminently honorable man, Arnold supplies the corroboration of good character to a body of religious belief which seems—for many reasons and to varying degrees—no longer credible to a significant number of English men and women. Far from being a new insight into a well-known religious crisis, this description merely casts in sharpened relief the conclusion which John Henry Newman suggested in his famous rejoinder to an Arnoldian interpretation of Scripture: Arnold answers for the interpretation, Newman observed, "But who is to answer for Arnold?" (151). Implicitly, the answer was that (according to Arnold's system) only Arnold answers for Arnold. And Arnold's character, remarkable as it may have been, was not sufficient authority for Newman.

Newman had the advantage of actually knowing Arnold, whereas most of the readers of the various literary vehicles which commemorated his life (biographies, reviews, novel, poetry) approached him only through the mediation of these texts. In a curious fashion, this situation enacts one of the tensions in Arnold's defense of the national English character: the attempt to steer away from matters of texts and interpretation and toward the life of action and practice seems, inevitably, to find itself all the more ensconced in the the printed word. Stanley's biography of Arnold is an emblematic and self-referential advertisement for a culture centered on books—not just the book—and thus what readers are meant to find in this life is the source of mediated *imitatio Christi*, the embodied image of a near-holy subjectivity produced by reading, by the cultural capital of classical and religious literature. Or, as W. C. Lake suggests, Arnold's biography presented "a character formed on Aristotle,

Thucydides, and the Bible" (468); a character that is "complete ... thoroughly leavened by moral nobleness" (507). Stanley's *Life of Arnold* went through seven editions in as many years, and it was hailed upon its appearance as a book "to be read and revered as the sacred memory of a great man" (Empson 233). Of the spiritual credibility of his life Florence Nightingale commented: "Our senses do tell us about the divine nature ... in the same way in which they tell me of the character of Dr. Arnold" (*Suggestions for Thought* 1: 111). And Charles Dickens, who early recognized the new supplementality of Scriptures, wrote to Forster requesting a copy of the *Life*: "I must have that book. Every sentence that you quote from it is the textbook of my faith" (Forster 2: 125).

Arnold's posthumous apotheosis was consistent with the importance Victorians assigned to their panoply of heroes. But while the cultural work performed by such exemplary individuals evaded the indeterminacy of texts, it did not do so without occasional reminders of the texts that were thus supplanted. Thus the memorialization of Arnold as a hero of the spiritual life was, paradoxically, both an escape from and a testimony to the problems of literary authority in a society dominated by the printed word. As Carlyle proclaimed to the readers of *Sartor Resartus*, with a brilliant inability to forget the hermeneutic frustrations that inspire incarnational thoughts, "Great Men are the inspired (speaking and acting) Texts of that divine *Book of Revelations*, whereof a Chapter is completed from epoch to epoch, and by some named *History*" (142).

CHAPTER 3

Christ and the Holy Family

Two Victorian Sites of Subject Constitution

Between 1845 and 1850, Dickens, Disraeli, George Eliot, Tennyson, and Browning produced works that invoke, in a variety of genres and with mixed success, the image of Christ. As either a literary allusion or a quasi-mythical figure, Christ appears in Dickens's *Life of Our Lord* (1848), Disraeli's *Tancred* (1847), Eliot's translation of Strauss's *Das Leben Jesu* (1846), Tennyson's *In Memoriam* (1850), and Browning's *Christmas-Eve and Easter-Day* (1850). That writers of a comparable stature from the previous and following centuries did not, with such frequency and in such a concentrated period of time, make similarly explicit uses of Christology should alert us to the overdetermined—or at least overextended—nature of this Victorian trope. At mid-century Hunt and Millais also turned their attentions toward the figure of Christ, representing him as child, worker, man, and God; in all instances, as an icon of the hopes and dilemmas of an artistic movement that aspired, in Hunt's words, to "resurrect" the moribund aesthetics and semiotics of British painting. Such interest in the aesthetic potential of figures that straddled myth and history was not uncommon in Victorian art: commenting upon Pickersgill's *Burial of Harold*, a prize-winning painting of 1847, a reviewer in *Punch* expressed hope that the mania in English art for finding the body of the last Saxon king had expended itself, and that "British artists would leave off finding [Harold's] body anymore, which they have been doing, in every exhibition, these fifty years" (Strong 118). The reviewer's hopes were rewarded; during the next few years, Harold became a less frequent subject in British painting. However, with the advent of Pre-Raphaelitism, the subject anticipated by this, one of Harold's last and most successful appearances, was just emerging: Pickersgill's Harold was based directly on a Lamentation over the Dead Christ.

The resurgence of interest in Christ was largely the result of the birth of the modern period in Christian theology, a period dominated less by supernatural articulations of faith than by scientific and historial ones.[1] The Higher Criticism, Comtism, philological and ethnological research, manuscript studies, and travel writings were among the influences that reintroduced European imaginations to Christ and mandated a realistic, sober approach, as if the style of treatment, whether literary or iconographic, could somehow confer historical verisimilitude on the subject. Hence the life of Christ became an important subgenre of the nineteenth century, one practiced by Strauss, Renan, John Seeley, F. W. Farrar, and, one might add, Nietzsche, although his work bears little resemblance to that of the others.[2] Throughout England and much of Europe, the life of Christ was one of the battlefields on which the pious contended with skeptics over the role that religion should play in modern society. But changing images of Christ also reflected another, ancillary battle over the perceived generational and gendered nature of religious authority.[3] As we saw in the previous chapter, there was the Christology of Arnold's Broad Church tradition, with its emphasis on a modern-day secular supplement to Christ, the manly English character. Approaching the topic of Victorian masculinity from a different angle, Herbert Sussman's study pays considerable attention to the dilemmas that a manly Christ posed to the artists of the Pre-Raphaelite Brotherhood. Norman Vance analyzes the specifically Christological tradition in more detail, exploring the nuances of the concept of manliness as it was appended to a practical ethic of male Christian behavior. And yet, even at the height of Kingsley and Hughes's manly Christian movement, the associations between Christ and femininity or (as we shall see in the next chapter) Christ and childhood were also quite visible in Victorian art and literary culture. The readiness with which Christ might be transposed onto images of women is evidenced by examples of a feminine Christology from the mid-nineteenth century—by Sarah Stickney Ellis's comparison of women to Christ in the conclusion of *The Daughters of England*, for example, or by Florence Nightingale's quite different vision of a female messiah with distinctly feminist inclinations. Indeed, the rhetoric of Muscular Christianity was partly a reaction against perceptions that Christian faith had become, via the influences of sentimentality and Evangelicalism, a mode of thought and behavior arguably more proper to women than to men.[4]

The subject of this and the following two chapters is Victorian Christology. Chapter 4 will explore a set of issues in Dickens's mid-century representations of women and children that I have framed around the figure of Christ. Chapter 5 will explore the ramifications of the Victorian alliance between Christ and femininity for one Victorian woman, Florence Nightingale. Consequently, it may be a source of some dismay to the reader that as much attention will be devoted in these chapters to the rhetoric surrounding women and children as to that surrounding Christ. In this brief chapter, I hope to make clear the reasons for frequently neglecting my announced topic. The previous chapters have narrated instances in which problems of scriptural interpretation are resolved with appeals to the incarnation as a revelation in the flesh, a distillation of the idea of truth into what was a definitive trope of nineteenth-century philosophy, the anthropomorphic form. In this uniquely Victorian cultural enactment of the incarnation, the body of the human divine functions less as a fulfillment of the Scriptures than as an attempt at a symbolic replacement for the Scriptures, and this implicit modification of traditional Christian theology occurs, I have suggested, because print culture dominates to an unprecedented degree, and in a manner that reveals its inability to supply the ideological coherence desired of it—an ideological coherence nostalgically, if illusively, associated with the Bible. The next chapters follow a different pathway, where the efficacy of the incarnation to resolve uncertainties of biblical meaning is undercut by problems raised by the idea of the incarnation itself. These problems arise once the authority of

Christ's image as the realization of the Word in a human identity is interjected into social contexts where authority is also managed by a careful but tenuous economy of gendered and generational roles.

As with so many dilemmas of the Victorian age, one way to narrativize the tensions inherent in the Christology of the period is to cite Carlyle. With uncharacteristic reserve, Carlyle omitted Christ from the list of luminaries touched upon in *On Heroes and Hero-Worship*: "The greatest of all Heroes is One—whom we do not name here! Let sacred silence meditate that sacred matter" (11). Such was a more pious but no less mystifying approach than the one he took in *Sartor Resartus*, where he proclaimed Christ the highest symbol of the godlike, albeit a symbol "whose significance will ever demand to be anew inquired into, and anew made manifest" (179). In both instances, Carlyle refuses to enframe the human divine, refuses to arrest a dynamic spiritual process that is ongoing in history in what must paradoxically be understood as a most material way. But the problem with this paradox as Carlyle presents it is that the idea of Christ resists iconic and narratological representation even as it incites the desire for such representation. The results become evident in Carlyle's response to *The Light of the World*. After William Holman Hunt used Christina Rossetti as a model for the painting, Carlyle accused him of selling out to Royal Academy tastes by making Christ "a puir, weak, girl-faced nonentity, bedecked in a fine silken sort of gown" when he should have made him in the image of a "Man toiling along in the hot sun ... tired, hungry often and foot-sore.... His rough and patched clothes bedraggled and covered with dust" (quoted in Hunt 1: 358).[5] And yet, even Carlyle, as the above quotation from *On Heroes* demonstrates, was unwilling to attempt such a depiction himself. As Sussman states, the image of Christ forced together two incompatible cultural standards, "the traditional representation of the life of Jesus" and "the norms of early Victorian bourgeois manhood" (120). In this regard, Hunt's feminization of Christ might be understood as a remedy for a dilemma that Carlyle had aggravated when he encouraged both an advance upon and a retreat from the idea of Christ as an adult male. The other remedy was to embrace a masculine but spiritually diluted Christ, as in the apotheosization of Arnold's character, or in F. J. Foxton's *Popular Christianity* (1849), which makes Christ the master type of other prophetic geniuses such as Shakespeare and Homer (160–61), or in one of Hunt's anecdotes of Pre-Raphaelite beginnings, in which during a studio break in 1848 the Brotherhood composes a "list of immortals" that distinguishes Christ from other personages by virtue of assigning him four asterisks instead of three (the number assigned to Shakespeare) or two (the number assigned to Chaucer, Keats, Browning, and King Alfred) (Hunt 1: 159). Such a Christ was hardly a god at all, so thoroughly was his story recontextualized into that of men gifted with genius in a rare but by no means exclusive way. He was, to quote Vance's adjectives, "vigorously" and "intensely" human (6). But he was also lacking in supernatural spiritual powers, powers which it seems could only be conveyed by the use of symbolism (as Hunt would do in *The Shadow of Death*), or, more problematically, by the use of a female model.

The source of ambivalence toward representing Christ as a man lay in a psychological effect of Christianity itself: human subjectivity of the nineteenth century was often predicated on guilt, and according to the plot of sentimental fantasy, guilt was a male prerogative, a dubious entitlement linked to sexual and monetary appetites that neither children nor women in their ideal forms shared. Hence the recurrent artistic attraction to the image of the prostitute, whose scandalous passage between the differential realms of a feminine and a sexual nature presented a unique opportunity for conferring fuller subjectivity on women characters, of allotting them the ontological status of a subject rather than an object in a salvation narrative. Hence also the artist's habitual withdrawal from the image of Christ as an adult male, an image which suggested a disturbing convergence of guilt and divinity, of dependency and power. Indeed, this convergence was all the more disturbing for being true, since it captured an impossible but efficient formula of authority in Victorian culture, the formula that wedded men to their images of women and children as purifying displacements of their own power and authority.

Carlyle's desire for the image of a working Christ, of an emphatically embodied Christ, is remembered as a call-to-arms of the proponents of manly Christianity, Kingsley and Hughes the chief among them. The relationship between Kingsley's Christology and his ideology of gender has been explored in detail, not only by Vance but more recently by John Maynard. Neither critic takes notice of a review of Anna Jameson's *Sacred and Legendary Art* that Kingsley contributed to *Fraser's* in March 1849—a forgivable omission, as the review does nothing to further our understanding of Kinglsey's ideas. However, because it sets Kingsley's thoughts on gender and Christology in the framework of aesthetic appreciation, and because in so doing it divides quite clearly, even simplistically, the symbolic functions of viewer and viewed, I would like to discuss briefly this review and the book that occasioned it.

Sacred and Legendary Art (1848) was the first in Anna Jameson's four-part study of medieval and early Renaissance European art. The second volume in the series, *Legends of the Monastic Orders*, was published in 1850; the third volume, titled *Legends of the Madonna*, appeared in 1852; and the last volume, *The History of Our Lord*, was published posthumously in 1860, after being completed by Lady Eastlake. Jameson's decision to undertake a volume on artistic representations of Christ at the culmination of her twelve-year attempt to mediate the iconography of Mary and the saints to the Protestant world was sensible enough; it is also, we might note, consistent with the Protestant tradition of avoiding a direct treatment of the human divine. In *Sacred and Legendary Art* Jameson establishes the objectives and approach that will inform her entire series. She presents herself as a critic who is anxious to defend Italian Renaissance painting, even as she acknowledges the need for caution in the study of Catholic hagiography. Frequently, she makes reference to the English commonplace that the idolatrous veneration of saints in medieval and early Renaissance Europe was a symptom of the religious perversions caused by withholding the Bible from the poor. But this, she argues, is no reason to deny the beauty and pathos of the art produced in Roman Catholic countries. The Catholic Church's management of Christ's divinity she considers more misguided than deliberately malevolent, suggesting that in their solicitude for orthodoxy, the church fathers altogether removed Christ's personal character "far away from the hearts of the benighted and miserable people ... into regions speculative, mysterious, spiritual, whither they could not, dared not, follow Him" (*Sacred* 3). And yet, these speculative, mysterious, and spiritual qualities are precisely what English Protestantism, she fears, misses entirely. Like the Pre-Raphaelites, she accuses English aesthetics of lacking the beauty and brilliance of early Renaissance art because of stale conventions, narrow prejudices, and repressive tendencies. In these habits, she suggests, the English art public are encouraged by their fear that religious superstition is a disease transmitted by familiarity. Thus the time has come to master this fear and decipher impartially the symbols of late medieval and early Renaissance art. For the English to do otherwise is to "seal up a fountainhead of the richest poetry, and to shut out a thousand ennobling and inspiring thoughts" (*Sacred* 12).

The review essay that Kingsley wrote upon the appearance of *Sacred and Legendary Art* is laudatory and discursive. The arguments of the essay typify the hybridity of Kingsley's beliefs, which included a faith in the propriety of gender roles, a faith in the evils of Catholicism, and a faith in the sanctity of sexual pleasure in married life. Thus he warns against the Catholic threat to English Protestant culture but, like Jameson, suggests that the best defense is a cautious appropriation of Catholic culture's superior sense of the beautiful. "The deepest cravings of the human heart" continue to be left unsatisfied by Protestant art, he states, reiterating Jameson's preface, and hence English youth "are looking for themselves at the ante-Raphaellic artists" (285). This should serve as admonishment to their Protestant elders for starving the imagination and the desire for beauty, all on the misguided assumption that "the Gospel had nothing to do with art, [that] art was either Pagan or Popish" (284). As a counterbalance to this erroneous tendency, Kingsley finds Mrs. Jameson's work irreproachable, because it "is enthusiastic but not idolatrous, discriminating but not captious" (289). If the separate identities of Protestant and Catholic Christians were to turn on nothing more than the difference between enthusiasm and idolatry, reactionary Englishmen might with some justification be alarmed. But Kingsley has additional reason to trust Jameson in this venture: because she is an "English wife and mother," she can approach the subject of Christian iconography with "tender and admiring sympathies" that are held in check by "her Protestant education to unsullied purity of thought" (289).[6] Kingsley's Christian beliefs, Maynard explains, were uniquely wedded to his endorsement of human sexuality, and two precepts that enabled him to accommodate both carnal pleasure and Protestantism were marital monogamy and the fulfillment of gendered identities.[7] The ideological axes that connected Protestantism to a sacramental sexuality in marriage and idealized gender roles could also be connected to national personality traits, and thus Kingsley lists among Jameson's qualifications not only a Protestant sensibility and a feminine nature but also "the birthright of English honesty" (290).

By invoking this ideological continuum in almost everything he wrote, Kingsley lent energy and a sense of exigency to the tradition that Thomas Arnold enlisted against the demons of rationalism and Tractarianism—the tradition of constructing an English national personality. However, these attitudes certainly extended beyond the Broad Church movement, and the pervasiveness of the associations that obtain in Kingsley's imagination is exemplified by their similar appearance among the Pre-Raphaelite Brotherhood. According to William Holman Hunt's retrospective account, he and Millais initially thought themselves capable of exploring early Christian art because they possessed an "English honesty" rounded out by certain inspiring qualities: their childlike approach to nature and their youthful, revolutionary stance toward the patriarchy of the Reynolds school. Moreover, it is worth noting that their seminal conversation occurred over Hunt's rendering of Christ in his painting *Christ and the Two Maries*.[8] Coming to the Brotherhood's defense in 1853, Ruskin took up the Brotherhood's conception of themselves as possessing a childlike genius, lamenting that of all great societies, "it is reserved for England to insult the strength of her noblest children—to wither their warm enthusiasm in patient battle" ("Lectures" 164). In the case of the Pre-Raphaelites, as in the case of Kingsley's review of Jameson's work, the future of English religious art is entrusted to sensibilities deemed not only English but also feminine and childlike. These examples signal the fact that the Catholic infection which Kingsley feared has already taken place; the English already have the disease, which in their case is an idolatrous treatment not of art objects but of discursive objects. For Kingsley's desperate attempt to distinguish between Catholic idolatry and Protestant enthusiasm is no doubt inspired by the even more tenuous distinction that it hides, the distinction between a Catholic worship of the Madonna and Child and the Protestant worship of mothers and children.

However, in what appears to be a diversion from the anti-Catholic bent of Kinsgley's rhetoric, the differences between Catholicism and Protestantism are made in his review to be less significant than the difference between Christianity and Paganism. To the peremptory importance of this latter distinction he is willing to sacrifice the grievances between the two main sects of Western Christianity. Paganism is a worship of power and evil, and hence the merger of Catholic iconography and Protestant belief is a less grievous error than that of "[tracing] malevolent likenesses" between a Cecilia and an Isis, or a Magdalene and a Venus (291). The separation of Christianity from religions that worship brute power is also metonymically connected to gender, for insofar as the chief Christian deity ennobles humanity, Kingsley suggests, he does so by imparting to it attributes that are presumably divine but also, within his discourse, gendered feminine. The first mention of Christ follows a discussion of Jameson's treatment of the story of Saint Dorothea:

Is there not heroism in it greater than of all the Ajaxes and Achilles who ever blustered on earth? Is there not power greater than of kings—God's strength made perfect in woman's weakness? Tender forgiveness, the Saviour's own likeness; glimpses, brilliant and true at the core, however distorted and miscoloured, of that spiritual world where the wicked cease from troubling, where the meek alone shall inherit the earth, where, as Protestants too believe, all that is spotless and beautiful in nature as well as in man shall bloom forever perfect? (292)

Of course, Kingsley acknowledges, the danger run by this religious aesthetic and religious sensibility is that it becomes, like the works by Giotto and Raffaello, "altogether effeminate" and wholly banishes the "masculine" Greek virtues "of sex, of strength, of activity, of grandeur of all forms" (294). The "passive spiritual faculties" (innocence, devotion, meekness, resignation) are all good, "but not the whole of humanity" (295). And yet, rather than including these missing attributes in the objects of artistic representation, Kingsley assigns them to the viewers of past history, men who are willful and brutal before they are ennobled by the alterior attributes in the masterworks they behold:

[Raffaello and Giotto] were faithful preachers of the great Christian truth, that devoted faith, and not fierce self-will, is man's glory. Well did their pictures tell to brutal peasants, and to still more brutal warriors, that God's might was best shewn forth, not in the elephantine pride of a Hercules, or the Titanic struggles of a Laocoon, but in the weakness of martyred women, and of warriors who were content meekly to endure shame and death, for the sake of Him who conquered by sufferings, and who bore all human weaknesses. (295–96)

Hence the subject who views works of high religious art is neither complete nor redeemable without the edifying and seductive virtues objectified therein. At the same time, the weakness and meekness of the women martyrs and Christian warriors portrayed in the paintings are—according to Kingsley's dichotomous definition of human nature—similarly incomplete without the brutal and martial subjects that stand before them. Not only is Christ unrepresented in the scene (his image only metonymically invoked as the original of the virtue of long-suffering), but the impossibility of his representation is also implied, insofar as Kingsley's desire to rewed power and meekness in an image of the Christian savior has been accomplished with great indirection, via the distribution of these qualities among viewing subjectivities and the glorified objects of their perception.

Christian identity, and with it the identity of Christ, is thus made into a necessarily social phenomenon, one which appears to privilege the individual but in fact depends entirely on the interdependent symbolic functions performed by a cast of characters.

Anna Jameson develops the concern with the gendering of the viewers and subjects of Christian art in a slightly different vein. In *Legends of the Madonna* she focuses on the subject of Catholic "Virgin worship," beginning her discussion by noting the theological difficulties that have historically accompanied the subject of Christ's gender. Adele M. Holcomb notes that Jameson's choice of subject matter for the third title in her series was probably influenced by two conflicting currents in women's history of the period: the rise of interest in Mariolatry that preceded Pius IX's proclamation of the doctrine of the Immaculate Conception in 1854 (the doctrine according to which Mary was conceived without sin in her mother's womb), and the advent of organized feminism in England and North America (113). The historical context goes some way in explaining the odd confluence of chivalric and feminist sentiments in Jameson's treatment of the role of women in early Christian history. She praises Christ for elevating the moral status of women (so does Nightingale in *Cassandra*), but she also wrestles with the tradition that God chose a male incarnation. Since true Protestant Christianity denies the divinity of Mary, Jameson laments, it is still troubled "by the want of a new type of womanly perfection." Jameson attributes this problem to what she considers the relatively recent historical preoccupation with gendered dichotomies. "Christ, as the model man, united the virtues of the two sexes," she conjectures, "until the idea that there are essentially masculine and feminine virtues intruded itself on the higher Christian conception" (24). And yet, there is no returning to the androgynous ideal of Christ, for the bifurcation of gender is also a sign of evolutionary progress. Consequently, she reaches a conclusion common to such dissimilar figures as Florence Nightingale, Sarah Stickney Ellis, and Auguste Comte: the future of the human ideal will manifest itself, Jameson proclaims, through women—women seen not simply as spiritual and physical conduits of the race, but as the embodiments of its higher nature.[9] Defending the iconography of the Madonna, she writes:

> Others will have it that these scattered, dim, mistaken—often gross and perverted—ideas which were afterwards gathered into the pure, dignified, tender, image of the Madonna, were but as the voice of a mighty prophecy, sounded through all the generations of men, even from the beginning of time, of the coming moral regeneration, and complete and harmonious development of the whole human race, by the establishment on a higher basis, of what has been called the "feminine element" in society. And let me speak for myself. In that perpetual iteration of that beautiful image of THE WOMAN highly blessed—*there*, where others saw only pictures or statues, I have seen this great hope standing like a spirit beside the visible form: in this fervent worship once given to that gracious presence, I have beheld an acknowledgment of a higher as well as gentler power than that of the strong hand and the might that makes the right, and in every earnest votary who, as he knelt, was in this sense pious beyond the reach of his own thought, and "devout beyond the meaning of his will." (*Legends* 22)

Unlike her reviewer Kingsley, Jameson stresses the attenuation of the act of worship across an evolutionary time frame that prophesies a more active role for the "feminine element." However, like Kingsley, she divides the Christian ideal of human nature into a masculine votary and an elevated feminine icon, the latter a source of ennobling and beneficent instincts for a human nature that is, at base, at once brutal, benighted, and male.

Once again, the Protestant suspicion of an iconography of Christ is corroborated for reasons more logical than pious. For in a culture preoccupied with the gendered division of signifying functions, the project of merging human and divine consciousness into one form is unthinkable. Or, more accurately, where it was thinkable, as in the Madonna or female Christ, it was dangerous, and this on three scores. First, the implicit deification of women resulted in a form of sentimental idolatry that could only function in Protestant culture as long as the fact that it was idolatrous was denied. Second, this deification could be turned into a challenge to the patriarchal order of Victorian belief, as it had been in Joanna Southcott's day, and as it would be again in Nightingale's *Cassandra*. Finally, the merger of sacred and profane powers into one human form defeats the ideological efficacy of a social construction of human nature, which maintains a patriarchal economy of power by distributing various forms of power and powerlessness among three symbolic participants: fathers, mothers, and children.

Another set of passages relevant to these aspects of Victorian Christology occurs in a better remembered art historical opus of the 1840s, *Modern Painters II*. In the second and final section, Ruskin presents his delineation of the imaginative faculty, the faculty that mediates to human perception the external forms of beauty, the forms which he analyzed in the preceding section under the rubric of the theoretic faculty. Nowhere, Ruskin suggests, do we observe the theoretic and imaginative faculties working together so completely as in representations of "the superhuman ideal." The problem with such representations, as Ruskin describes them, echoes the problem of divine incarnation, since they "attempt at realization to the Bodily senses of the Beauty supernatural and divine" (314). Because their powers are not equal to God, Ruskin withholds from artists the ability to portray Christ successfully. In human works the supernatural ideal necessarily diverts from its perfect culmination, manifesting itself instead in various indirect and peripheral means of representation: the depiction of God assuming a nonhuman form, such as the dove or the lamb; the depiction of a form properly belonging to the supernatural ideal, but not necessarily seen, such as the risen Christ appearing to his disciples behind closed doors; and the depiction of the supernatural ideal's operation on human forms, such as in the shining of Moses's face (315). Through these metonymic representations artists have gained greater success than in their portraiture of Christ, Ruskin determines, and indeed "all who are acquainted with the range of sacred art will admit not only that no representation of Christ has ever been partially successful, but that the greatest painters fall therein below their accustomed level" (317).

As in the passages from Kingsley and Jameson, Ruskin's opinions here are no doubt assisted by a residual Protestant conviction that Catholic iconography is idolatrous. However, what is for our purposes more striking is that Ruskin explicitly averts the artist's gaze from the body of Christ and fixes it instead on certain peripheral means of representing the superhuman ideal—pictures of angels, for example, or, what is by now a familiar substitute, of the Madonna: "We need reason no farther, but may limit ourselves to the purest modes of giving a conception of superhuman but still creature forms, as of angels; in equal rank with whom, perhaps, we may place the mother of Christ" (318). The passage exemplifies Paul Sawyer's diagnosis of a tendency that connects the first and second volumes of *Modern Painters*: "The acceptance of human imperfection produces the vision of a transcendent feminine Other" (81).[10] It also exemplifies a tendency that connects Ruskin to a broader cultural discourse, since by turning away from Christ and toward the secondary embodiments of God, Ruskin demonstrates the tendency of his generation to deify images of women—or, perhaps more precisely, of women and children, since the Madonna alluded to here is identified with her function as the bearer of a child. And yet, these secondary representations of an incarnational ideal are hardly an escape from the paradoxes of the primary incarnation, insofar as deified women are models at once preferable to a male Christ (for Victorian culture enforced, often at the expense of masculine sanctity, a direct bond between femininity and Christian holiness) and regrettably inferior (for within this discourse female images cannot fully realize the incarnation of God into man).

Here and elsewhere in *Modern Painters II*, the hidden face of God is the absent center of Ruskin's eschatological narrative of Renaissance art, a narrative that traces one thread of the *res extensia* of God through creation, even as it looks forward to the return of God and man to a *res cogitans* of heavenly apprehension. Throughout, the voice of the narrator imparts certainty that the study of beauty and the structure of aesthetic perception are not unlike the study of God and the structure of heavenly worship. For the reader ensconced in the above concluding details of Ruskin's epistemology of beauty, this certainty is likely to be an encouragement, all the more so since Ruskin has already reached his true conclusion some chapters before.[11] At the end of section 1, Ruskin explains how "theoria" or the theoretic faculty works in the service of a beneficent Deity, and as if to prove the point he conveys with the virtuosity of his scripturally resonant prose a foretaste of his imagined heaven:

We cannot say how far it is right or agreeable with God's will, while men are perishing round about us, while grief, and pain, and wrath, and impiety, and death, and all the powers of the air, are working wildly and evermore, and the cry of the blood going up to heaven, that any of us should take hand from the plough; but this we know, that there will come a time when the service of God shall be in the beholding of him, and though in these stormy seas, where we are now driven up and down, his Spirit is dimly seen on the face of the waters, and we are left to cast anchors out of the stern, and wish for the day, that day will come, when, with the evangelists on the crystal and stable sea, all the creatures of God shall be full of eyes within, and there shall be "no more curse, but his servants shall serve him, and shall see his face." (217–18)

In a sense, this conclusion is a visionary resolution to a question that Gary Wihl affiliates with the entire volume of *Modern Painters II*—a continuation of the first volume's attempt to decide "between the externally given and the internal, imaginative modification" (43). For if, at the culmination of time we are, as Ruskin paraphrases Revelation 22.3-4, "full of eyes within," it is unclear if the God we behold is within ourselves or without.

Importantly, the collapse of subject and object is here situated in an apocalyptic moment, as it was in Coleridge's prose, and as it was in the Irvingite glossolalists' belief that the possession of their bodies by God signaled an imminent Second Coming. We cannot know to what extent those earlier visionaries found in their self-shattering experiences an efficacious sense of escape or renewal. We can determine, however, from the textual record, that their experiences were tightly situated within the social and political structures of their lives, and that the heavenly impulse toward a catastrophic surrender of their identities also worked as a weapon in their contestations of and for religious authority. Set in this context, the ambiguous difference between the subject and object of worship in the above paragraph is far from being a momentary nuance of Ruskin's prose; it goes to the heart of mid-Victorian concepts of humanity, and to the divisions of power (social, sexual, and psychological) that structured those concepts. For, as we know, once Ruskin turns (in the following chapter) to the subject of this-wordly visions of the divine, the nondifferentiated apocalypse wherein sacred beauty extends both inward and out will divide itself into the more distinct and socially provocative form of a holy family.

In this way, the social and psychological patterns of Victorian worship were structured by the impossibility of the condition that Ruskin defines as heaven—the perception of a God at once internal and external, of a ubiquitous God who claims all space, both social and psychological, in the name of divine beauty. Likewise, one of the modern Christs of the nineteenth century was a character split internally between an awareness of his godhead and the awareness of himself as a mortal man. Versions of this psychologized Christ appear in the biographies of Renan, Strauss, and Farrar. Arguably, it is also a concern of some Pre-Raphaelite depictions of Christ—of Millais's *Christ in the Home of His Parents*, for example, where the boy Jesus displays a wound in his hand, a signifier in the flesh of his shocking corporal vulnerability, but also a typological reference to the antitype of his crucifixion, of the uncanny certainty of his sacrificial destiny as a god. His divided consciousness is the center of the painting, defining as it does the positions, attitudes, and functions of those who surround him.[12] It might also be understood as the social and psychological predicament with which an imagined male viewer of the nineteenth century most readily identifies. Separated from perfection by a materiality that was the condition of his being, male Victorian Christians had a primary prerogative to assign moral and psychological qualities to the various members of society, to institute the nuclear family as the whole embodiment of human traits, and to sequester this communal economy of human attributes within an individualistic paradigm of the soul in a state of (so Ruskin would have it in 1846) expectation and deferral, a state of seeking the habitat of its redeemer.

CHAPTER 4

Emasculating Christ, Mediating Authority

The Sentimental Logic of Literary Influence in Dickens's 'The Life of Our Lord' and 'Dombey and Son'

In March 1848 an essay appeared in *Fraser's* titled "Childhood and its Reminiscences." Like so many of the other, often forgettable essays of the prolific Victorian periodical press, there is no record of the author of this essay. But it offers a consummate depiction of one Victorian version of childhood—not the Evangelical version, where the state of childhood is one of innate depravity, and children are morally tractable only when terrified into obedience—but rather the sentimental version, the quasi-sacred child descended from Wordsworth. Children are "a deep mystery," the author writes, "the relics of another order of things.... Born, as it were, before sin had taken universal possession" (266). It is obviously inaccurate to describe such language as secular in orientation, even though the religiosity of the author's description of childhood conforms to no sect and pays heed to no doctrine. Most readers would identify the style of this description as sentimental, yet the imagery invokes Catholic iconography. Freezing a picture of the reified child who is the subject of his essay, the author conflates him with Christ: "The round lustrous eyes are wide open, which, like the eyes of the Divine Child in the Sistine Madonna, seem to look at nothing, in gazing at all things" (268).

I begin with these quotations because they express in striking fashion an inclination we began to observe in the previous chapter, the inclination of much of the literature and art of the early Victorian period to represent childhood and femininity as sacred categories. By invoking the image of the Madonna and Child, the *Fraser's* essayist only takes to its logical conclusion the tendency of Victorian sentimental rhetoric to treat women and children as spiritually privileged subjects. If the Romanist affiliations of his iconography did not disturb Protestant readers of the essay, it is perhaps because the ideological utility of the image of Madonna and Child overrode its uncomfortable theological ancestry. The image perfectly encapsulates the division of signifying functions in sentimental narratives, where religious power and moral authority are contingent upon powerlessness in other areas. Victorian women and children shared a degree of sexual, political, and economic disfranchisement that made them uniquely qualified to carry out the ministry of moral and religious duties. This predicament is exemplified in the rhetorical turns taken by the *Fraser's* essayist, who no sooner deifies childhood than he disempowers it: "We have dubbed the baby feminine. Babyhood seems so, with its beauty, its helplessness, and its waywardness,—ladylike in each of its extremes" (269).

The ideological burdens placed upon women have been analyzed at length in Victorian studies, as has the notion of a widespread feminization of British culture instigated largely by the novels of the early modern period. The role of childhood within these cultural conditions has also received critical attention, notably by Thomas E. Jordan and more recently in the intriguing interpretations offered by James R. Kincaid.[1] As these critics help us see, the material and symbolic duties assigned to men, women, and children in nineteenth-century sentimental narratives of family life are at once highly interdependent and rigidly segregated. Thus the cultural categories of motherhood and childhood share the attributes of helplessness and sanctity, and this symbolic similarity is reinforced by the other bonds (biological, economic, social) which connect mothers and children. On the other hand, the father figure of this emblematic family triad is less visible in many Victorian texts and images and less theorized in most of the twentieth-century criticism. Provisionally, I will offer two observations on the role of this father figure, observations that recapitulate possibilities developed in the previous chapter: the father figure is outside the sentimental iconography of mother and child because he occupies the position of the subject who regards them, imparting to them their sacred attributes, and he is outside the holy sphere of their iconic image because he participates in the profane activities of commerce, property, and politics. Implicitly, the male subject of Victorian sentimentality carries a burden of guilt, inadequacy, or spiritual incompleteness which is alleviated by the augmenting purity of his domestic deities.

This scenario is complicated by questions of narrative voice. If gender and age define the parameters of authority for the subjects of sentimental culture, to what extent do the gender and age of the authors of such narratives impinge upon their attitudes toward authorship? Or, if the author is male, can he divorce himself from the paradoxical conditions of masculine authority in his society, conditions which render him simultaneously inadequate and in charge? In the instance of the *Fraser's* essay, our ignorance of the author enables us to dismiss this question, and to pose the following observation in its place: the viewer of the Madonna and Child is also the speaking subject of the narrative, and speaks in a way that announces a masculine subjectivity, for it is a subjectivity which confesses its own inadequacy in the face of a sanctified mother and child. Consequently, his worshipful narrative is an act of both creativity and parasitism, for this subject projects images of childhood and femininity so as to reabsorb a mediated form of his own authority. As a morally and spiritually disempowered figure in the domestic economy, the male subject of "Childhood and its Reminiscences" needs the mystified alterity of women and children in order to borrow from their signifying potential.

While this description cannot be simply transposed to other writers of the nineteenth century, it does have, I believe, a particular relevance for Dickens, who of all Victorian novelists was the most inclined to use images of childhood and femininity as vehicles of a secular gospel of feeling. Dickens is the most influential practitioner of Victorian sentimentality, and yet the most remarkable aspect of his writing is not his ability to express its ideology but rather his almost compulsive exploration of its tensions and contradictions.[2] One example, albeit a minor one in his corpus, is his textual treatment of Christ. In the 1840s, Dickens was more attracted to this trope than at any other time in his long career. From 1845 to 1848, he wrote several Christmas books; the gold-edged, generously illustrated editions made attractive presents and as such were a sensible device for the seasonal market. They also encouraged Dickens to explore Christology in several of the stories composed for the occasion. Possibly the Christological thoughts and allusions appended to Tiny-Tim struck him as uniquely effective; he repeated the approach with Paul Dombey, the beatified boy-child of his major novel of the period. Indeed, as he began *Dombey and Son*, Dickens was composing a life of Christ addressed to his own children. The resulting *Life of Our Lord* is not a remarkable achievement in either theology or children's literature, but it testifies to the strength of the author's belief in the religiosity of childhood. As a consequence, perhaps circumstantial but also apparently desirable, the savior in this text is redeemed from any taint of manhood: the Dickensian Christ is a perfectly childish hero.

By employing Christology in his works of the 1840s, Dickens was participating in a larger cultural trend of the period. As we saw in the previous chapter, the bonds of spirituality, Christ, childhood, and femininity were forged in the first half of the nineteenth century within a sentimental discourse of the family, and the *Fraser's* essay is but one example of this discourse. Dickens's literary treatments of Christ decidedly belong to this early stage of Victorian Christology, when images of Jesus as a sentimental hero were common in popular culture, and the outcry against his subsequent effeminization had not yet become the *cause célèbre* of Arnold's and Carlyle's descendants. Consequently, the complications in Dickens's mid-century images of Christ result not from a desire to masculinize him, but rather from the convention of using Christology in highly affective and hence often emasculating narrative circumstances. Dickens's employment of Christ as the insignia of a consummate rhetorical moment is further complicated by his self-reflexive habits, by his tendency to encode his narratives with ambivalent expressions toward his own authority as a Victorian sage of the fictional arena. Frequently this ambivalence is both expressed and resolved in his writings by the segregation of potent masculinity from religious and moral sources of power. For example, Dickens's sentimental gospel is typically mediated by the purifying vehicles of child and female characters; thus Nell and Tiny-Tim are distanced from their masculine creator by a purifying childishness and femininity, even as their behaviors, beliefs, and habits of feeling embody Dickens's rhetorical presence and intentions. The character of Christ thematizes this predicament by bringing into the realm of representation a male authority who must be shrouded in childish and feminine attributes. My argument in this chapter will address this predicament: the images of Christ figured in Dickens's writings, I believe, show the novelist in the act of working out his vexed relationship to the deities of his imagination and the powers of conversion claimed by his written word. Ambitious in the resolutions it seeks, and provocative in its failures, Dickens's Christology reveals the blurred, unstable, and fluid boundaries between the objects and subjects, the saviors and sinners, of Victorian sentimental discourse.

In the following pages, I will develop this thesis in an analysis of three texts: *The Life of Our Lord*, *Dombey and Son*, and Dickens's letters to Miss Burdett Coutts on the topic of their joint venture in the reform of "fallen women."[3] My initial examination of the representation of Christ in *The Life of Our Lord* will lead to discussions of two other topics: Victorian attitudes toward literary entertainment and Dickens's attitudes toward prostitution. While neither of these topics seems immediately relevant to Christology, I hope to demonstrate a relationship based on Dickens's attitudes toward the sentimental and didactic powers of his prose. In *Dombey and Son*, he thematizes a tension that Victorian critics perceived to be fundamental to novels as a genre—namely, the tension between a literature that entertained its readers and a literature that improved them. Christ appears in *Dombey* as the validating original of certain child and female characters who resolve this tension by demonstrating a beneficent as opposed to a prurient interest in the stories of others. The novel transposes this moralized form of interest onto its ideal readers; at the same time, it transposes Christic authority onto Dickens. But the irreproachable nature of such authority is unsettled by the fact that *Dombey and Son* demonizes adult masculinity as the source of sexual appetite and monetary greed. A similar problem also troubles the textual record of Dickens's involvement in Urania Cottage, the home for reforming prostitutes which he sponsored in the 1840s and 1850s. If the Gospels disturb social and religious hierarchies by presenting their incarnate male God in intimate proximity with fallen women, Dickens repeats the pattern by aligning his own authorial voice with Christ and then addressing that voice to nineteenth-century prostitutes. Thus at Urania Cottage, Dickens claims for himself the role of author of events, texts, and circumstances that will inspire the women's conversion experiences. However, he also proclaims his interest in their scandalous stories and his heartfelt anxiety on their behalf, and as we shall see, such interest and anxiety are normally the affective states adopted by the sinful objects rather than the spiritually assured agents of a conversion experience. In this way, interest and anxiety become the fundamental affective states which bind the author in a web of symbolically overdetermined relationships. Beneath the surface clarity of moral vision and authorial stances in *The Life*, *Dombey*, and the correspondence with Burdett Coutts, the diction and the rhetorical strategies of the texts betoken signs of a mimetic confusion of the emotions and attributes which supposedly separate the cast of characters involved: Dickens and his Christ, Dickens's Christ and his women and child characters, Dickens and his readers, and Dickens and the prostitutes he desired to reform.

The Christ Child of 'The Life of Our Lord'

The Life of Our Lord is Dickens's only attempt to put into narrative form explicitly theological material.[4] He wrote this brief text for his children, and because such material invited criticism from the Evangelical press, he insisted that it not be published either during his life or after his death. The manuscript was a family text and a childhood privilege. With its sentimental style and juvenile diction it offers yet another example of the Victorian convention of embellishing domesticity and childhood with a rhetoric of the sacred. But *The Life* supersedes other works which practice this convention by, in a sense, practicing what it preaches; it not only represents the sacred power of children within the home but also performs it in its unique textual history. Until after Dickens's death, the manuscript of *The Life of Our Lord* never left the family circle.

The Christ of *The Life* is childlike and tenderhearted, a votary of the nursery. Likewise, the tone of this work is secure and reassuring, almost complacent; it evokes a haven of sentimentalized childhood carefully sealed from the outside world. Allusions to the reader's unworthiness and guilt—hallmarks of Evangelical literature for both children and adults—are absent from this text, and the doctrines which Dickens casually hints at are consistent with the Broad Church religion of the heart to which he subscribed. These veiled theological positions are adjusted to a young readership by the use of simple syntax and diction: "He will teach men to love one another, and not to quarrel with one another, and His name will be Jesus Christ" (13). If such faux childish platitudes infantilize Christianity, they do so on the premise that the most essential teachings of Christianity are accessible to a child's mind. Consequently, a return effect of Dickens's attempt to render Christ clear to children is that Christianity is infantilized. Of course, to a certain extent Dickens treats religion as a childish subject because of the nature of his audience; but considering the tendency of his other works to associate religious insight and clarity with childhood, it also seems true that—to a certain extent—he chooses a young audience for this subject because of the nature of his attitudes toward religion. Hence *The Life of Our Lord* is arguably more effective at deifying its child reader than its Christ. For the text bears the mark of Dickens's affinity with Unitarianism in that it refrains from announcing Christ's divinity. And yet, taking liberties with his Gospel source, Dickens has Christ conclude the Transfiguration with a sermon on the sanctity of children, culminating in a benign but unorthodox declaration: "All of the Angels are children" (59). The heavenly worshipers of Christ are, like the earthly ones who read this book, angelic children. But in regarding the Dickensian Christ—a character who has been distanced from his own male adulthood by a sentimental and childlike style—these angelic children in effect face a reflection of their own idealized selves. The child readers of *The Life* are cast in the role of worshiping an image of what their author would have them be.

In this way, the narrative voice of *The Life of Our Lord* nostalgically constructs and identifies with an image of child sensibility which his text then worships for its spiritual desirability. *The Life* differs in this regard from the literary fabrications of sentimental children which Dickens wrote for an adult readership. Here Dickens attempts to relinquish the position he occupies vis-à-vis Nell, or Tiny-Tim, or Paul Dombey, characters whose subjectivities he imaginatively occupies even as he retains an adult perspective, thus remaining outside of childhood. Moreover, he literally denies adult readers access to *The Life*. Admittedly, the sensibility of the adult observer is preserved by the manner in which the text conceives of childhood as innocent, wise, and free of rancor or vindictiveness. But the very repression of this fact is, in itself, revealing; *The Life*'s denial of its own adult perspective completes a pattern wherein Dickens attempts to banish all forms of adulthood (the narrator's, the characters', the style's, and the readers') so as to render the text hermetically secure for a nostalgic infantile gestalt.

On the level of plot, this security is further ensured by the inconspicuousness of God. At best, God the Father in *The Life of Our Lord* is an aloof patriarch; at worst, he is the distant agent who requires, in remuneration for human sins, the crucifixion of his son. Consequently, it might be that the Dickensian Gospel refrains from more studious references to its God not only because such a Father would spoil the childish ambiance but also because the logic of this gospel would inevitably draw him as a devil. For this God is in keeping with Dickens's often noted ambivalence toward father figures, although in this case what comes to mind is not the pathetically irresponsible version (Micawber, Dorrit, Skimpole), but the powerful fathers who control events and pursue their desires with cunning efficiency—characters such as David Copperfield's stepfather; or Fagin, the surrogate father of thieves; or the senior John Harmon; who wills his son's unhappiness from beyond the grave. Or, for an instance which is contemporaneous with *The Life of Our Lord*, we might consider Paul Dombey.

If *The Life of Our Lord* creates a refuge for idyllic childhood by banishing adult masculinity, *Dombey and Son* casts some light on the question of why adult masculinity needs to be banished. Departing from the hermetic security of *The Life*, Dickens places two beatified children in perilous circumstances. The senior Dombey wants a male heir who will be a reproduction of the man he imagines himself to be: competent in business, influential, his attentions desired by men and women alike. At the same time, he refuses the image of himself as an affectionate father, the image which his daughter harbors in her imagination and summons forth with her desire for his love and approval. Dombey is the hated paternal ego-image imagined from the perspective of a self-hating paternal ego-image: he imposes soul-deforming priorities—money, pride, power—on an epoch of childhood which is itself the only source of an ego-ideal. And yet, despite the scorn he elicits from the narrative, Dombey is eventually redeemed via a series of typically intricate events. One means to his redemption, perhaps the crucial one, is provided by his agent Carker, whom the novel employs as a vehicle of displacement for Dombey's sins. Carker comes to embody Dombey's sexual and monetary appetites in an exaggerated, more actively malevolent form; once displaced, these attributes of the malevolent patriarch can be removed, and the remaining shell of the man reanimated with the affective attributes imparted by his daughter. Florence shatters Dombey's remaining reserve with a self-deprecating lie, begging for his forgiveness when, by all accounts, it is he who should apologize. The fundamental moral structure of Dombey's life culminates in this moment; his ambition for a financial dynasty built on male primogeniture gives way to the salvific, humbling embrace of his daughter.

While Florence redeems her father with a loving gaze, it is also true that, in a sense, her gaze symbolically castrates him. Redemption and castration appear to be the same thing, if indeed the logic of Dickensian sentimentality is such that masculine potency cannot coexist with the sanctified state of affective simplicity. The importance of underlying sexual tensions is borne out by the fact that throughout the novel Florence's sexuality is carefully but imperfectly elided. While she bears what may be a symbol of sexual taint in the bruise she carries from her father's hand, Florence proves she never deserves the stain of such guilt on her character, and thus in the end she becomes a living icon of saintly womanhood, an image likened to a masthead on her husband's ship, which presents "to the roughest men on board an image of something that is graceful, beautiful, and harmless" (908). The symbolic chastity of her marriage to Walter is suggested by the fact that in name the insemination of no new bloodline occurs, for Florence reproduces the Dombey children who initiated the story, giving birth to a little Florence and a little Paul.[5] But such perfect closure also echoes the note of incest that has haunted the novel, and indeed the closing vignettes dwell more on Dombey's presence in this nuclear family than on Walter Gay's. The point to be emphasized is that Dombey is now emasculated; his finances, his sexuality, and his mental capacities have all been stripped away, leaving him a dependant whose senility renders him like a child. Now it is Dombey, and not the toddler Paul, who "repeat[s] the childish question, 'what is money?'" (957). Meanwhile, Carker has been eliminated by the combined forces of women he has wronged and the narrative device of an avenging train; Walter Gay, another potent male adult, is mostly off at sea, and even when "safe at home" he is absent from much of the action.

Thus the novel retreats from images of male power and concludes with a sketch of the nuclear family without a formidable patriarch. Moreover, the manner in which it does so suggests that the need for emasculation stems from the taints of sexual lust and financial ambition with which unneutered masculinity is associated in the narrative. In this regard, Captain Cuttle's vision of the seafaring trade undone by marriages (934) is indeed prophetic, because marriage in *Dombey and Son* challenges the symbolism of the sea as the primary locus of male trial and self-discovery. While young Paul is captured by the plaintive sound of something "the waves are saying" and Walter proves himself in his offstage conduct during a shipwreck, for the protagonist Dombey all trials, changes, and oracular voices are experienced at home. Young males like Paul Dombey are—through death, senility, domestication, or desexualization—destined by the sentimental logic of this narrative to one or another form of absorption into a feminized ethos. Thus "what the waves were saying," one of the choral lines of the novel, might be answered by another choral line, that "*Dombey and Son* is indeed a daughter after all." *Dombey and Son*, begun as Dickens was writing *The Life of Our Lord*, is another fashioning of the Dickensian sentimental religion, where the innocence of spiritual power is maintained by segregating it in realms that are coded infantile, feminine, and domestic.

However, the crucial difference between these texts which we must return to is that Dickens emphatically refused to publish *The Life of Our Lord*. There are several possible explanations for his discretion, not least among them, as I mentioned before, Dickens's fear of sectarian criticism. But in the context of this discussion there is another possible explanation, which is that Dickens sequestered his textual Jesus for the same reason that he might have been drawn to him in the first place. Dickens's religiosity was typically Broad Church in its emphasis on the centrality of Christ—his example, his teachings, and his ambiguous divinity—to Christianity. And yet the very centrality of Jesus was at odds with the narrative logic of much of Dickens's own fiction, specifically as we have observed in *Dombey and Son*, where masculinity is aligned with characters who plot to achieve sexual and monetary advantage. As the original and definitive locus of authority in Protestant Christianity, the idea of Christ calls attention to the empowering prerogatives of male adulthood which *Dombey and Son* as well as *The Life of Our Lord* work so hard to obscure or eliminate. Thus the Christ of *The Life* is a sequestered figure symbolically as well as materially. The style and textual history of *The Life* transform him into an occasion for celebrating an infantilized religiosity within the privacy of the Dickens family home. The secrecy and infantilization which thus shroud the masculinity of the Dickensian Christ reflect his status as a displaced symbol of the shrouding of male authorial power in the published narratives of Dickensian sentimentality.

Literary Interests, Prurient and Christ-like

Thus far, I have outlined an approach to two of Dickens's mid-century sentimental narratives based on the belief that an ideological logic governs the distribution of behaviors and attributes among characters. The various duties (ethical, economic, sexual, spiritual, emotional, and intellectual) which bind together the families of these narratives are divided between characters according to the cultural proprieties of gender and age. Given the simultaneous importance and fragility of these proprieties, it is not surprising that the more studied of the narratives, *Dombey and Son*, both undermines and confirms them. Indeed, part of the Victorian reader's interest in *Dombey* undoubtedly stemmed from a fascination with the various threats, internal and external, which beset the desired subjective proprieties of the characters construed as family members—as son, mother, father, wife, daughter, nephew, or husband—and which are eliminated at the novel's close by the reinstatement of a sentimental domestic regime. Similar tensions between scandal and moral sensibility are standard fare in the plots of most sentimental novels. But, as we shall see, *Dombey and Son* rises to another level of narrative complexity by thematizing this tension, recasting it as one between two forms of interest, the prurient and the sympathetic. The tension between prurient and sympathetic interests is not only staged in the imaginations of the novel's characters but also imparted to the novel's readers. Thus this dimension of the novel recapitulates one of the effects we observed in *The Life of Our Lord*: it brings an implied reader into the realm of the narrative and casts that reader in a role which completes the novel's internal interpretation of itself as moral cultural fantasy, a quasi-religious, quasi-ethical literary performance. Later in this section, I will discuss the formal aspects of *Dombey and Son* which encode its concern with the types of interest people take in literature and stories. However, it is important to note that this concern was part of a larger cultural preoccupation with the perceived schism between a literature which entertained and a literature which presumably elevated the characters of its readers. The founding text for this preoccupation was the Victorian Bible—not the Bible per se, but rather the specific Bible of the nineteenth century, situated as it was among various cultural forces, among them the influence which religious spokespeople and literary critics exerted over an expanding reading public, itself the consequence of religious educational efforts and cheap print. Consequently, before returning to *Dombey*, I would like to review some of the attitudes which Dickens and his contemporaries shared toward the literary appeal of the Bible and of popular novels.

The Life of Our Lord is based primarily upon events recorded in the Gospel of Luke, which in England was widely (and wrongly) considered to be, along with Matthew, one of the two earliest Gospels. By selecting Luke's Gospel as the basis for his children's testament, Dickens not only demonstrated a predictable preference for a synoptic, highly narrative gospel but also, as Janet Larson notes, expressed his belief that a sufficient understanding of Christianity could be gained from the New Testament alone (12). Indeed, Dickens's preference for the New over the Old Testament was well known: Forster comments that he had "a profound conviction of [the New Testament's] self-sufficiency" (xv), and Edgar Johnson treats as common knowledge Dickens's disdain for the Old Testament (332). This attitude is reflected not only in the religious education he provided for his children but also in that which he recommended for trade schools and reforming prostitutes. The curriculum of "schools of industry," Dickens wrote, should reinforce "the sublime lessons of the New Testament," for these are the "only means of removing the scandal and the danger that beset us in this nineteenth century of our Lord" (Johnson 341). And in regard to the religious instruction provided at Urania Cottage, he cautioned Miss Burdett Coutts to draw solely from "the *New* Testament" because he feared the harm that could be done to "this class of minds by the injudicious use of the Old" (*Letters* 5: 181–82).

Behind Dickens's injunction to Burdett Coutts was a sizable debate about the relative virtues of the two Testaments and the different divine personalities and ethical systems associated which each. Textual evidence that the Jewish Yahweh and the various civilizations chronicled in the Old Testament were cruel and vindictive—even at times barbaric—troubled religious and secular readers alike. To some minds this made it difficult to accept the Old Testament as a commendable text for developing character. Thackeray responded to divinely ordained acts of bloodshed such as the slaughter of the Canaanites with enraged satire: "Murder them Jehu smash run them through the body Kill 'em old and young" (Chadwick 1: 529). Richard Carlile, the radical atheist, sounded a similar note of concern as part of his anti-Christian campaign: "The infant reader of the Bible is trained to ideas of violence, blood, rapine, murder, and all other human violences. The slaying of Abel, the drowning of the world, the attempt of Abraham to make a sacrifice of his son Isaac, the rite of circumcision all] are, or should be, shocking to an infant mind, and is a mass of the most improper reading for children or any other person" (434). Evangelicals might have been less troubled by the wrathful God of the prophets, but they shared in the tendency, almost universal in British Christian culture, to demote the theological importance of the Old Testament. Hence in the first half of the nineteenth century, when foreign and domestic missionary efforts were particularly energetic, the tract societies printed many more editions of the New Testament and the Psalms than of entire Bibles. Of course, the popularity of Psalms was due in part to their exceptional merit, but their specific literary reception was also shaped by the fact that British readers were accustomed to typological interpretation, and hence approached the Psalms as prophetically Christological poems and as lyrics of the *Christian* soul in moments of trial or celebration. On the other hand, the ability of Evangelical publishing organizations to treat the New Testament as an autonomous text seems at odds with the supposed prevalence of typological interpretation, which proceeds by connecting an incident or appellation in the Old Testament with one in the New in such a way as to make the meaning reciprocally revealed between the incidents. In such an exegetical practice, the two Testaments could not sensibly be promulgated separately: the fact that they were reflects the heightened emphasis which Victorian Evangelical Christianity placed upon personal salvation and the necessity for a powerfully experienced encounter with the life and teachings of Christ. It also reflects the historical climate of belief in which it was conceivable for Dickens to write a paraphrase of a Gospel that takes only negligible notice of Old Testament prophecies. Despite his antipathy toward Evangelicalism, indeed toward any aggressive form of Protestantism, when it came down to the religious education of prostitutes, technical students, and even his own children, Dickens shared with the Evangelicals a belief that the fundamental Christian conversion was exclusively contingent upon textual communions with Christ.

However, the belief that the Gospels were the most edifying books of the Bible was unsettled by the similarly common opinion that for dramatic intrigue and narrative interest, the Old Testament far surpassed the New. In *Jane Eyre*, the young heroine incriminates herself in conversation with Rev. Brocklehurst by voicing a preference for "Revelations and the book of Daniel, and Genesis and Samuel, and a little bit of Exodus, and some parts of Kings and Chronicles, and Job and Jonah" (35). Jane's childhood affinity for Old Testament literature reflects the Arnoldian belief that the stages of moral development take one through an Old Testament ethics of vindication on the way to a New Testament ethics of forgiveness. Thus Jane becomes disillusioned with the pleasure of vengeance ("as aromatic wine it seemed, on swallowing, warm and racy: its afterflavour, metallic and corroding" [41]), and eventually takes up the New Testament under the influence of Helen Burns, who does not recommend its good stories but rather its good lessons. The notion that the Old Testament provided more engrossing reading than the New is similarly a theme in *The Bible the Best Book*, one of Charlotte Tonna's popular Evangelical tracts for children. As the story begins, two children, Thomas and Ellen, sit down to read the Bible. They turn to their favorite parts, the Old Testament histories, only to learn from their mother that these histories are insignificant if considered without reference to Christ. This provokes from Thomas the confession that when he reads the Bible, he forgets "everything but the pleasure of the story" (7). As a result, Thomas and Ellen receive from their mother a lesson in typological interpretation which enables them to redeem the interesting pleasures of the Old Testament by referring them to the sublime mysteries of the New. Like Brontë, Tonna illustrates the different levels of interest aroused in young readers by the two Testaments in such a way as to advocate a hermeneutics of interdependence. Hence, for Tonna, the tension between interest and edification is resolved simply enough by resorting to the respectable theological position that there is a dialogue between the prophets and the gospels which makes them, in effect, an interwoven text. For Brontë, as for Dickens, however, the perception of a division in the Bible between the testament of scandalous and bloody interest and the testament of wholesome and morally sound edification was of greater consequence. It invoked the question of their own novels' literary interest, and the much-debated relationship between sensationalism and moralism in popular fiction.

As is well known, Dickens's sales had fallen off somewhat with *Martin Chuzzlewit,* and in the later 1840s he stood, to his own mind, in need of another resounding success. It was perhaps for this reason that when the sales of *Dombey and Son* reached an impressive 33,000 a month, Dickens expressed to Forster both relief and enthusiasm: "Meantime thank God, Dombey is, out of all question, the most popular book, in the best sense of the word, I have ever written. And I assure you, I take enormous pains with it" (*Letters* 5: 42). Richard Altick suggests that the "pains" Dickens took with *Dombey* "imply a more acute concern than before for his readers' satisfaction and comfort" (122). And yet their satisfaction was not unproblematically connected to their perceived moral benefit, for as Altick also notes, contemporary dramatizations of Dickens's works suggest that the scenes readers found most "agreeable" were not those which reviewers found the most edifying. Thus a writer for the *North British Review* comments that "in the process of [dramatic] transmutation, the better and more sober parts necessarily disappear, and the striking figures, amusing low life, smart vulgar conversation, and broad farce, are naturally preserved with care" (Altick 121). More pointedly, David Masson took both Dickens and Thackeray to task for not setting higher examples of artistic and moral integrity. Surveying the "fictitious literature" of England in 1851, Masson concedes that while the aim of all such literature "is primarily to interest the reader," the writers of the day have failed their calling by pursuing only "that special kind of interest which consists in mere amusement." The motives of fiction-writer, he argues, have become vitiated by greed and market forces; "the spirit of craft and money-making has crept into our artistic literature," and hence writers of fiction "candidly own that they write to make money and amuse people." A premise behind Masson's argument is that material and immaterial "interests" are in conflict and almost mutually exclusive—almost, but not quite, for in a gesture typical of the period's popular aesthetics, Masson proposes an ideal of art wherein "no kind of literary composition whatever is valuable that is not interesting" (88). The hope that the best kind of popularity could also be the most profitable rationalized literary work in an economic and discursive environment which organized itself around perceived conflicts and alliances between financial interest, moral interest, and "low" or "vulgar" interest in sensational material.

Thus, like the Victorian Bible, Victorian novels such as *Dombey and Son* were thought to struggle in a breach between their readership's lurid desires and spiritual needs. Indeed, nineteenth-century literary critics and commentators discussed this aspect of popular fiction almost as much as they discussed plot, characterization, and description. In this light, we might ask to what extent Victorian styles of fictional narrative were determined by assumptions not only about the nature of literature but also—and inseparably—about the nature of nineteenth-century readers.

Dombey and Son thematizes the issue of readers and their literary tastes by offering several instances of characters who show different kinds of interest in the stories of other people's lives. An untoward curiosity is displayed by Miss Brown and Alice when they pin down Rob the Grinder, demanding "to be told all about" the activities of the invidious Carker (826). An even more excessive curiosity is demonstrated by the muckraker Perch, who disseminates in print the scandalous details of Dombey's private affairs. And yet these instances of curiosity simply encode within the narrative the positions of curiosity and ignorance occupied by the readers, who are also complicit, albeit at the level of illusion, in the penetration of Carker's and Dombey's hidden lives. Like "the Jew and Christian auctioneers," and like the footsteps that reverberate in Dombey's mind, the narrative pursues with relentless energy—and, in part, for the purposes of profit—its excavation of Dombey's "private property," leaving at the end "not a secret place in the whole house" (928). What saves the novel, and the readers, from this internal condemnation of curiosity in thrilling and scandalous stories are the alternate images of interest found in the characters Florence Dombey and Harriet Carker. Ideally, the interest of the novelist and his readers is to be likened not to Perch but rather to Floy, whose invasion of her father's house brings compassion, sympathy, and forgiveness. Or, in a less prominent but more telling moment, their curiosity might be likened to that of Harriet Carker, whose kindly interest in the story of Alice Marwood's life brings about the conversion of the prostitute on her deathbed.

Alice's deathbed scene returns us to the subject of the Dickensian Christ, for this is one of the only moments in *Dombey* where Christ is explicitly mentioned.[6] Dickens here employs a standard Evangelical trope as he has Harriet read to the dying convert from the New Testament:

> Harriet complied and read—read the eternal book for all the weary, and the heavy-laden; for all the wretched, fallen, and neglected of this earth— read the blessed history, in which the blind lame palsied beggar, the criminal, the woman stained with shame, the shunned of all our dainty clay, has each a portion ... read the ministry of Him who, through the round of human life, and all its hopes and griefs, from birth to death, from infancy to age, has sweet compassion for, and interest in, its every scene and stage, its every suffering and shadow. (923)

Harriet is here revealed to be a type of Christ—his imitator as well as his mediator in that, like him, she shows a "sweet compassion for, and interest in" Alice's life. As such, the Christ of this passage is the distant original of a salvific curiosity which the narrative seeks to distinguish from its examples and enactments of pernicious curiosity. Harriet Carker's compassionate interest in Alice Marwood ignites in "the fallen woman" an interest in the text of Scriptures that brings her together with the saving interest of Christ. The narrative extends the chain of female associations with Christ-like curiosity in the next chapter, where Miss Tox reemerges as a newly sympathetic character, her formerly self-serving interest in the events of Dombey's life transformed into a "sympathy [that] is such she can scarcely speak." By an act of narratorial fiat, she is suddenly and somewhat arbitrarily altered: "[Miss Tox's] heart is very tender, her *compassion* very genuine, her homage very real" (933; italics added).

Thus the novel distributes among its characters examples of both noble and ignoble interests. The opposition of "vulgar" to "sober" forms of entertainment which concerned Dickens's critics is thus reconfigured as a function of both reception and literary style. In this regard, the above passage from *Dombey* replicates the efforts of *The Life of Our Lord* to inscribe a reader who is more than ideal—a reader who is, like Harriet, like the Dickens children, yet another *imitatio Christi* insofar as she is assigned the attributes of the Christ represented in the text. And yet, insofar as the Christian deity appears in *Dombey* as the ultimate and originating model of an "interest" which is also a "sweet compassion," this appearance is, admittedly, very mediated, arguably gratuitous, even buried.

On the one hand, this adds to our reading of the novel the irony that compassionate interest is assigned to the highest Christian authority in a passage which most readers would not find very interesting. Indeed, if the Victorian reader's interest in the novel survived this passage, it was possibly due to the proximity between Harriet's recitation of the crucial but notoriously dull New Testament and the other, more sensational story which this chapter relates, that of the prostitute Alice's scandalous connections to the house of Dombey. Prostitutes in Dickens's novel are numerous, and not in all cases does he exploit the opportunity to allude to the prostitutes of the Gospels. By doing so here, he simultaneously redeems his character and his narrative concern with her story: both are placed in textual proximity to the purifying image of Christ.

On the other hand, the fact that Christ is *so* mediated should alert us to the similarly buried presence of the author in his role as the authoritative mediator—of Christ, of the story, and of the story's intended literary appeal, both high and low. For there are at least three layers of mediation: Harriet reads from the Evangelist's report of Christ, and the Dickensian narrator presents a synopsis of what she reads. The narrator thus draws upon the irreproachable motives of a saintly woman character, and the two male figures of authority—Dickens and Christ—are distanced from the scene of a feminized redemption even as their authoritative presence is obliquely invoked. Moreover, despite the perfunctory fashion in which this moment of Bible reading is narrated, the possibility that it evidences a more general if subconscious desire on Dickens's part to confiscate the power of the Gospel is strengthened by the fact that he was, as we know, simultaneously writing another paraphrase of Scripture, *The Life of Our Lord*. In this regard, Dickens seems to supersede his own Christ. While we may acknowledge the passage to be, at best, a lesser example of Dickensian virtuosity, we must still see the author as the superior presence in that his prose is meant to induce a readerly experience of the sentimental aesthetic. Alice's conversion to Christ accompanies an attempted enactment of the reader's conversion to the Dickensian religion of the heart, an enactment that is occurring in and through the moment of reading. Thus, not only are Alice and the text at stake in this redemption, but also the reader. All three are brought together in a moment of symbolic narration, wherein the representation of reading the Gospel vies with the star of the Gospel for the power to impart a transformative grace, a grace that changes interest into compassion and, in Alice's case, heartfelt remorse. The present agent of this grace, concealed beneath the veils of Harriet, of Christ, and of the Gospels, is Dickens himself, acting through the agile powers of his prose.

In summary, the two scenes of Christian enlightenment which we have considered thus far—the enlightenment of Alice which is represented in *Dombey* and the enlightenment of Dickens's children which is enacted by *The Life of Our Lord*—cloak adult masculinity in ways that register Dickens's concern with his own literary influence: its legitimacy, its relationship to the perceived dispositions of Victorian readers, and, most uncomfortably, its origins in a male consciousness which his own sentimental precepts held in abeyance. Both of the scenes we have considered conflate the Gospels with the word of Dickens in such a way as to make the Dickensian text the source of a quasi-sacred literary power. Both scenes reflect in their language their particular relationship to their readers; Alice's deathbed scene completes *Dombey and Son*'s inquiry into the moral valence of literary interest, while *The Life* precludes the compromising issue of the marketplace by banishing it and its adult readers altogether. And in both instances, the mediated appearance of Christ simultaneously calls attention to adult masculinity as the ultimate source of a salvific literary influence and to the necessity for a deflection of this influence through the represented others of women and children. As such, the Dickensian Christ is a nodal point of tension in the organization of power and authority in sentimental narratives.

Masculine Dilemmas and Feminine Resolutions

As a popular and influential author, a man whom critics identified as the spokesman of a sentimental gospel, of a social reform based on empathy, Dickens shared in the predicament of his Christ. For if, as one critic stated the familiar Victorian cliché, "in spite of the vaunted superiority of men, there are heights of moral elevation, and even influence, which woman may claim as peculiarly her own" (Olmstead 1: 553), then the problem handed to Dickens was how to claim and justify access to those heights as a male novelist.[7] Implicitly or explicitly, Victorian reviewers of Dickens called attention to this problem. Margaret Oliphant, David Masson, Walter Bagehot, and George Stott—a sampling of reviewers with diverse literary and political affiliations—shared some distinctive tendencies in their approaches to the rhetorical methods of Dickens's prose. They all identified a latent religious or ethical content in his novels which they referred to as a gospel, a moral philosophy, or a system; they all considered the idealistic or sentimental style of his writing to be the most important factor in the communication of this religious and ethical content; and finally, they all described Dickens's literary persona as that of a child or a feminine genius, thus aligning him with the represented spiritual and moral authority figures in his own texts. Moreover, these reviewers indicated that Dickens's mastery of a sentimental style rendered him incapable of either expressing or successfully representing a mature, gentlemanly masculinity.[8]

There are passages in Dickens's fiction which might be read as encoding an awareness of the critical dialogue surrounding his work. Certainly he was cognizant of the moral authority which many popular authors of the day claimed with a seemingly unflinching confidence, and this cognizance gives a symbolic resonance to many scenes in his works where moral authority is either corroborated or undermined. For our purposes, there is one passage in *Dombey and Son* which is particularly telling. This passage relates an interaction between Harriet Carker and Mr. Morfin, "the hazel-eyed bachelor." At the culmination of his oblique courtship of Harriet, Morfin accedes to Harriet's wish to have her inherited fortune secretly rechanneled to Dombey, and thus he relinquishes his influence upon the outcome of events. As Morfin imagines it, his concession to Harriet's will is a kind of erasure of his obtrusive presence from the story of Harriet's and her brothers' lives: "I have no right to mar the great end of a great history, by any obtrusion of my own weak self. I have every right to bend my head before what you confide in me, satisfied that it comes from a higher and better source of inspiration than my poor worldly knowledge" (916). This male humility before a woman's act of self-sacrifice epitomizes the moments of secular worship which are so frequent in Dickens's novels: the object of worship is female and immaculate, while the worshiper is a man who gestures toward his own inadequacy. But in the context of this discussion, Morfin's self-abnegating gesture might additionally be read as an expression of the Dickensian narrator's self-consciousness before the specter of his own displaced and feminized authority. Harriet has been invested with power over a sexual and a financial situation: she possesses Alice's confession, deserves to possess it, and mediates forgiveness; in addition, she dictates the conditions by which Dombey's fortune is returned to him. Alice's confession of sexual taint thus passes through Harriet and is returned to Alice in the form of absolution; in parallel fashion, Dombey's wealth passes through Harriet and is returned to him in the form of a secret gift—it becomes, via the impress of her generosity, money laundered of the taint of capitalistic acquisition. By thus assigning Harriet limited agency over a sexual and a monetary crisis—two areas of activity inappropriate to women's sphere per se—the narrative channels these issues through a woman who serves to purify them. In much the same way, the Dickensian narrator passes his own authority through characters like Harriet and Florence and reabsorbs that authority in such a way as to preserve the feminine alterity which is the condition of its validation. *Dombey and Son* bespeaks the powers of domesticating influence and salvation by sentiment. And yet, like

Morfin, the narrative voice of the novel demotes, even theatrically erases, the masculine origins of its projection of female authority.

There is another detail, however, which further complicates this picture. As the novel recounts the manner in which Harriet takes charge of events, it makes some effort to protect her from the charge of willfulness. Hence, oddly enough, even as she dictates the terms of Dombey's financial future, Harriet preserves her demeanor as a quiescent and long-suffering woman. In related fashion, one of the salient features of Harriet's bedside manner with the dying Alice is her passivity. In the scene where she reads to Alice from the Gospel, the narrative reiterates that she neither glosses nor comments but simply "reads." Rather than urging Christian beliefs upon the fallen Alice, Harriet merely "complies" with the prostitute's wishes. Ironically, given the narrative concern with forms of interest in human stories, the hallmark of an ideal mediator of the divine story seems to be what I have previously described as benign curiosity, but what might also be described as disinterestedness.

The significance of this disinterestedness, of this passive concern, is illuminated by the epistolary records of Dickens's attempts to reform the real-life prostitutes of Miss Burdett Coutts's "home for wayward women." In his correspondence with Miss Burdett Coutts, Dickens stressed the importance of pursuing spiritual regeneration slowly, because the main danger lay in alienating a woman before the seeds of change had taken root. The quiescent demeanor that Harriet Carker displays in *Dombey and Son* is consistent with the methods that Dickens recommended for approaching the real-life prostitutes at Urania Cottage. Hence it was of the utmost importance for reformers to refrain from didactic reprimands and maudlin piety; the "unfortunate creatures are to be *tempted* to virtue," Dickens writes, "they cannot be dragged, driven, or frightened" (*Letters* 5: 183). The letters in which he made these recommendations were contemporaneous with *Dombey and Son*, and indeed the narratives of imagined conversion in both the novel and the letters proceed along similar lines, with the prostitute lured gradually to a point of anxious receptivity, while the agent of her conversion forces nothing from her and nothing upon her. However, as we shall now see, the record of Dickens's involvement in Urania Cottage also tells another story, wherein the distinction between saviors and sinners is neither so clear nor so singular in purpose.

The Prostitute's Redemption

From a nineteenth-century perspective there was nothing unusual in Dickens's literary and philanthropic preoccupation with prostitutes. Judith Walkowitz, in her important study of Victorian prostitution, observes that it was a "public and private obsession"; Gladstone, for one, acknowledged that it was "the chief burden of my soul" (Walkowitz 32). As always, prostitution was objected to on religious, moral, and hygienic grounds, but there was never any doubt that it presented an ideological more than a hygienic threat to Victorian society. Prostitution disrupted quite visibly the boundaries which demarcated the public standards of female subjectivity. By bringing femininity into simultaneous contact with sexuality and commerce, the prostitute challenged the well-defined roles of symbolic and material exchange which women played in Victorian culture. However, even the ideological motives do not fully account for the overdetermined nature of her social presence; if the prostitute aroused as much philanthropic concern as the working poor or the non-Christians of other lands, it was probably because of the exciting nature of her story. Scandal as well as ideology were instrumental in keeping her at the center of the middle-class Victorian consciousness. The prostitute presented an interesting phenomenon as well as an ideologically vested interest.

All these factors help fill in the backdrop against which Dickens's religious and sentimental engagement with prostitution played out. Although Dickens thought it best to approach prostitutes with a kind but detached manner, the two emotions which he most frequently expresses for them are "anxiety" and "interest." He writes to Miss Burdett Coutts of the "unspeakable interest" he has in saving "fallen women" (*Letters* 5: 188); an unusual case history he finds to be "interesting and touching in the extreme" (178); and on several occasions he alludes to the "great anxiety" he feels in connection with the Urania Cottage project. One letter begins on a particularly urgent note: "My dear Miss Coutts, I am in a state of great anxiety to talk with you about your 'Home'" (177). Such pronounced interest and anxiety sharply distinguish Dickens from the ideal agents of conversion described in his correspondence and in his portrayal of Harriet Carker. Ostensibly, he recommended restraint to the reformers at Urania Cottage because it was effective, but the recommendation seems to have run counter to his own feelings for this project, his abiding and somewhat dubious fascination with the prostitutes he hoped to see transformed. The possibility that his relationship with these women provided him with rich literary material has been suggested by Joss Lutz Marsh, who analyzes the manner in which Dickens recorded and controlled the prostitutes' personal accounts (409–12).[9] Certainly Dickens's paradoxical stance toward the objects of his conversion betokens an overdetermined relationship, one that confounds his attitudes toward the recipients of his philanthropy with his attitudes toward the pleasures of his literary art. For by confessing himself to be a man interested in the stories of prostitutes, Dickens aligns himself with the characters in *Dombey and Son* who are driven by a prurient curiosity. He also aligns himself with the readers who are reflected by this thematic aspect of *Dombey and Son*, readers who are requested to vindicate with benevolent motives their attraction to his fiction's "striking figures, amusing low life, [and] smart vulgar conversation."

Moreover, Dickens's project to reclaim wayward women is, like *Dombey and Son*, protected from the uncertainty of its motives and goals by the talismanic image of Christ. Both the reformers and the reformed at Urania Cottage stand in need of the chastening influence of the Lord, whom Dickens seeks to impress upon their memories. Hence he reminds Burdett Coutts that the reformers' treatment of the prostitutes should resemble that of Christ (*Letters* 5: 7), while at the same time, in a letter to the prostitutes, he recommends Christ as an inspiration for holding fast to the path of improvement. But if inspiration and spiritual wisdom come from

Christ, it is also true that they come from Dickens. Literature played a key role in Dickens's scheme for the psychological makeover of the prostitute, and among the authors whom he recommended for the purpose were Jeremy Taylor, Wordsworth, Crabbe, and himself (*Letters* 5: 185, 186n). In the living room of Urania Cottage, Dickens directed that two devotional inscriptions he had composed be displayed; additionally, a copy of his "Appeal to Fallen Women" was distributed to the inmates for private study, and he later wrote an address that was read to each woman upon her admission (179, 186). Despite the emphasis placed on Christ, it is not clear who is the originator of the inspired word and who is the intermediary. Does Dickens convey the message of Christ to the fallen women of his age, or does Christ serve as the displaced accreditation of the message of Dickens?

In this light, we can see how the feeling of interest in the prostitute's condition might readily usher in the other emotion which Dickens ascribes to himself—namely, anxiety. The project at Urania Cottage reflects the depth of the Victorian faith in the written word, the belief that texts are capable of an ambitious mission, the thorough refashioning of an individual's subjectivity. To a certain extent, then, Dickens's anxiety might be a response to his own powerful influence, an expression of misgiving for the hidden knowledge that, beneath the layers of mediation through the images of Christ or of sainted women and children, the instigator of these conversions is a man who is himself complicit in the suspect interests of his reading public no less than the suspect desires of his adult male characters. If so, it is fitting that although Dickens's anxiety was most pronounced when he approached the potential converts among "wayward women," it was also present when he faced the unconverted among his own family, as suggested by the opening sentence of *The Life of Our Lord*: "My dear children, I am very anxious that you should know about the History of Jesus Christ" (11).

Dissimilar as the inhabitants of Urania Cottage might be from Dickens's children, the two are in a similar predicament vis-à-vis the author of their salvation. The fallen woman who reads "An Appeal to Fallen Women" and the tractable child who reads *The Life of Our Lord* consume the word of Dickens as the author of their ideal subjectivities, their ideological destinies as the proper woman or the proper child of sentimental culture. And while any explanation for the emotions which he expressed in his nineteenth-century diction can only be speculative, it seems plausible that Dickens's feeling of anxiety is a symptom of this basic solipsism which haunts his philanthropy, the desire to better society by reproducing individuals whose inner and outer behavior fulfills the typology of a sentimental religion.

This description gains some credence insofar as it reflects the problems of authority and intersubjectivity that haunted the pattern of conversion in Victorian Evangelicalism. Dennis Walder has showed how Dickens's lifelong assaults on Evangelicalism originated in an intimate and emotionally charged familiarity, the result being that he reproduces aspects of the Evangelical tradition even as he seeks to distance it, publicly and psychologically, from himself.[10] Additionally, the vexed intimacy between Dickensian sentimentalism and Evangelicalism might also reflect the extent to which both ideologies are shaped by the historical conditions of a print-based society, and they both reproduce the premises and problems of that society. Consequently, in his expressions of anxiety for the objects of his proselytizing, Dickens instances the operative paradox which drives Evangelical religion; the agent of conversion needs the sinner almost more than the sinner needs him. In Evangelical discourse, this need is encoded by its opposite, the projection of anxiety upon the sinner who is also a potential convert. Anxiety is typically the insignia of the unregenerate, the man or woman who has yet to attain assurance in Christ. In many conversion narratives, it is the emotion which marks the liminal state between sin and salvation; the unregenerate's redemption begins with the feeling of anxiety for the state of his or her immortal soul. Indeed, one could say that anxiety was a crucial, almost obligatory, in fact, almost ritualized condition of the Evangelical psyche. And it was, in all its manifestations, an insignia of the inescapability of doubt, of unworthiness, and of utter dependence upon Christ. For anxiety could be quieted by the assurance of Christ, but even after salvation it lingered on as a useful residue in the Christian, guarding her, as Wilberforce said, from complacency (34). Dickens was no Evangelical, but his habits of diction expose the concealed logic of this predominantly Evangelical trope. As a philanthropist, he is the mediator of salvific knowledge, and yet he takes on the qualities and emotional state typically projected onto the recipients of such knowledge; he becomes the anxious one, the needy one, the one who is interested to hear and learn more. He becomes, in this fashion, the one who is truly anxious for reassurance, the one who desires to see his beliefs validated by the conversion of others. Along with the cast of characters involved—Christ, the prostitute, and the reformers—Dickens finds himself in a web of projected emotions and mediated authority; the relationships among them, almost of necessity, blur the lines between the mediators and the recipients of salvation. Thus the agents of Dickensian reform graft sinners on saviors, converters on converted; the fluid boundaries between them are the suppressed confusion of the outwardly distinct boundaries between the author, the objects, and the agents of a sentimental conversion.

Conclusion

In the preceding pages I have explored the possibility that in the 1840s, Dickens was drawn to the dissimilar figures of Christ and the prostitute for similar reasons. In 1848 he wrote *The Life of Our Lord* for the purpose of his children's religious education, but the text served another purpose as well, adjusting the character of Christ to fit the sentimental logic that informed all his fiction of the time. By infantilizing the Gospel story, Dickens banished adult masculinity from the scene and rendered Christ more akin to the child readers who were already perceived to possess a monopoly on sacred privilege. In a similar vein, his efforts to reform the inhabitants of Urania Cottage were arguably driven by a desire to adjust these women to the same sentimental logic—in effect, to control the representational status of women, rendering them capable of the sanctified roles which women were expected to fill in Victorian society. Thus while the image of Christ in the nineteenth century transgressed the boundaries separating spiritual authority from adult masculinity, the image of the prostitute posed a parallel threat by transgressing the boundaries which separated a sanctified feminine sphere from sexuality and commodification. Consequently, if prostitutes were, as Dickens referred to them, "tarnished and battered images of God" (*Letters* 5: 183), the mission to renovate their womanly souls, like the project of writing a child's life of Christ, was one of creating emasculated images of God.

Such issues of representation had significant ramifications for Dickens's literary art, which also straddled, somewhat uncomfortably, the perceived boundaries between gender roles and between literary entertainment and edification. As a male author writing in a sentimental mode, Dickens sequestered his literary persona behind a style which was understood to be feminine and childlike, a style which complemented the spiritual prerogatives allotted to the women and children portrayed in his fiction. And as a literary sage who thus appropriated a feminine spiritual authority which he sold in novel form, Dickens violated the separation of immaterial from material value which purportedly ruled the lives of women as well as the production of art. Insofar as these several cultural operations overlap—the rules governing the Victorian woman, the Victorian Christ, and the Victorian author—they do so under an overarching logic that divides purity from sexuality, authority from guilt, and sanctity from monetary exchange. Through the self-reflexive dimensions of his fiction, Dickens manages to register both the imposing ideological façade of a sentimental culture built upon these divisions and the contradictions and tensions which existed just under its surface.

Of Dickens's *Life of Our Lord* it is certainly true that, as Ruskin pronounced of Italian portraits of Christ, "the greatest painters fall therein below their accustomed level" (*Modern Painters II* 317). But as we have seen, the reasons for his failure reflect the complex interactive symbolism of the positions of childhood, adult femininity, and adult masculinity. The adult male of Victorian sentimentality is distinguished from the women and children of his culture not only by the condition of his implicit spiritual and moral inadequacy, but also by the tacit acknowledgment that the women and children he worships are both the products of his own imagination and the displaced vehicles of his own promulgation of truths. Thus within the various rituals of Victorian worship, adult masculinity is not and cannot be a condition of the successfully represented object of worship, because this implies godhead, the unity of the subject and object of creation. This reluctance to emulate Christ in his ultimate act of presumption—in Saint Paul's words, to emulate him in the "robbery" of his father's divinity—informs the interactive symbolism of the gendered and generational characters of Dickensian sentimentality. Divinity feminized or infantilized was divinity contained and vicariously borrowed. And it was divinity free from the taint of self-doubt, insofar as it differed from the male subject who could not claim the same for himself. Thus, the male subjects of Dickens's paradigms of worship do not create deities in their own images because it is not in their interest to do so. They need the difference between themselves and their gods to maintain the order of their theology, wherein the anxiety of authority is translated into the anxious neediness of the recipient of salvation, the worshiper of ministering angels.

CHAPTER 5

"But Do We See One Woman Who Looks Like a Female Christ?"
The Messiahs of Florence Nightingale

It is well known that an enthusiastic mythology arose around the figure of Florence Nightingale during the Crimean War. In a war best known for bureaucratic ineptitude and negligence, it is appropriate that the greatest popular hero was not a leader of the battlefield but rather a hero of the hospital, a self-proclaimed vigilante on a mission to correct the hygienic mismanagement of Her Majesty's Army. And, given the coupling of femininity and worship which we have just seen exemplified in *Dombey and Son*, it is also appropriate that this hero was a woman. For in her inexhaustible ministry to the wounded soldiers of the Battles of Balaclava and Inkerman, Nightingale fulfilled Victorian England's sentimental ideal of womanhood, and in so doing she presented the lyricists and printers in Seven Dials and Soho with the raw materials for a living legend. She became an object of public reverence, celebrated in penny ballads such as "The Nightingale in the East" and "The Shadow on the Pillow." Monkton Milnes, a family friend and onetime suitor, quoted a politician's observation that "Florence in the Hospital [made] intelligent to him the Saints of the Middle Ages" (Cook 1: 238). The distillation of such accolades into public culture was not a trend that Nightingale encouraged, but even her retreat from fame was incorporated into her hagiography; the author of the ca. 1855 penny-edition of her biography noted that the Savior, likewise, instructed his followers not to publish abroad the accounts of his works (*The*

Only and Unabridged Edition 12). Lytton Strachey, in his narrative of Nightingale's part in the Crimean War, ridiculed the English ambassador to Constantinople for suggesting that the *Times* fund be spent on a Protestant church at Pera instead of medical needs. But in the person of Florence Nightingale it appears that England got both, since as Strachey writes, in the hospitals of Scutari "a passionate adoration spread among the men.... 'Before she came', said a soldier, 'there was cussin' and swearin', but after that it was as 'oly as a church'" (136–37).

Nightingale herself had a fascinating and complex relationship with the discourses of religion and gender available in her day. Not surprisingly, the hagiography and Christology of her private life are at once more psychologically complex and more intellectually progressive than those of the sentimental celebrations of her which were popular during the height of her fame in the mid and late 1850s. Scholars such as Elaine Showalter and Mary Poovey have thematized such discrepancies between Nightingale's public and private personae. They find her to be an intriguing, albeit unwilling feminist ancestor for whom Victorian conceptions of religion and gender interacted in illogical but ideologically useful ways.[1] In this chapter, I wish to add to recent investigations of Florence Nightingale by reassessing the private life of her ideas and spirituality, a life dominated by her diverse Christology. My analysis draws from three textual sources: *Suggestions for Thought to Searchers After Religious Truth*, the three-volume work of religious philosophy that Nightingale privately published in 1860; *Cassandra*, the semi-autobiographical feminist manifesto that she salvaged from an abandoned novel; and her diaries, letters, and marginalia.[2]

Surveying the references to Christ that appear in the disparate personal records which span a roughly sixty-year period of her life, I have been struck by the consistency of the story that Nightingale tells and tells again; her life is unendurable, and death is preferable to the depression and frustrations that she sustains; her savior calls her to a better existence founded on public usefulness, and through her work she becomes a savior herself; but somehow this apparent resurrection falls short, for Nightingale periodically returns in her private books and diaries to her wish to die. This skeletal plot-line she invokes and echoes at several points in her personal writings; the tropes of death, Christ, and work are the primary materials she uses to tell the stories of her life, stories that are at times interpretive, at times prophetic, but always repetitions of an inward crisis that is resolved by the will to emulate Christ in her work. The plot-line also informs her philosophical opus *Suggestions for Thought*, although here the triad of death, Christ, and work is deployed in a metaphysical and not an individual narrative. Work becomes the resolution to problems of spiritual authority, not personal despair, and Christ becomes the reified insignia of mankind's divine potential.

The moralistic imperative of work was of such importance to Nightingale that she had difficulty reconciling it with her literary proclivities, with the pleasures and satisfaction she derived from reading and writing. Her ambivalent engagement with a work that was not work, with literary habits that consumed her time, will be discussed in the last section of the chapter.

Having committed herself to the Victorian metanarratives of historical positivism and religious reconstruction, Florence Nightingale felt the tension of her gendered exclusion from these narratives in every dimension of her life: emotional, familial, social, and public. Consequently, as in the Christology of Dickens's works, the Christ of Nightingale's imagination is a matrix of Victorian concerns with gender and authority. But her textualization of his image, as we shall see, is shaped by her unique predicament not only as a nurse and a hero but also as a female intellectual who wished to engage in some of the most pressing and male-dominated intellectual and social issues of her day.

Early Life: Death on the Nile, Resurrection in Crimea

Florence Nightingale received the first of several calls from God in 1837, the same year in which Victoria ascended the throne. It is an attractive coincidence, since Nightingale's vocation epitomizes the earnest, moralistic, and socially directed energies that provide one definition for the epithet "Victorian." Years later, Nightingale claimed that her call had always been specifically to nursing. Whether or not the memory was accurate, her family adamantly opposed her wishes for a career from the beginning, and in the more than fifteen years between her initial intimations of a life of public service and her success in the Crimea, she faced enormous resistance from her mother and her sister. Between battles with her sister, Parthenope, and her mother, Fanny, Florence made educational pilgrimages to hospitals and escapist excursions to Rome and Egypt. She also waged a personal war with depression. Commentators on her life tend to single out the years 1850–52 as her most difficult emotionally, but in fact Nightingale had depressive episodes throughout her life. In November 1845, for example, in the midst of conflict with her family, she prayed to God—as she frequently did— to take her life away: "Forgive me, O God, & let me die—this day let me die and it is not for myself that I say this." And here, as so often in her life, Nightingale turned to thoughts of Christ as relief for her mental anguish: "Oh if our Saviour walked the earth how should I not go to him, & would he send me back to live the life again which crushes me into vanity & deceit, or would he not say Do this" (*Ever Yours* 28–29).

The Savior appealed to here typifies the private Jesus of Nightingale's life: a trusted confidant whom she calls upon in psychologically painful moments; a strong male God who offers salvation by demanding work; a sympathetic interlocutor to whom she expresses the suicidal thoughts that she seems to have trusted to few others. Elsewhere the association between her secret wish for death and the Christ of her interior life takes a more austere form; in the marginalia of Nightingale's copy of *De Imitatione Christi*, Nightingale responds to a caution against the wish for death by chastising herself: "Woe to me if I so long for death, when I have not yet learnt the first lesson of forgiveness, long suffering." A few pages later, she glosses the line "when it is morning, think thou wilt not live till evening" with the ironic rejoinder, "Oh how glad I should be" (Papers). The struggle to live a life of Christic imitation entailed the problem of correctly interpreting the life of Christ; Nightingale's interpretation, like that of many of the Victorian readers of Thomas à Kempis's book, pitted introspection against activity. If the former led, by some ineluctable logic, to various forms of mental malaise—in Nightingale's case, to a near suicidal depression—the latter offered relief in the form of chastening hard work. The true imitation, so it was commonly felt, held these two tendencies in equilibrium.[3]

The topics of Christ and death were much in Nightingale's thoughts in 1849–50, when she accompanied her friends Charles and Selina Bracebridge on a journey up the Nile. Throughout the tour, Nightingale remained in dutiful correspondence with her family, and after her return to England they privately published her letters so as to memorialize her vividly rendered impressions of Egypt. Many of the impressions she records are of tombs and of ancient Egyptian attitudes toward death. She also, and increasingly in the course of the voyage, turns to the specter of Christ, whom she conjures with intense necessity. What the specter provides is suspiciously akin to what the tombs provide; while the tombs suggest the possibility of a spiritual practice centered on the consecration of the physical body, the divine presence summons her to a vocation in which spiritual mission entails care of the material world.

Nightingale was not the first to dwell on the topics of Egyptian tombs and mummies, but she dwelt on them almost exclusively, and with unabashed mystical zeal. Indulging in a romanticism she denied herself at home, she exclaims of a funeral papyrus, "I never saw anything more interesting than this supernatural novel, this romance beyond the tombs" (*Letters* 40). Entering the graveyards outside Cairo, she is overtaken by her enthusiasm for the company of the ancient dead: "You pass through the gate, and come, oh change! oh wondrous change! from the city of the living into the city of the dead. I never saw anything so wonderful as this: as far as the eye can reach you see nothing but tombs!" (*Letters* 33). The sight of modern Egyptians does not elicit such pleasant feelings, however, and as John Barrell has observed, Nightingale's letters are quite typical of English travel writing on Egypt in their expressions of revulsion and disgust for the country's living inhabitants. In Barrell's words, Nightingale "is troubled by impossibility of deciding whether the modern Egyptians are human or animal." These horrifying encounters appear to be, like other inconveniences faced by the tourist, difficulties that must first be experienced before "the true Egypt" reveals itself—the Egypt of unpeopled landscape, of antiquity, and of the evocative tombs (106-9). Hence it is only after leaving Cairo and finding herself in an environment of uninhabited ruin that Nightingale's enthusiasm for the spiritual tradition of Egypt flourishes. Significantly, it is the ancient Egyptians' attitudes toward death (or rather those attitudes that she attributes to them) that strike her as a sign of their superiority over modern-day Christians:

> Much more interesting than all, you see a nation so spiritualized that death was to them more interesting than life: or rather, death did not differ to them from life, it was such a small fragment of the whole to them ... with their faith in [the evidence of the senses], the Egyptians seem to have gone farther than other civilizations, seem to have said "we will consider this life interesting only in its connection with the whole of which it is a part". I have often thought how Christ's life showed us this more advanced stage of civilization which we call heaven; how we have persisted in calling him "the man of sorrows", instead of calling him the man who is already in a state of blessedness, the man who has progressed and succeeded. (*Letters* 74)

The harmonic integration of living and dead identities, the assurance of immortality inspired paradoxically by the lifeless body—it is all a far cry from the oppressive reality and desire for oblivion that moved the diarist of 1845 to pray for death. Whether Nightingale's aestheticization of ancient Egyptian death signals a retreat from her suicidal wishes or an accentuation of them is unclear. In either case, the ambiguity leaves open the possibility that the notion of a "death that does not differ from life" not only made thoughts of dying more tolerable but also—and for Nightingale this was the more difficult task—thoughts of living more tolerable.

The above quotation we might pose as Nightingale's first attempt to transform the energies of her personal *Thanatos* into the signifiers of a messianic alternative. Frequently she portrays herself in the letters from Egypt in a state of expectation for the working vocation that might save her from the painful idleness of her life thus far. If the tone of these letters differs from that of her other letters and personal writings it is only in their sense of patience for this deferred destiny, their contentment to dwell passively upon Egypt's ancient proofs that empirical reality is haunted by mystical dimensions. The meditations of her Egyptian tour were important, because in future years she conceived of her career as an attempt to put such meditations into practice, and hence nursing became, like the proposed theology of ancient Egypt, a coupling of mysticism and empiricism. In this way, the personal discoveries of Egypt were channeled into her later work, and without a doubt the ultimate alternative to suicide that Nightingale embraced was work. Indeed, in the second half of her life, the various projects and duties that she chose for herself consumed her imagination along within her time to a point where heaven itself became unthinkable without certain chores: "Father, I do not in the least care whether I die or live," she wrote in 1857, confined in illness to her sofa, "I do not suppose that there will be any less work for us in any future state of existence.... Thou wilt send me where most work is wanted to be done. Lord, here I am. send me" (*Ever Yours* 191). What makes this ominous prayer so interesting is that it evidences the preservation of Nightingale's death instinct even in her working alternative; suicide and nursing, it may be, were both forms of self-annihilation—not true alternatives so much as flip sides of the same coin. If Florence Nightingale couldn't kill herself, then she would resurrect herself in a new form, as a working goddess, a female deity of reform.

The notion of work as a resurrection into a godly form, although not drawn from Nightingale's own imagery, is in keeping with its spirit. Both her English diaries and her letters from Egypt contain contemplations of death that are attended by the proximate presence of Christ, who in the course of the tour of Egypt became so of a piece with its spiritual tradition that he visited Nightingale five times among the tombs. It is not always clear in what sense he visited her—visually, aurally, or as a felt presence—but in any case the nature of the encounters between Nightingale and Christ undergoes a change. While in the diaries and the early letters Nightingale conceives of Christ as an external authority with the power to change her life, if only by ending it, in the course of her journey the tenor of her Christological imaginings becomes at once more hopeful and more strongly willed. At Philoe, she comments: "The myths of Osiris are so typical of our Saviour that it seemed to me as if I were coming to a place where He had lived—like going to Jerusalem; and when I saw a shadow in the moonlight in the temple court, I thought, 'perhaps I shall see him: now he is here'" (*Letters* 114). This was as close as Nightingale's parents came to learning of her visitations from her letters; it was only in autobiographical notes that she recorded "a call from God to be a saviour" (Cook 1: 43). With such concerns frequently on her mind, it is unfortunate that Nightingale's itinerary did not include the Holy Land, although she compensates for this by imaginatively transposing New Testament images onto Egyptian scenery. After her visit to the Temple of Abu Simbel, Nightingale describes the sensation of watching the light of the rising sun enter the sanctuary: "The Marys could hardly have been more surprised when they saw the angel whose countenance was bright as snow, and knew that He whom they sought had risen, than we were when we saw the resurrection which had taken place there" (*Letters* 103). Resurrection, at this the southernmost point of their voyage, begins to assume the former importance accorded death, and in this way Nightingale's letters construct her journey as a recapitulation of the Christian story of a passage through death to life. At the same time, a subtle transformation takes place in Nightingale's subjective position toward Christ, and Florence the supplicant begins to see through the eyes of her savior: "I thought how Christ, if he had been there, would have felt" (*Letters* 200).

The comment would be insignificant except for the fact that Nightingale's sense of the psychological immediacy of Christ continued for at least the next few years, and when history offered her a duty commensurate with her own ambition, she identified with Christ as often as she prayed to him as a savior. This was, then, her personal resurrection, one that she seems to have relived more than once in her life: in periods of productivity, Nightingale feels her powers and destiny, as well as her trials and suffering, equivalent to those of Christ. Thus in her letters from the Crimean War, we find her appropriating Christological references to herself: "The cup which my father hath given me shall I not drink it?" (*Ever Yours* 92). Or, in a letter to her mother, she offers the following comments on the Christ-like nature of her schemes for reform:

> I have often thought in early life ... that I should throw my body into the breach, that I should bridge the chasm to reform,—that I must be an Originator, a Promulgator, an Executor, to each Reformation, Christ said, I am the way *and* the life—in general, there is the way (the thinker), the truth (the speaker), the life (the actor), separate persons to each great step.... I remember thinking, so perish those who pioneer the way for Mankind. But they may perish, but I shall endure. I shall not break my heart of disappointment, though even mine own familiar friends turn against me. No, dearest Mother, I shall do nothing, the originator never does, but greater things than these shall others do—the Army shall be reformed, the Army Medical Board, the military Hospitals—those three sinks of jobbery & official vice—& I have done all I hoped by representing these things. ("*I Have Done*" 86-87)

Nothing could be farther from the truth than Nightingale's representation of herself as the originator and not the executor in a reform movement. Her ability to work long hours, and to expect the same of others, was reportedly unequaled in the hospital at Scutari. Some years later it was said that by extending the demands she placed on herself to her closest male advisors, Sidney Herbert and Arthur Hugh Clough, she accelerated their early deaths. Nightingale was hurt by these allegations, all the more so because she mourned them deeply. But in the privacy of her diaries she also confided an angry sense of betrayal, and in this regard, as well, she found parallels between her predicament and Christ's: "Who has ever had a sadder experience than I? Christ was betrayed by one. But I have been betrayed by everyone—ruined, betrayed, destroyed alas! ... Wear, Clough, Salisbury, Stanley *et id genus omne*, where are they?"

("*I Have Done*" 165). Nightingale drew solace and self-confidence from her meditations on Christ; she also acquired, it seems, a messiah complex, complete with feelings of persecution.

The Crimean War would give Nightingale a mission, but in its valleys of the dying, the fervent mysticism that she had discovered in the Egyptian valleys of the dead was challenged by the enormous demands and appalling sights of her daily routine. Death here was neither a theoretical nor a nostalgic affair, and with the abundance of death around her Nightingale no longer wished for her own but rather immersed herself in the work of preventing that of others. To accomplish her new duties she felt it necessary to wean herself from the pull toward autobiographical and introspective writings. That objective would pose some problems in her later life, but in the Crimea it was a temptation she seldom had the luxury to feel. In Egypt, others had done the work of cooking, cleaning, carrying; in the Crimea, such tasks became Nightingale's own as she occupied herself with the chores of cooking, cleaning, dressing wounds, and organizing details. Similarly, in her correspondence, where she had formerly exercised her rhetorical skill in fusing the Egyptian "worship of the body" with a Christian worship of the purged soul, she now discussed more pedestrian and pragmatic concerns. She writes to Sidney Herbert, the secretary at war, about critical shortages of basic supplies and petty disputes among the medical corps, and to her parents about the moral passions that bent her soul on victory. To Herbert she lists shirts, sheets, soap, mops, candlesticks, toothbrushes; explains her scheme for equitably dividing the meat in meals; recounts debates about cleaning wounds, dishes, linens, floors; notes the rises and declines in frostbite, amputations, and fevers; and worries about the exceedingly high rate of mortality among the wounded, reaching thirty in one hospital in twenty-four hours, and "seventy-two burials in one day from all Scutari hospitals" ("*I Have Done*" 82–93). And yet, to her parents she lapses into a somewhat different story, of a "baptism of fire, what words those are! [that] must baptize all those who would be 'Saviours' of mankind" (131). During her journey up the Nile, Nightingale had associated Christ with a mystical merger of life and death, with a landscape and a history that aestheticized death. Under the chastening horrors and demands of war, the Christ of her imagination was redivided into the moments of his passion, appearing as death on the suffering bodies of men, and as resurrection on the liberated woman attending them.

The Composition and Critical Reception of 'Suggestions for Thought' and 'Cassandra'

The private Christology of Florence Nightingale's early life, so clearly a source of inspiration and of empowering, sometimes unsettling messianic identifications, is at once illuminated and complicated by the comments on Christ she made in *Suggestions for Thought*, her three-volume work of spiritual philosophy. Nightingale's stated purpose in writing *Suggestions for Thought* was to divert the working classes away from atheism, to win them over to a progressive, post-Christian spiritualism. Conceived as a multivolume work that divides itself according to the divided social classes that it addresses, *Suggestions for Thought* might have been inspired by Coleridge's similar (and similarly abandoned) plans for the *Lay Sermons*. No doubt it was also inspired by the results of the 1851 census, which revealed a staggering decline in religious observance among the general population of England, and—from the middle-class perspective, what was most alarming—a decline in piety among the poor. Hence Nightingale undertakes to present a palatable and sensible spiritual philosophy, one which, rather than depending on the vexatious apparatus of clergy and doctrine, can be reached by "the spirit of truth" that guides any thoughtful inquirer. However, although volume 1 is dedicated and addressed to "the artizans of England," the nature of Nightingale's imagined audience changes as the work progresses, becoming less specifically working class and more generally British. The focus of her philosophical narrative changes as well, moving from questions of religious authority to issues of free will, historical design, and gender politics. When Christ appears in these various discussions, he is seldom in the guise of supernatural hero or spiritual confidant; rather, he is presented as a religious teacher whose vision was distorted by both his own errors and the mistakes of the church that followed him. With stunning self-confidence, Nightingale undertakes to set those errors right.

Her treatment of the topics discussed is provocative, at times radical, and one wonders what effect *Suggestions for Thought* would have had on Nightingale's reputation had it been published for a wider audience. However, as critics have observed, the power of the text's ideas is diminished by its haphazard and repetitive arrangement. Given the history of its composition, there is little wonder that it is such an erratic work. Nightingale wrote the first draft of what would become *Suggestions for Thought* between 1850 and 1852, after her return from Egypt. She then rather brusquely put the manuscript aside in 1853, when a long-awaited opportunity for a hospital appointment arose, and she became the superintendent of London's "Institution for the Care of Sick Gentlewomen in Distressed Circumstances." Within a year, she departed for the British army hospitals at Scutari. Upon her return to England, despite compromised health, she set about assisting the reform of the army hospital administration, which consumed most of her attention, and then in 1860 became a best-selling author with her terse guide, *Notes on Nursing*. During the late 1850s, she also revised *Suggestions for Thought* and, in 1860, had it printed in a still unpolished, small-run edition. Without revealing herself as the author of the work, she arranged for its submission to several well-known men of letters, among them Benjamin Jowett, whose warm praise was to some degree offset by the extensive revisions he suggested. Partly because of the daunting nature of the changes Jowett recommended, partly because of other, more pressing commitments, Nightingale never undertook to gain *Suggestions for Thought* a wider circulation.

Jowett expressed enthusiasm for the intellectual acumen of Nightingale's manuscript even before the name of the author was revealed to him. Unaware that *Suggestions for Thought* had any association with the celebrated "lady with the lamp," he wrote to Clough that the manuscript had imparted to him "the impress of a new mind"

(Cook 1: 471). The remark is telling, coming as it does from an Oxford disciple of Hegel who was destined to become Balliol College's best-known master. Jowett felt that Nightingale "wanted to know more," and for that purpose he took her into his confidence. Even so, they were beginning from high ground, since *Suggestions for Thought* bears witness to Nightingale's extensive reading; the book is nothing if not learned in its scope of philosophical reference. Its theology is a distillation of many scholarly influences, among them, as Calabria and Macrae explain, Plato (whom she read in Greek), Comtian positivism, the burgeoning discipline of social statistics, and contemporary Western studies of Hinduism and Buddhism (Calabria and Macrae, *passim*). The list of influences that Nightingale absorbed into her theology also includes medieval Christian mysticism, although it seems that this area of exploration was not as important for her in early life as it became in later years. Additionally, Nightingale had, as a young woman, read German philosophy, history, and theology, and these, too, left an impression on her religious beliefs and attitudes toward Scriptures.[4]

Suggestions for Thought is thus clearly the product of a well-versed participant in the European intellectual climate of the nineteenth century. However, the spiritual philosophy that comprises most of the three-volume work has not received nearly the attention accorded a brief section of the book, commonly known as *Cassandra*, which appears at the end of the second volume. Nightingale originally drafted this section in 1850 as part of a novel and later inserted it into *Suggestions for Thought*. The *Cassandra* section is a fierce indictment of the constrictions placed on middle-class women's lives. Since Ray Strachey made it an appendix to her *The Cause: A Short History of the Women's Movement in Great Britain* (1928), it has been recognized as a significant piece of feminist writing. Likewise, for the first readers of *Suggestions for Thought* it was the *Cassandra* fragment that seemed to make the strongest impression; Mill alluded to it in *The Subjection of Women*, and Jowett dwelt on its arguments in his initial correspondence with Nightingale.[5] However, *Cassandra* is not representative of the overall philosophy in *Suggestions for*

Thought—indeed no section of this eclectic book could be said to represent the whole—nor is it representative of Nightingale's ambivalent and politically uncooperative attitude toward the question of women's rights.[6] Because it stands out from the body of *Suggestions for Thought* in several regards—its subject matter, its narrative voice, its tone, and its Christology—I will first outline the arguments of *Suggestions for Thought* and then turn to the different matter of *Cassandra*.

Arguments and Implications of 'Suggestions for Thought'

Like so many works of speculative philosophy of the nineteenth century, *Suggestions for Thought* is both a psychological and a historiographical treatise. Nightingale builds her system on several premises that she considers unassailable: the universe is organized by divinely mandated laws, the spirit of these laws is beneficent, and one of the laws stipulates the evolving perfection of human individuals. Indeed, the individual's recognition of his own divinity—his realization, as Nightingale liked to repeat, that "the kingdom of God is within you"—is, she believes, the ultimate purpose of creation. In the spiritual practice that furthers this teleological plan, the individual must at all times listen to his best self, for in such moments he exercises the inner essence that connects him to the ordering principle of the universe, the will of God. "Are not all men 'incarnations' of God," Nightingale writes, "as they think His thought, partake His consciousness, are one with Him?" (1860, 1: 50). The male gender of this idealized subject is allegedly a shorthand for a genderless rational subject; such is a given of the philosophical discourse that Nightingale enters into in *Suggestions for Thought*. And although in volume 2, Nightingale questions this assumption, throughout much of the work she assumes an unspecified similitude among the members of a reified humanity. Hence the chief player in her scheme of history is an abstract human subject, and history will be completed when this subject fully internalizes the will of God (variously called "the unlimited," "the Father," and "the All-Wise") and becomes one with him (1860, 3: 373).

The theology of *Suggestions for Thought* might thus be described as incarnational positivism. Despite the considerable attention that she pays to Christ, most of Nightingale's points in *Suggestions for Thought* go to diminish his stature; the Christ of history is relatively insignificant in this work, while the idea of the incarnation, as Nightingale interprets it, is supremely important. From her late historical perspective, Christ is simply one of many great souls that populate the historical progress which will culminate in a unity between mankind and the divine. "But there are many things [Christ] said, which are very beautiful, and yet not true," she states at one point (1860, 2: 164); elsewhere she suggests that once God's laws in history have been successfully traced, "Christ will no longer be considered as supernatural authority" (1994, 53).

Having jettisoned the weight of the Gospels, Nightingale replaces it with works of secular knowledge—science, statistics, philosophy, and ethics—for it is in such works, she believes, that we recognize the immutable laws through which God reveals himself and his plan for creation (1860, 2: 187). In fact, so strongly does she believe in the inviolability of God's laws that she assesses Christ's belief in miracles as evidence of his primitive misconception of the divine nature. Obviously, the majority of British Christians fail to understand either God or Christ in this manner, and this Nightingale attributes to the unfortunate bibliolatry of their religious practices. Indeed, the Protestant Christian's tendency to displace personal wishes onto the ever-illusive texts of Scriptures has, in Nightingale's mind, resulted in a sadly distorted image of the human divine: "It is truly remarkable, indeed, how some have believed that Christ said to them what they said to themselves, and this with the printed book before them. Little, indeed, does that book probably represent Christ—as little as other books of men's sayings and doings represent *them*. Still, it assures us that he did not think what he has since been said to think" (1994, 50–51). The Bible is no more inspired than other sacred texts of the major religions, Nightingale claims, and in any case all beliefs garnered from books are inferior to those gained immediately through the human faculties of observation, analysis, and feeling. In this light, Protestantism's dependency on books is stagnating, an encumbrance on the ever-improving, ever-evolving human spirit. Once freed from this culturally imposed arrested development, she predicts, English men and women will begin to cultivate the seeds of their divine potential. Throughout *Suggestions for Thought*, Nightingale presents this egalitarian understanding of the incarnation as intuitive knowledge, as in the following statement: "Can we deny this, that every human being, born into this world with the ordinary human faculties, has capabilities for a divine nature? Is not this our experience?" (1860, 2: 346).

Building upon her understanding of the incarnation, Nightingale replaces the authority of the Bible with that of an enlightened individual who is qualified for this trust by virtue of the divine component in his or her understanding. That divine component is key, for it enables Nightingale to differentiate between "private judgment"—a concept she detested—and the personal apprehension of objective laws. It is on this basis that Nightingale distinguishes her position from latitudinarianism, from the spirit of theological tolerance which she feared gave rein to the implication that truth was nothing more than an amorphous body of ephemeral and relative beliefs.[7] As for Coleridge and Thomas Arnold before her, right understanding proceeds from an incontrovertible core of good conscience; it is a matter of personal congruity with abiding principles. However, Coleridge and Arnold were careful to maintain a role for the Bible as the text that forms this conscience; their religious hermeneutics theorized a reader of Scriptures, not of the world. Nightingale preserves the personal impetus of the Protestant religion, but in a manner consistent with her dismissal of scriptural inspiration, she diminishes the importance of Bible reading in character formation: "That people should be satisfied to take their belief upon the most important of all subjects, the subject which embraces every other, from a Book—for which, too, there is so little evidence, extrinsic or intrinsic, and knowing hardly anything even of what extrinsic evidence there is—that they should do this, instead of all mankind striving to find out truth for themselves, seems extraordinary" (1860, 3: 85).

While the words of Scriptures might aid in the discovery of truth, they do not, in Nightingale's estimation, fully contain it, nor are they a more privileged vehicle of sacred learning than the evidence of the senses, of experience, of other inspired works, or even of the human accomplishments of secular wisdom. By thus placing the evidence of the senses and of reason above the evidence of a text, Nightingale recognizes, certainly more than Arnold could, the implications of scientific methodology for religious faith. At same time, she secures this methodology to a familiar and comfortable belief in innate moral wisdom, in a divinely instilled grid of perception through which men and women recognize in scientific discoveries the hidden pattern of a sacred design.

However, although she relegates the authority of the Bible to that of reason, Nightingale still conceptualizes the mind after the fashion of a book. In a manner that recalls the biblical philologist's quest for a pure manuscript, she believes that the answers to her questions reside in an ability to distinguish between the contents of consciousness that are pure and original and those that are superadded and corrupt. But whether the Bible is at issue or the seemingly more imminent voice of conscience, the distinction between inherent and imposed meanings remains difficult to draw. And for this reason, having replaced the testimony of Scriptures with the underlying moral conscience of an enlightened, improving humanity, Nightingale still faces the problem of potential distortions. The question of validation is simply deferred, for even the voice of conscience cannot be certain of its origins:

> It is said that those who do not admit "authority" do not know *when* it is God that speaks, and when it is the excitement of a cup of coffee—that they cannot tell whether their vessel be pure. Swedenborg's was pure, and St. Francis of Assisi's was pure, yet they came to different conclusions. We may naturally be mistaken in what God says to us, because we have to construct for ourselves and each other the vessel into which the Holy Ghost enters, and often inevitably it becomes occupied with other ghosts. (1860, 1: 51)

As this passage suggests, Nightingale's concept of the self as an empty vessel to be filled is haunted by the familiar uncertainty of inspirational sources. Her resolution to this dilemma is much like that of Coleridge and Arnold, for she wishes to contain the subjectivist implications of a belief in personal conscience by appealing to an eternal law or ethical wisdom that all individuals inherently, at some level of their private depths, understand. To know yourself, in other words, is to recognize that your true conscience, beneath the distortions that have accumulated around it, is at one with the objective and unchanging laws of God.

It is a striking feature of *Suggestions for Thought* that the crisis of poisoned subjectivity, so aptly described in the above passage, does not trouble the narrative for long. Unlike many other nineteenth-century affirmations of transcendent wisdom—unlike those of Coleridge, Edward Irving, and Dickens—Nightingale is not compelled to weave complex validations or mediations of her inspirational sources. Uncertainty about the inner voice seems to be a dilemma limited to her readers; she sympathizes with their qualms, offers advice, but does not herself partake of their unease. She has, it seems, little doubt that her moral and religious opinions are mandated by God. As indicated by the following quotation, her earnest sense of mission seems void of self-doubt:

I could not understand God, if He were to speak to me. But the Holy Spirit, the Divine in me, tells me what I am to do. I am conscious of a voice that I can hear, telling me more truth and good than I *am*. As I rise to *be* more truly and more rightly, this voice is ever beyond an above me, calling to more and more good.

But you have to invent what it says. (1994, 127)

It is an intriguing aspect of Nightingale's writing that she can quite calmly let this opinion slip: interpreting a divine voice is an act not of mediation but of invention. What at first appears to be an unexpected admission that God is absent, a blank to be filled by her own creativity, is in fact something quite different—an admission of what might strike the reader as the momentous fragility of her faith, which is poised on the certitude that she has an empathic understanding of God's will.

The burden of such self-confidence was no doubt alleviated by the fact that most of the divine messages which Nightingale received took the form of a call to action. Her sense of moral and spiritual certitude was strengthened by her internalization of the work ethic, which informed her that action was not only a remedy for depression but also the true test of faith and a reliable antidote for theoretical uncertainty. In Carlylean fashion, the narrator of *Suggestions for Thought* asserts that "it is more in accordance with [God's] purpose to work than to meditate" (1994, 139); here and elsewhere, work is the quintessential Victorian virtue that ultimately saves the theology of *Suggestions for Thought* from foundering on any of the several threats to faith that it acknowledges: subjectivism, sectarianism, or religious despair. The point to be stressed here is that work, which in her private writings provides Nightingale an exit from depression, also provides her a pragmatic and confident answer to the question of inspirational sources. In useful activity, she assures her audience, the individual distinguishes, naturally and unequivocally, the divine voice of conscience from voices that are satanic, polluted, or merely human: "Work your true work, and you will find His presence in your self—*i.e.*, the presence of those attributes, those qualities, that spirit, which is all we know of God. If we recognize this spirit within us, when ever man is well at work, may we not say 'He is in us, and we in Him?'" (1994, 143). Thus, work appears on the scene in *Suggestions for Thought* as a *deus ex machina* that resolves by fiat the impasse between subjectivism and divine truth. It is heralded as a means of immediate interior clarification, precisely because it takes one outside one's self.

In this way, *Suggestions for Thought* replays the paradox of spiritual epistemology that we encountered in Chapter 2. The inquiring subject of Victorian spiritual growth is a problematic locus of religious knowledge, necessary to the phenomenological process of faith but also necessarily held in check. As a source of authority, the inquiring subject not only interrogates revelation but also his or her own inner purity, a purity which, ironically, amounts to freedom from subjectivism, the very condition of its coming to knowledge. Nightingale's resolution to this paradox differs slightly from the irresolution of Coleridge and Irving, from their uneasy acceptance of the need to simultaneously dissolve and preserve the self in the act of apprehending divine truths. She poses, as an alternative for such dissolution, a work wherein one finds the sublimating escape from self-consciousness.

Nightingale does not explain how work enables the self to know itself and its divine elements in this enhanced fashion. But then again, neither did Carlyle, in many ways the progenitor of this faith, actually explain how work provides the assurance and equanimity that he accredited to it.[8] In Nightingale's case, the call to work provides a philosophical conclusion for *Suggestions for Thought* that returns us to the book's beginning. As I mentioned earlier, the first volume of *Suggestions for Thought* opens with a dedication to "the artizans of England," as this was the readership that she believed would most benefit from her progressive notions of religion. Even though she changed her notion of the book's audience in the course of writing it, the fact that she began with the working classes in mind raises two questions which are important to the entire plot of her philosophical narrative. First, what are the political ramifications of the ideas espoused in *Suggestions for Thought*? And second, what is the relationship between the various forms of work which the book invokes: that of its specified audience, of its philosophical conclusion, and of the effort that Nightingale put into writing it?

Jowett objected to the dedication of the first volume on the grounds that there was much in *Suggestions for Thought* that could benefit all readers, regardless of class. He might also have thought it preferable to avoid the volatile implications of addressing such teachings specifically to working-class readers. However, his caution was unnecessary, not only because the book was not widely published, but also because *Suggestions for Thought* defuses its own radical charge. For one, Nightingale's ideas are couched in a philosophical and theological discourse that holds its political subtext in abeyance. An intellectual benefactor of Hegel, if only at secondhand, she is drawn to the same project which preoccupied other second-generation Hegelians, that of delineating a new approach to the incarnation. Like Strauss and Feuerbach, Nightingale argues that the incarnation includes not Christ alone, but all humanity. And, like Strauss and Feuerbach, she is too firmly entrenched in historical idealism to render this thesis solely in material terms. Consequently, although she defends the claims of physical life and empirical evidence as components of an evolving humanity, her defense stops short of inquiring into the social and economic ramifications of such claims. It is, in the final analysis (as Marx observed of Feuerbach), part of an idealist and not a materialist discourse.[9]

Another restraint on the political ramifications of Nightingale's work involves her notion of agency. The primary actor in her philosophical narrative is not the race, the nation, or the species, but rather the heroic individual. Agency for her is concentrated in certain stalwart individuals whose habits of self and social improvement win them the mantle of saviors. Hence her working-class readership—boldly specified by the first volume, abandoned by the second volume—is addressed as a mass of individuals and potential individualists, not as a social group with shared interests shaped by economic and political disadvantage. The book thus bespeaks an outlook that is poised on the ambiguous boundary between heroes and hero worshipers. Its views are inhospitable to Christian Socialism, insofar as *Suggestions for Thought* stipulates neither a role nor a rationale for the clergy or the Established Church. But it is also inhospitable to Chartism (which for the most part had dissolved by the time Nightingale began to write *Suggestions for Thought*), insofar as her incarnational positivism does not position the agency of change along the axis of class-based coalitions.

As this prognosis suggests, Nightingale's relationship with the working classes, while informed by much textual familiarity (blue books, hygienic reports, statistics) was in part imaginary—a theoretical affair. Approaching the "artizans of England" as a cultural concept, an audience to be elevated by her theology, she seems in the course of writing *Suggestions for Thought* to abstract from them the attribute of work and assigns this attribute a peremptory significance in its own right. Work is not conceived of in the text as an oppressive or alienating necessity, and one might argue that this makes *Suggestions for Thought* complicit in an ideology of submissiveness and resignation. But it is important to remember that the author only knew work as a privilege, not as a necessity, and for this reason I believe her manipulations of the term signal something different. *Suggestions for Thought* is an intellectual venture in which the working classes save Nightingale even as she is trying to save them. They provide her with a means of objectifying the grounds of her belief in divine identification, and they provide this means in two regards: as the audience of minds that she originally wished to work upon with her writing, and as the social mass that her text metonymically reduces to glorified activity. In the first regard, the working classes transform Nightingale's writing into work because it is through their imagined conversion and improvement that *Suggestions for Thought* will become a socially useful undertaking. In the second regard, the working classes are themselves transformed by the text, because they are ultimately destined by the theoretical bent of this book to become tropes in its narrative. They contribute the signifier "work," a term that signals Nightingale's desire to materialize an immaterial system, or, in what in this case amounts to the same thing, to externalize the deified interiority produced by her philosophical narrative. Thus *Suggestions for Thought*'s abandonment of the working classes as an audience is consistent with its appropriation of their activity as a theoretical position, as a soul-saving regimen recommended to the members of all classes. And just as work is an abstraction that signifies an escape from abstraction, a material resolution to a spiritual quest, so is it an escape from the disembodied and isolated interiority of the author in the act of constructing a philosophy. Both as an audience and as a trope, the working classes provide the assurances that the narrative voice of *Suggestions for Thought*, alone, unmediated, and dependent on its own psychic resources, could not achieve.

The Feminist/Feminine Christology of 'Cassandra'

The *Cassandra* segment of *Suggestions for Thought* is a feminist jeremiad, Nightingale's attempt, as Showalter and Landow have suggested, to appropriate sage writing against itself by making Victorian attitudes toward women's knowledge the object of attack.[10] As I mentioned earlier, Nightingale originally wrote *Cassandra* as part of a quasi-autobiographical novel, and the truncated version that she appended to volume 2 introduces some formal and thematic disarray into the overall scheme of *Suggestions for Thought*. Prior to the *Cassandra* section, the narrative of *Suggestions for Thought* becomes increasingly concerned with the woman question and the enforced idleness of middle-class women's lives. And then, with *Cassandra*, the text shifts from philosophy to something approximating autobiography; at the same time, the speaker divests herself of the voice of impersonal rationality to become a female visionary. The difference between *Cassandra* and the chapters that precede it is one of genre, obviously, but in this case the abrupt apposition of two disparate narratives is testimony to a schism that also divided Nightingale herself. *Cassandra* originates in the personal conditions of her life, conditions wherein the values and conclusions of *Suggestions for Thought* are absurdly untenable. While *Suggestions for Thought* reifies work, detaching it from the social class that is predicated upon it, *Cassandra* concretizes work as a political reality pertinent to gendered rather than class oppression. The work of "moral activity" and "spheres of action" (227)—those activities through which the Enlightenment subjects of *Suggestions for Thought* come to recognize God's nature in themselves—are thematized in *Cassandra* as precisely those activities that are most cruelly denied to middle- and upper-class women. Approaching the enforced idleness of women in this way, she greatly increases the stakes. For insofar as she is prohibited from all forms of meaningful work, the middle-class woman of Nightingale's spiritual philosophy is alienated from her divine potential, her natural destiny in an incarnational telos.

Although purporting to speak of women in general, most of the concerns addressed in *Cassandra* are specific to women of the middle and upper classes: women have nothing to do, and are allowed nothing to do; they must conform to the demands and entertainment of society; they must be devoted to their families; they are, in fact, slaves to their families, and are repeatedly tricked by romance or desperation into marriage, which is only a false liberation into the constraints of another family. They are coerced into the duty of having only "leisure time," of perpetual passivity, of always being available for the company of others. Thus the women of the upper and middle classes are allowed no time to pursue their own projects in a sustained fashion. Above all, Nightingale protests, they are doomed by this custom of life to "incurable infancy" (216). And so adamantly does she disown the sentimental privileges ascribed to the feminine and childish spheres—the pristine intuitions, the insipid empathy—that she begs for suffering as a reprieve: "Give us back our suffering, we cry to Heaven in our hearts ... better have pain than paralysis!" (208).

Writing in a state of frustration and despondency, Nightingale now gives a somewhat different picture of the incarnational positivism that she described in *Suggestions for Thought* with such remarkable equanimity. Her gender, misused as it is by society and family, presents a painfully real barrier to the mission of socially oriented self-improvement that was previously conceived in an ungendered or implicitly male-gendered theoretical arena. Situated within the constraints of middle-class femininity, Nightingale no longer relates to Christ as an equal who is subject to the scrutiny of her rational analysis. Rather, he is partially restored to his supernatural status, and this in two regards. First, Christ is the central locus of authority whom Nightingale cites to disprove the efficacy of the status quo, as in the following passage: "Jesus Christ raised women above the condition of mere slaves, mere ministers to the passions of men, raised them by his sympathy, to be ministers of God. He gave them moral activity. But the Age, the World, Humanity, must give them the means to exercise this moral activity, must give them intellectual cultivation, spheres of action" (227). Here Christ is a rhetorical ally, a means of castigating her family and society for the "paralyzing" demands they make of her. Indeed, the deep affinity Nightingale feels with Christ enables her to appropriate his image in a recklessly uninhibited manner: the annoyance of meddling family members is an annoyance that Nightingale imagines Christ must have felt; the desire to complain is a desire that she believes would have consumed him—as it consumes women, as it consumes Cassandra—if he had not been a man and thus free to take action against the miseries of the world.

The second function that Christology performs in *Cassandra*, although related to the rhetorical function, is somewhat more complex. It concerns what might be called the savior function, that is, Nightingale's invocation of Christ as a past and future hero who transcends the oppressiveness of society. In keeping with the messianic hopes and identifications of her letters, and in keeping with the incarnational positivism of *Suggestions for Thought*, Nightingale imagines her Christian liberator not only as a supernatural other who saves her from social incarceration but also as an emergent individual upon whom she projects her own desires for self-perfecting pursuit and philanthropic activity. Speaking in the voice of her prophetic narrator, she anticipates a future wherein "there shall arise a woman who will resume, in her soul, all the sufferings of her race, and that woman will be the Saviour of her race" (*Cassandra* 227). Or, in something of a more hesitant forecast: "The next Christ will perhaps be a female Christ. But do we see one woman who looks like a female Christ?" (230). As always, it is not a passive salvation that Nightingale wishes for but rather the privilege of being a savior, the privilege of acting for others. However, this privilege seems more inaccessible than it does in her correspondence from Egypt and the Crimea, no doubt because in England Nightingale felt her sources of oppression to be both immediate and insurmountable. Hence the prophesied second Jesus of *Cassandra* is not Cassandra. Rather, it is a woman removed into the future, a woman from whom an impossible achievement is expected, for she must emulate Christ by overcoming a complacent English social order that makes it impossible to emulate Christ. Between the appearance of this salvific woman and the social freight of a frivolous Philistinism there are gaps that *Cassandra* fails to bridge. Consequently, the text ends not in the speaker's Christological resurrection but rather in her death, and the narrative drives home its growing hopelessness by paratactically placing this scene next to a passage in which Cassandra contemplates Christ. Having imagined one last point of sympathy between herself and Christ—the liberated man who is God, savior, and woman—the speaker arranges her own demise: "Free—free—oh! divine freedom, art thou come at last? Welcome, beautiful death!" (232). At every level—social, psychological, temporal, and even syntactical—Cassandra's narrative encodes the barriers between herself and the perfect woman whose subjectivity signifies her liberation.

The gaps and barriers that divide *Cassandra* are the consequences of Nightingale's position within a Victorian philosophy of gender. Her vision of a female Christ is a logical if heterodox consequence of her culture's deification of woman, not uncommon really, since as Barbara Taylor notes, faith in a female messiah was a persistent heresy within millenarian sects in the late eighteenth and early nineteenth centuries (161). However, Nightingale undoes the social formula that licenses this deification by desiring women to have access to all forms of development, not just spiritual and moral. In the previous chapter, I suggested that the religious and moral authority which Victorian culture ascribed to women was contingent upon their sexual, political, and economic disfranchisement. Nightingale at once appropriates and disassembles this ideological arrangement. She desires a society wherein women may evolve into totalized human subjects, fulfillments of what she deems human and not simply gendered potential. To this end, she disabuses her contemporaries of their misinformed notions of middle- and upper-class women; their most noble longings and capacities, Nightingale argues, can only be fulfilled if certain world-redeeming job opportunities in the public sphere are made available to them. However, she also believes that one of these women—the female Christ whom she prophesies, the female Christ whom she wants to be—will supersede other human subjects because of a unique potential that might be construed as a vestige of her feminine cultural role. In short, Nightingale maintains the ideological advantages of her gender even as she tries to remove the social disabilities that are, ideologically speaking, the conditions of these advantages.

This arrangement has ramifications for the question of narrative authority, ramifications which become apparent when we compare the maneuvers of *Suggestions for Thought* to those analyzed in the previous chapter. Dickens, as we saw, mediates his spiritual and ethical authority through the feminized and infantilized deities projected by his sentimental beliefs; Nightingale, in contrast, declares war on the sacrosanct boundaries that encircle these deities, boundaries that enforce women's separation from the purposeful and practical activities of a male-dominated public sphere. Indeed, her narrative voice would probably do away with mediation altogether, if only it could collapse into one totalized subject the segregated economies of power—the masculine activity and intellect, the feminine moralism and spiritual insight—that sustain the Victorian social imaginary. However, in this endeavor, the narrative voice of *Suggestions for Thought* is not successful, or at least not always successful. As we have seen, Nightingale at times speaks with great self-assurance, with a conviction born of the ideological association between femininity and spiritual intuition. However, as we have also seen, she suspends her philosophical quest for the authoritative origins of her beliefs by presenting work as an ultimate resolution, even though this resolution is arguably only a declaration of faith supplanting other declarations of faith. When Nightingale borrows from her specified "artizan" audience the reified and redemptive phenomenon of work, she is borrowing a phenomenon that was, initially at least, as inaccessible to her as the condition of feminine and infantile purity was to Dickens. Through this narrative movement, she implicitly underscores the inadequacy of her own spiritual authority, its structural dependence on the differentiated male realm of work. Like Dickens, Nightingale in effect tries to mediate herself; having begun by addressing the other of the working classes, the other who holds the right to the sanctifying principle of authority in her philosophical system, she seeks to incorporate this conceptual source of their authority into herself. But in Victorian terms this totalized subject is impossible; it would entail the realignment of gendered social functions and attributes along the axis of individualism. Nightingale contests these terms without abandoning them, and consequently the economies of power which, in *Dombey and Son*, create a story of disturbance and restored equilibrium, create in *Suggestions for Thought* an eloquent yet alienated narrative, a text divided between its philosophical positivism and its autobiographical despair.

For these reasons it is fitting that the totalized human subject described and prophesied in *Suggestions for Thought* is postponed to a utopian future. The predicament of the book is one in which socially enforced differences of gender preclude the emergence of an individual who integrates all forms of virtue. Elsewhere in her writings, Nightingale lamented the ways in which society divided human properties between the sexes, and, interestingly enough, one such division concerned the relationship she perceived between genre and modes of knowledge. Women, she observed in a letter to her father, are socialized to assume only a personal mode of discourse:

Why cannot a woman follow abstractions like a man? ... Is it not because *the habit* of never interesting herself much, in any conversation, printed or spoken, which is not personal, of making herself & her own feelings the subject of speculation—(& what is the good of studying our own individuality, save as the reflection of the generality)—of making all she says autobiographical, & being always in a moral *tête-à-tête*, of considering her own experiences as the principle part of her life, renders her powerless to rise to any abstract good, or general view. (*Ever Yours* 30-31)

Excluded from the objective voice of the philosophical treatise, women confine themselves to the autobiographical. In effect, this confinement is epistemological, for women learn to access only those ways of knowing that they can situate in personal experience. On the one hand, it seems that Nightingale did not consider herself limited in this way to subjective habits of thought, since in much of

Suggestions for Thought she practices the philosophical mode of discourse which (so it is implied above) couples the masculine with the objective. On the other hand, her assumption of a highly personalized voice in *Cassandra* leans toward what she thought to be a feminine form of knowledge, the woman's voice which "mak[es] herself & her own feelings the subject of speculation."

Jowett and Nightingale corresponded about precisely this issue, and Jowett confirmed Nightingale's earlier assessment of the problem: "The reflections on the family" in *Cassandra* should not take "the form of individual experience," he suggested, as it "lessen[s] the weight of what is said" (4). Nightingale responded by claiming that *Cassandra* was not as autobiographical as it seemed, although for many readers other than Jowett it continues to invite such interpretation. To his credit, Jowett saw great value in the *Cassandra* fragment, and his proposed remedy for its disorderly appearance in *Suggestions for Thought* was to publish it separately, restored to its original novel form (Jowett 8). Nightingale's failure to do so reflects a certain genius of ideological intuition: by blatantly failing to integrate its component narratives, her book mimics formally the historical conditions that frustrate its philosophical dream of a fully realized, fully integrated human subject.

From this standpoint we can perceive a logic in the structural heterogeneity of *Suggestions for Thought* as a whole. For it is possible that Nightingale could not or maybe would not integrate *Suggestions for Thought* and *Cassandra* into a homogeneous document for the reason that her own subjectivity was divided between the narratives of incarnational positivism and feminine subordination. The former held sway in a world of ideas and imagination; the latter interrupted—interrupted her psychology as it interrupts her text—with the reminders of a more constrained reality. Thus *Suggestions for Thought* represents Nightingale's interpolation into a male world of ideas, her internalization of and entry into a philosophical discourse wherein Christ is a signifier not of himself but of universal human potential. But the universality of this potential is belied by the buried premises of that discourse's male pronoun, premises that are revealed when Nightingale assumes the female pronoun of *Cassandra*. The female pronoun is for her both a privilege and a handicap; it bespeaks the ideological underpinnings of her image of a female messiah, her ready alliance of Christ and woman, but at the same time it situates her within material social conditions that preclude this image as anything other than imaginary. In this way, *Cassandra* differs from *Suggestions for Thought* in a manner that is also a trenchant commentary. It signifies her exclusion from the imaginary world represented in that discourse, a world wherein everyone is free to work toward, and through work discover, his divine self. Hence, in *Cassandra*, Christ represents potentials that society denies the speaker, and her frustration is so great that death looks preferable.

But this is a familiar story, for as we saw earlier, Nightingale has already described, in her private writings, her willingness to embrace death. In this light, we might interpret the death speech in *Cassandra* as an echo of the private self beneath the public philosopher; we might also recognize it as a transformation of Nightingale's death wishes from an emotional into a political trope. Whatever description we wish to give it, the death figured in *Cassandra* is more about figuration than death. The prophetess's invocation of a "beautiful death" is a rhetorical gesture, an interruption; in both cases, an awkward allusion to the fact that this death is no ending, for the philosophical narrative and its philosopher survive into a third volume. Likewise, the encounters with death staged in Nightingale's psyche always saw her reemerging at the end more bent on her existence as a public servant, a public voice, an incarnation of the gospel of work. By the very repetitiveness of its appearances, death in Nightingale's corpus becomes a trope of almost comic familiarity, as if its several appearances serve to announce that the overarching narrative of positivist, linear development simply cannot accommodate the oscillations of her emotional life. Nor did the positivist precepts of *Suggestions for Thought* prove adequate to the tests of her many years. "O my Creator, art Thou leading every man of us to perfection?" Nightingale questioned in 1873. "Or is this only a metaphysical idea for which there is no evidence? Is man only a constant repetition of himself?" (Cook 2: 243). And similarly, she observed of her own life at roughly the same time that she could see "no consecutive path growing out of one's own deeds, but only a succession of disjointed lives and unconnected events . . . Now in old age I never wish to be relieved from work, but only to have it to do" (Cook 2: 214). Of the various convictions claimed and defended in *Suggestions for Thought*—the belief in historical progress; in the divine nature of the individual, synchronically unfolding through a lifetime of improvement; in the necessity of education and careers for women; and in the urgent importance of work—only the last conviction seems to have survived, and this because it provided comfort for the disappointments and shortcomings of the others.

The Writing Cure, the Working Cure, and the Zymotic Cure

The narrative of messianic self-fashioning that Florence Nightingale took to herself was a self-fulfilling prophecy, conveniently offering a structure for her failures as well as her successes, a structure which cast into relief the ideological tensions that intersected in her life, the tensions between her godly ambitions, her inner disquiet, and the limitations placed on her by her gendered predicament. More specifically, the trope of Christ was itself, in Nightingale's manipulations of it, an entanglement of other tropes, specifically of death and work. Let us recapitulate briefly the biographical narrative suggested by the preceding exploration of Nightingale's multivalent Christology. As a young woman, Nightingale kept occasional company with Christ, the savior who called her to a vocation but took his time intervening on her behalf, and during this period of deferral she expressed an attraction to death, a willingness to die if no other escape was possible from her life as a female member of the leisured class. During her tour of the Nile, death temporarily ceased to be a personal preoccupation born of despair and became a phenomenon beheld from a historical and aesthetic distance. Confronted with the tombs of Egypt—death in the form of a tourist's itinerary—Nightingale imparted to the builders of these ancient memorials a mystical wisdom that she imagined was shared by

Christ, and the traces of her suicidal thoughts became the medium for a journey narrative that resuscitated her hopes for a messiahship. A more abstract but still discernible variation on her Christology occurs in *Suggestions for Thought*. Here Nightingale presents a philosophical metanarrative of incarnational positivism and salvation through work. The trope of death disappears beneath the genderless utopia presumed by this discourse, but it reemerges at the conclusion of *Cassandra* as the only action possible for the woman who would be Christ, if it were not for the illegitimate strictures of a society that denies her the freedom to try. Finally, in the Crimea, and afterwards in her domestic-based labors, Nightingale found liberation in the work of preventing the deaths of others—not only the literal deaths of soldiers, of the English poor, and of Indian subjects of the Imperial Crown, but also the metaphorical deaths of those women who, like herself, wished desperately for meaningful work or, in more prosaic terms, for an improvement of their limited career options. As a reclusive female Jesus of the latter nineteenth-century, Nightingale submerged her former identity as a lady of society beneath the alterior and presumably godlike consciousness of working for others, for herself, and for more work to be done.

This biographical plot can be also be expressed as a biographical enactment of a certain strain of Victorian intellectual history. Amassing a variety of cultural voices into a creed of disciplined labor, Nightingale fostered an image of herself as divine, at least within one nineteenth-century tradition of imagining divinity. She articulated and exemplified a strain of Hegelian religious thought, wherein work is a vehicle for self-objectification, specifically for a self that, in so working, identifies with the mind and purpose of God. In this way, work—and it should be clear that we are speaking of the idea of work as much as the act of doing it—offered Nightingale a resolution to the problem of ascertaining the sources of her astonishingly confident religious beliefs. The origins can be judged, so it is implied, by the results; labor at once silences the inner questioning voice, a voice that seems to lead the self away from the self, and crystallizes the true self in an austere, expurgated form. Her relationship to her career as a health missionary and a founder of modern nursing can be construed in terms of what Hegel calls a "determinate negation," since the enormous tasks that she set for herself came about not only as death's alternative but also, ironically, as its surrogate. For the nurse's duties annihilated the woman's personal thoughts and desires, putting an end to energies spent on the self. Work annihilated this woman so as to create another in her place, the woman who could see her divinity, her oneness with God, objectively, in the form of her actions upon the world. In this way, it is conceivable that Nightingale enacted in her work a self-annihilation that was another form of the suicide which her work saved her from. Work legitimized herself as other than herself; it objectified her in the unassailable form of tangible contributions to the grandest work of all, the teleological narrative of mankind's advance toward perfection.

When it comes to the subject of the literary life, however, Nightingale's relationship to work becomes puzzling. Because she defined work as activity that tangibly benefits society, she devalued her time spent in literary engagement, in writing and reading, and especially in introspective, autobiographical writing. This opinion she held throughout her life; literary labors were always inferior in her opinion to projects that improved the lives of the poor or infirm. Thus, in a letter of her youth Nightingale asserted that "one's feelings waste themselves in words; they ought to be all distilled into actions" (Cook 1: 94). Her biographer Cook speculates that Florence looked upon her skills in writing not as "gifts to be cultivated, but rather temptations to be subdued" (1: 93). As late as 1873, when she was 53 years old, we find her prefacing a collection of medieval mystical writings with a disclaimer that reiterates this sentiment: "It may seem a strange thing to begin a book with:—this Book is not for anyone who has time to read it—but the meaning of it is: this reading is only good as a preparation for work" (Cook 2: 233). Only those words that she could bring to bear on the world as activity found approval in Nightingale's judgment; everything else was either shameful self-indulgence or an impotent waste of speech.

"Words, words, words," she wrote in 1857, "and truly all this generation is Words, words, words. And while I write I am under the empire myself of words" (*Ever Yours* 177).

As a remedy for the loquacious but immaterial tendencies of the interior life, Nightingale reworked the trope of Christ much as she had reworked the trope of death. To her mind, the emerging vocation of nursing realized *Cassandra*'s prophecy of a female Christ, and in such a way as to hold meditation and introspection accountable to utilitarian ends. Late in her life, she painted a picture of the successful nurse that recalls the incarnation of John's Gospel: "A good nurse must be a good woman," she wrote in 1890, "she cannot be a good nurse without. A good woman cannot be gauged by words. She must be *herself* THE WORD—a name made divine to us by our great Master, and which He expects each one of us women particularly, to embody in her own duty, each in her own tiny sphere" ("Introduction" xviii). On the one hand, the intransigent idealism of this statement must be placed in context; Nightingale spent much of her later life trying to repudiate the growing professionalization of nursing because it encroached upon her vision of it as an all-consuming vocation, and thus she increasingly employed religious language in her addresses to the student nurses of St. Thomas's. On the other hand, it is noteworthy that Nightingale resorts, in this example, to a quite familiar image in her corpus, as if the most viable weapon against the pedestrian fragmentation of modern life is the weapon she has wielded all along against anyone who would contain her—family, society, or bureaucracy: properly understood, a woman who works is a modern-day incarnation, and the faultless nature of her judgment is apparent in the beneficent effects of her actions upon the world. Moreover, this woman is an incarnation in the specific sense that she materializes and contains the ephemeral and irresponsible language of the mind; her flesh, her thoughts, her actions, every corner of her being are bent upon improving the world around her. Hence the importance Nightingale assigns to "confidentiality": the good nurse must be "no gossip, no vain talker," as these attributes are of a piece with the other virtues of her character—her religiosity, self-respect, delicacy of feeling, and skills of observation (*Notes* 125-26). Thus the "words, words, words" that Nightingale disparaged in 1857 were recuperable, as she recuperates them here, in a censored edition, as the woman who perfectly obeys the voice that summons her to a unified ideological subjectivity, the voice which, as she frequently inscribes it in her writings, reverberates with Logos, the Word of God.

At least, this is the official story. Such an absolute taming of consciousness does not strike a modern reader as particularly desirable, and indeed it is easy to interpret Nightingale's ongoing struggles with the enticement of literary introspection as evidence of her inability to reconcile herself fully to her own creed of productive behavior. Showalter suggests that writing was therapeutic for Nightingale, in spite of her ambivalence toward it, and that *Suggestions for Thought* was "the bridge by which [she] made her escape from hysteria into feminism" ("Miranda and Cassandra" 320). Similarly, for Barbara T. Gates, *Cassandra* exemplifies a typical Victorian remedy for suicidal wishes, much like Mill's and Carlyle's autobiographies of despair and its overcoming (78). It is certainly true that having finished the introspective task of *Cassandra* and the first draft of *Suggestions for Thought*, the near-suicidal depression that Nightingale had suffered for several years ended, if only temporarily, and she rose to the occasion of the Crimea, with its respectfully physical exigencies. And even though Nightingale did not think of writing as a cure so much as a symptom, her behavior was not entirely consistent with her beliefs on this matter. Despite what she said about the moral and mental hazards of a text-based existence, Nightingale repeatedly turned, in moments of depression, to writing and reading. The marginalia in her religious books are a record of the ongoing emotional darkness of her life and of her melancholy dialogues with the authors, with herself, and with her God. Indeed, the importance and perhaps the shame that she attached to these private emotional expressions is borne out by the fact that she initially willed that all her religious books be destroyed. To some extent, that wish probably proceeded from her circumspect nature; to some extent, it might have proceeded from a sense of guilt that she so often relied on what she might have called the crutch of literary introspection.

Certainly she did her best to organize her textual endeavors according to her espoused principles. After the Crimean War, Nightingale immersed herself not only in philosophy but also, and increasingly, in more strictly utilitarian projects—in blue books, sanitary suggestions to India and to English cottages, provisos for student nurses, and proposals for Poor Law reform. And yet, to show that these projects were themselves fundamentally literary in nature it is enough to point out that Nightingale undertook all of them from one of two places, her bed or her sofa. Confined, arguably by a form of manipulative convalescence, to her private quarters, she refused to entertain more than one visitor at a time, and she only left her house to visit another of her family's properties. From these reclusive spaces she wrote, read, studied, consulted, and oversaw the agents who carried out her schemes. In this way, she arranged the best possible compromise between her creed of work and her ambivalence toward the literary life. Physically incapable of the former, drawn to the latter, she constructed an interior world inhabited by vast, even global, sanitary and hygienic projects, all of them executed—as far as her involvement went—on paper.

Nightingale's ambivalence toward the literary life exemplifies a pattern that has been repeatedly encountered in this study, namely, a tendency to disparage writing and reading in favor of work and action. It is a striking paradox that a culture so dependent upon print and literacy would promote such anxiety about the ramifications of print for one's mental well-being. On the one hand, the discomfort expressed by Carlyle, Thomas Arnold, and now Nightingale is not entirely alien to modern beliefs about language and psychology; her feeling that writing was a "temptation to be subdued" is a part of the culture that eventually produced the talking cure insofar as both treat language as psychoactive pharmacology. Hence for Victorians such as Nightingale, linguistic self-examination was too strong to be indulged to excess, while with the emergence of psychoanalysis in the next century, linguistic self-examination was construed as something akin to an antibiotic regimen that must be followed through to completion. On the other hand, something undoubtedly has changed between Victorian and modern conceptions of the relationship of life, language, and health. The change is visible simply in the fact that, from a modern perspective, it is difficult *not* to see Nightingale's principled reticence as an instance of repression, as a tactic for avoiding psychological formations too painful to be confronted. But it must be stressed that Nightingale articulated her situation in the somewhat different terms of a desire to integrate all areas of her life. The preponderance of print in her society not only facilitated a distinction between interiority and exteriority but also made it possible to develop one's interiority in a manner that was felt to increase its distance from external reality and physical existence. From Nightingale's perspective this discrepancy disrupted the necessary balance of the interwoven attributes of one's identity: physical health, spiritual understanding, and social usefulness. For similar reasons, Nightingale did not and perhaps could not separate the pragmatic problem of limited career options for women from the larger spiritual and philosophical problems that troubled her times. The very notion of compartmentalizing aspects of life and knowledge was anathema to her beliefs, wherein the disciplines of science and theology were not only compatible but fundamentally related, and progress depended on the discovery of principles that would obtain in both.

This conviction was something of an intellectual prejudice in Nightingale and helps explain her resistance to germ theory. It was in keeping with her notion of a benevolent nature to believe that disease ensued from disorder—from pollution, filth, and the mismanagement of noxious fluids discharged from the body—rather than from organisms that had a life of their own. Disease was, as she termed it "a reparative process"; the symptoms themselves indicated that nature was already setting right an imbalance between the body and its immediate environment, an imbalance brought about by factors such as "want of fresh air, or of light, or of warmth, or of quiet, or of cleanliness, or of punctuality and care in the administration of diet, of each or of all of these" (*Notes* 8). That biological existence could harbor life forms which were mutually destructive, as in the relationship between a parasitic virus and its host, was inimical to Nightingale's outlook, wherein the laws of nature could will no evil. Thus Nightingale, the intransigent miasmatist, a proponent of Dr. William Farr's zymotic theory of disease, argued that smallpox "grew up" in overcrowded wards and poorly ventilated chambers; it was not a specimen descended from some primordial strain, but rather a specimen emitted spontaneously by vile conditions (*Notes* 32). Holding these beliefs, Nightingale imparted to nursing a great potential for controlling nature, for one had only to be an attentive student "of those laws which God has assigned to the relations of our bodies to the world" to gain mastery of public and domestic health (*Notes* 11). Consequently, the nurse was a guardian of both physiological and ethical conditions, since in Nightingale's spiritually and scientifically interwoven universe, it was a sensible principle that filth was a moral as well as a hygienic failing. Even as late as 1890 she argued against germ theory because it implied the pessimistic view that human behavior was determined by "original innate sin," and in her post-Edenic but anti-Calvinist Britain, nursing entailed the nurturance of "germs of *health* ... original virtue—innate morality" ("Introduction" xiii).

At this point, however, even Nightingale must have been aware of how antiquated this sounded, of how far she had become habituated to her role as a holdout for a dying tradition in both the etiology of disease and in the profession she had helped create. Only a few years before she wrote these words, Pasteur was deploying the anthrax and rabies viruses against themselves, employing in his work on vaccination a Darwinian notion of contagious disease as a competitive rather than a reparative process. Diseases were now conceived as discrete living entities whose defeat depended on specialized immunity, such as that which developed, paradoxically, after introducing into the system a portion of their own dead or weakened selves. In such a light, the war of illness was waged inside the blood, and the significance of a recuperating patient's surroundings, while still important, was only secondary. It was a defeat of Nightingale's philosophy that had been prepared for years before: *Notes on Nursing* had appeared in the same year as *Origin of Species*, and perhaps it initially outsold the latter because it appeared to be as scientific as evolution theory but in a more comforting way; it betokened a kind of Paleyesque optimism, radical in its vision of a public profession for women, but highly traditional in its approach to nature and to the feminine essence of nurture that made it possible for it author to state that, under the right conditions, "every woman is a nurse" (*Notes* 3).

Nightingale's faith in the beneficence of a spiritually diaphanous natural order is entirely consistent with her beliefs in the perfectibility of self and society. As we have seen, her faith in the interdependence of spirituality and empiricism had been tested and confirmed in Egypt and the Crimea, and this faith formed the substructure of her medical, social, and philosophical convictions. Her ideal nurse was thus a minister in and of a principled universe—from Nightingale's perspective, the perfect modern scientific subject; from our perspective a strange amalgam of Victorian Christianity and Victorian scientism. For on the one hand, the nurse's authority was radically empirical, based on her well-honed powers of observation and her practical familiarity with the reliable laws that order natural processes. But her authority also stemmed from religious principles and stereotypes, from the necessity that she "be a religious and devoted woman" (*Notes* 126), and from her quintessentially Christian feminine habit of "abnegation of the self" (Holton 63). Thus Nightingale disparaged book learning, for it could never be a substitute for practice, fieldwork, empirical education, and self-discipline. Thus, also, she feared literary and philosophical indulgences, for they pulled the nurse away from her duties, from action, and into the isolated, socially nonproductive wards of private consciousness. One of Nightingale's achievements was to imagine an early version of the modern scientific female subject, an identity predicated on empirical more than textual authority and on various forms of inner and outer control. But the origins of this subject were deeply ensconced in her Christology, specifically as it wedded her to a passion for self-improvement dictated by messianic energies and teleological designs.

CHAPTER 6

The Holy Books of Empire

Translations of the British and Foreign Bible Society

[My word] shall not return unto me void, but it shall accomplish that which I please, and it shall prosper in the thing whereto I send it.
> Isaiah 55.11, quoted by the Madras Auxiliary
> Bible Society, in defense of the Mahratta Bible

In the preceding three chapters, we have considered instances wherein the authority of the Bible is in dialogue, at times in debate, with the authority of Christ. For Nightingale, Christ signified a religious epistemology that privileged empirical evidence and personal experience over exegetical dependence on a flawed and antiquated text. For Dickens, Christ became, during a fairly brief period of time, a literary figure charged with his own hopes for and anxieties about the cultural authority of his novels and his narrative persona. In both cases, the image of Christ promised a superior revelation, a connection to sacred powers and sacred truths that eclipsed the connections provided by the Bible because it situated authority in a single, sacralized individual, because it figured the immanence of God in a coherent personality that could be transposed onto other human images, be it of the self (as in Nightigale's case) or of a sentimentalized other (as in Dickens's).

And yet, in no instance is the image of individual authority free of social contingencies. The economy of gendered and generational attributes in Victorian culture secured a patriarchal hierarchy, but it did not always or only do so with images of noble Christian manhood. Equally important was the decentering of cultural authority across a social spectrum, across a triumvirate of balanced powers and interwoven dependencies that was, symbolically speaking, the nuclear family—one might say, the secular holy family. The intersubjective nature of this cultural authority, its intransigently social mechanisms, was obscured by the belief (or, where that failed, the desire for belief) in a transcendental authority that structured the family, the nation, the colonized globe, from beyond. For the spiritual powers represented in many Victorian narratives—the powers to convert the soul, to move one to tears, and to fix this internal drama in a transpersonal and transhistorical ideology—were not allegories of transcendence so much as by-products of the narratives themselves. A large-scale cultural confrontation with the disappearance of God was, to a certain extent, circumvented by sentimental narratives that assisted faith, creating an illusion of sacred forces via the circulation of affective powers through the structural positions occupied by the symbolical characters of masculinity, femininity, and childhood.

In this chapter, we will trace the integration of this sentimental narrative into the Victorian ideology of empire. The histories of the British and Foreign Bible Society were, in several regards, anything but histories; it is more accurate to say that they were cultural fantasies of a global religious hegemony instigated and maintained by the Bible. If Christ does not appear in Bible Society stories as often as he does in the national literature of the period, it is perhaps because his symbolic function is, in these settings, not required. Distributed across the imagined social landscape of Asia and Africa, the Bible can elicit uniform interpretations and uniform transformations of character because the dissonance of domestic sectarianism has been muted. Muted, but not eliminated: Edward Said suggests what he terms a "contrapuntal" reading of the cultural archive, by which he means reading with a simultaneous awareness of Western cultural forms and of "the dynamic global environment created by imperialism." The objective of such reading is to uncover the structures of feeling and reference that appear in metropolitan Western culture as accompaniments to the political, economic, and militaristic history of imperialism (*Culture* 51–53). Approached in this spirit, the fantastical histories of the British and Foreign Bible Society register not only the theological crises of Victorian Protestantism but also the translation of Evangelical faith into a dialect of international commerical capitalism. An artifact that is an articulate emblem of this translation appears late in the nineteenth century; it is a collection box in the shape of a Bible. Vacated of their textual content to make a space for small monetary donations, such miniatures testify to something more subtle than the Bible Society's practical combination of religious and financial plans. They bespeak what no one who used them seemed consciously to recognize; that Evangelical theology, in the process of globalization, had been absorbed into an enterprise which pressed to an extreme its ever-present potential for political and economic uses.

The Bible Famine, the Bible Society, and the Histories of the Bible Society

Early in 1802, Rev. Thomas Charles, a Methodist minister, approached a group of London Dissenters and Evangelicals with the problem of a "Bible famine" in his native Wales. Rev. Charles had spent more than a year encouraging the Society for Promoting Christian Knowledge to begin a program for supplying the poor people of Wales with Bibles. He found the Society, which was the official Anglican organ for the distribution of religious literature, difficult to move and finally unsatisfactory in its response. In contrast, the London Evangelicals and Dissenters whom Rev. Charles approached were immediately incited to action by his pleas. After making further inquiries and circulating a questionnaire in Evangelical magazines, they decided that Wales was only symptomatic of an alarming shortage of Bibles among the poor, both in Britain and abroad. Encouraged by promises of foreign cooperation and confident that theirs was a divinely inspired task, they decided to organize a Bible Society that would encompass both national and international needs. Thus the British and Foreign Bible Society was founded in March 1804 for the purpose of sponsoring translations and cheap editions of Bibles, Testaments, and Psalters in "all the languages spoken by man."[1] As one charter member reportedly said, in a spirit of naive enthusiasm that would largely account for the Society's success, "If for Wales, why not for the world?" (Smit 1–3).

The British and Foreign Bible Society was the third great society for conversions inspired by the Methodist and Evangelical revivals and the millenarian excitement of the previous decade. The other two societies were the London Missionary Society, which was mainly a Dissenting enterprise, and the Church Missionary Society, which had an Evangelical and patriotic character. Over the next fifty years, the B.F.B.S. would claim full or partial responsibility for the distribution of more than 250 million Bibles, in whole or in part, around the world. These included 125 new translations into languages or dialects in which the Bible had never before been printed. Several factors assisted the Society in this remarkable achievement. First, innovations in the print industry made it possible to mass-produce inexpensive editions of standardized texts. Second, the Society's aggressive methods of proselytizing, in spite of early opposition from the East India Company, proved to be increasingly suited to England's changing colonial policies.[2] Third, the Bible Society developed an elaborate hierarchical national structure that allowed its middle- and lower-middle-class members, many of whom were women, to exercise control at the regional level.[3] And finally, the Bible Society owed its success to missionaries in India, Africa, and Asia—men like Henry Martyn, William Carey, Robert Moffat, and Robert Morrison, who assiduously applied themselves to the work of translating the Bible into languages they barely knew, and for people whom they were simultaneously teaching to read. Aided by the Society's donations of paper, type fonts, and money, these missionaries, most of them Dissenters with little formal education, devised orthographies for oral languages, compiled dictionaries and grammars for languages with alphabetic scripts, and, assisted by native speakers of the language whom they employed for a minimal sum, composed and often printed and distributed their own Bible translations.

In Rev. George Browne's two-volume *History of the British and Foreign Bible Society*, letters from missionaries provide the chief source for sensational depictions of the Bible's purportedly unequivocal effect on people in diverse cultural, environmental, and political circumstances.[4] The inhabitants of India, Africa, and Asia become, in Browne's history, products for an English home audience, images of benighted heathens who acquire, via the agency of the Bible, the familiar attributes of Protestant belief, Victorian domesticity, and biblical literacy: "Friends of the Bible will rejoice to hear that the poor Namacquas, whose days were formerly spent in roaming over mountains and deserts, have learnt from the Sacred Scripture to assemble together to hear the Word of God" (Browne 2: 243). The purpose of Browne's history was to update an earlier work, *History of the Origin and First Ten Years of the British and Foreign Bible Society*, which had been written in 1816 by Rev. John Owen, a prominent Evangelical minister and the Society's first secretary. Whereas the bulk of Browne's work focuses on the operations the Society carried out in Europe, Africa, India, and Asia between 1815 and 1850, most of Owen's account focuses on the accusations and controversies that troubled the Society in the first decade of its existence.

In this chapter, I will develop three arguments that pertain to the histories produced by the British and Foreign Bible Society. The first argument primarily concerns Browne's history, which interpolates letters from missionaries and Bible Society workers in such a way as to transform cultural difference into an opportunity for large-scale cultural displacement. The Bible Society based and justified its existence on the belief that the exposure to Holy Scriptures created an abstract Christian subject with similar attributes of behavior and belief regardless of cultural conditions, material environment, or preexisting religious beliefs. In this regard, Browne was a good candidate for the job of Bible Society historian because he had never been a missionary, nor had he traveled to the Asian or

African missions whose histories he chronicled. Consequently, although his mediated depictions of Africans, Indians, and Catholic Europeans reading the Bible for the first time provide very little in the way of ethnographic observation, they do provide narrative vehicles through which problems central to English Protestant culture are acted out and resolved. Some of these problems are familiar from previous chapters; they include religious sectarianism, the competing integrity of public and private reading, and the difficult predicament of masculine authority in sentimental narratives. However, there is an additional problem broached by Browne's history, one that gives a new valence to those other religious dilemmas of British domestic culture: it is the threat that differences of language and culture posed to Protestant faith in the Bible's univocal and universally translatable meaning.

Second, I will argue that the driving force in the Bible Society's narratives was the desire to believe that English Evangelicalism did not insert itself as an interpretive authority between the Bible and its newly extended world readership. This desire was evidenced in three ways: by both Owen's and Browne's relative inattention to the details of translating and preaching the Gospel, by their appropriation of economic metaphors, and by Browne's use of the motif of sentimental child characters. Both Owen and Browne use economic metaphors to depict England as the "agent" of a divinely monitored "circulation" of the text of Christian revelation. Their reiteration of the terms "agency" and "circulation" works to obscure the several ways in which English missionaries were the authors of that revelation—they devised alphabets and orthographies for oral languages, they translated the Bible in such a way as to make it consistent with a particular brand of English faith, and they projected a vision of early Victorian British expansionism as a postmillenarian fulfillment of Christian teleology.[5] Additionally, Browne's history more completely erases the missionaries' presence by transferring their proselytizing functions to foreign children, whom he portrays as the innocent, honest, and willing disseminators of a Book whose authority comes from God, not England.[6] Moreover, when these children are girls, which is often the case, they become symbols of the conflicted conscience of Evangelical imperialism: while their appearance as innocent proselytizers veils the problematic power of the missionary endeavor, their gender veils the patriarchal structure of the Bible Society's relationship to its foreign beneficiaries. In this way, Browne's missionary vignettes attempt to structure the missionary encounter according to an economy of sentimental literary authority similar to the one we investigated in Dickens's midcentury writings.

My third argument concerns Owen's and Browne's histories of the Bible Society in their capacity as fund-raising exercises. The method of composition that Owen and Browne used in their texts created a direct and persuasive correspondence between English contributions to the Bible Society and foreign conversions to biblical literacy. By interweaving the missionaries' accounts of conversions with statistics, lists of new Auxiliary Societies, new translations, and records of donations or subscriptions, Owen and Browne inserted their targeted readers (the largely middle- and lower-middle-class members of the Society) as characters in their texts. Consequently, their histories both enact and epitomize the Bible Society's most important function, which was to create a hegemonic cultural practice that offered middle-class Evangelical men and other, more marginalized citizens (women, Dissenters, and members of the lower middle classes) a means of identifying with the English state as a beneficent agent of God's will. Apart from the question of how the Society's translations were actually received and interpreted in non-Christian societies, and in spite of the animosities that frequently arose between colonial agents and religious missionaries, the Bible Society abetted and reflected Victorian nationalism and imperialism by offering English men and women at home a means through which they could imagine themselves to be active participants in the establishment of a Christian empire.

These arguments reflect the degree to which the English Evangelicals and Non-Conformists who created the Bible Society invested an entire and complex ideology in a single commodity. The translated Bibles that Owen and Browne tracked around the world returned to their English sponsors reassuring reflections of converted and grateful communities, proof that the coalition of English religion, culture, and technology could indeed divide the world into the providential symmetry of a "British" and a "Foreign" society. When members of foreign communities are depicted displaying an anxious desire for Bibles, they seem to confirm the innocence and integrity of English Evangelicalism's own anxious desire for the millenarian expansion of its Christian society. They seem to confirm the reciprocity of that desire, but not without occasional recognitions of unfamiliarity, displays of what Homi Bhaba calls hybridity—a misrecognition of discriminated subjects that returns a distorted and contestatory image to the eye of the colonial observer (112-15). A Muslim sends his servant thirty miles to buy a Bible, and the Society's colporteur momentarily wonders if their mutual fetishization of this book truly betokens similar motives—"What makes the Mahomedans so desirous to possess the Bible, is not clearly apparent" (Browne 2: 161). As we shall see, that momentary glimpse of the horrifying commodification of sacred writings was a destiny inherent in the Bible Society's project. For, even in the early stages, as long as foreigners wanted the Society's books and were willing to pay a nominal fee for them (the Society never gave Bibles away), their actions were consistent with the Society's mystical valuation of this good. Alongside the Society's members, foreign purchasers of the Society's Bibles were assigned a fixed role in the new continuations of the Bible, the Bible Society histories. These books depict a world being transformed by books, and they cite as their authority for this transformation scriptural passages like the one from Isaiah quoted at the opening of this chapter. For the readers of the Society's histories, the figural affiliation that Isaiah draws between prosperity and divine intentions had found a new manifestation in the anticipated alliance between capitalist expansion and Protestant evangelism. To their minds this new alliance was more than literary; like the translated Bibles themselves, it represented the literalizing word-play of God's ongoing authorship of history.

From Babel to the Mouths of Babes: Problems in Translation and Their Fictional Resolutions

In 1844, Rev. Barnabas Shaw, a Wesleyan missionary in South Africa, wrote a letter to the British and Foreign Bible Society containing this description of how the Word of God was carried to a tribe of so-called Bushmen or San in southern Africa:

> Two little girls went from my station in Namacqualand to visit a tribe on the borders of the Bushmenland. They carried their Testaments with them, and read among the people. The natives were so interested in what they heard, that they allowed the two children but little time for rest. Day and night they were under the necessity of reading out of the "Great Word", by which several persons of that tribe were brought under the sound of the Gospel. Thus, "out of the mouths of babes and sucklings, he has perfected praise." (Browne 2: 255)

Without trying to gauge how much of Rev. Shaw's account is fact and how much is fiction, we can still marvel at the simple, anecdotal, and reassuring manner in which it casts a text-based culture's mediation of its symbolic book to a society with very different linguistic practices. There are, in fact, more mediators lurking in this passage than there are messages communicated. The Bible is the primary symbol of communication, since it bestows with magical irresistibility the message of Christian revelation. But the young girls are responsible for this communication as well, since they are the ones who, armed with a missionary-school education, purportedly go out and read the Bible to the San for several days in a row. And since this is a translated Bible, there is also the past intermediary of the translator, who in this case must also have devised a system of orthography for the San's speech. Finally, there is the concluding quotation of the Bible, which with an innocence as great as the babes and sucklings to which it refers, filters out the immense labor and cultural gaps suggested by these other agents, and mediates to an English readership the image of more heathen souls brought into the Christian fold.

The presence of the young girls is crucial here for several reasons.

First, the fact that they become the teachers of their elders infantilizes the San—the only adult in the story is an absent narrator, the Rev. Mr. Shaw. Consequently, the young girls provide a vicarious innocence for the English missionary, who imaginatively participates in their role as child-preachers and thus is separated from the aspects of his vocation that, from an English point of view, were controversial and disturbing. (What exactly is Rev. Shaw teaching—Anglican or Non-Conformist doctrines? How do the Africans interpret what he says? How can they be apathetic in their own need for salvation and Western enlightenment, if indeed these gifts are clearly desirable?) Childhood becomes the pristine space wherein Christianity and the San meet, a space distanced from the adult world of the mission, where the missionary's presence is more problematic, for himself as for the native population, and less clearly illustrative of divine guidance. In a gesture that became a commonplace in the Bible Society histories, the story displaces the agency of conversion from an English missionary—the single most important mediator in the Evangelical encounter—to native children, and the question of interpretive interference in the communication of the Bible is dissolved with a biblical symbol of inviolable immediacy to God's inspiration—the mouths of babes.

Like most stories contained in George Browne's *History of the British and Foreign Bible Society*, Rev. Shaw's account does not dwell on insurmountable obstacles posed by the prospect of converting oral cultures to biblical literacy. In part, this is because Browne has reduced the missionaries' experience to propaganda, deflecting attention away from the long years missionaries often had to spend in Africa before they could claim any converts, and from the immense frustration they sometimes expressed in their correspondence and memoirs. Robert Moffat, for instance, spent five years in Namacqualand before he could report a single baptism, and Anne Hodgson, the wife of a Methodist missionary, wrote home of the disillusionment of finding herself "among a people who have never heard the Gospel, and 'are dead in trespasses and sins;' and whose principal requests are 'give me meat—give me tobacco'" (William Shaw 171).[7]

And yet, in the Society's published accounts, the missionaries present an optimistic picture of recent or imminent progress, and never attribute setbacks to the cultural and epistemological differences between their own language and those of the societies they wish to convert. As the Comaroffs comment on Moffat's efforts in South Africa, the missionaries' "'fever for translation' ... flowed from a growing conviction that language, a human creation, could be made into a global medium of communication." Moreover, this conviction was based on the epistemological belief in the indexical properties of language, in its malleable transparency to empirical and cognitive signifieds (215–16). Their writings predate, of course, anthropological debates about the underlying differences or similarities between oral and literate languages, or between phonetic and pictographic or hieroglyphic writing systems.[8] What is clear from their writings is the degree to which the missionaries' perceptions were shadowed by their own ambivalence toward the relative benefits of bringing Asians and Africans within the sound of the Gospel and bringing them to read it. For the missionaries, the problematic division was not between orality and literacy—their mission centered, after all, on a Book—but rather between the competing integrity of oral recitation and silent reading in the transmission of the text they regarded as divine revelation.

Their anxiety over the various rhetorical ways that the use of language could distort its message was indigenous to a post-Enlightenment, empirical, and phonetic conception of language, and in this case, specifically to the impact of that conception on Protestant attitudes toward the Bible. Like their supporters in England, the missionaries who preached and translated the Bible believed that revelation was singular in its original and ultimate meaning, and that oral reading and private reading were as necessary to communicating the Bible's divine intentions as they were capable of distorting it.[9] But both oral and private reading allowed an unfortunate liberty of interpretation, of either inflectional or typographic interference with the meaning of Scriptures.

Within England, the Evangelical community increasingly valued private reading of the Bible as the supremely accurate and unmediated form of communication between God and humanity, although paradoxically, the high value that early-nineteenth-century Evangelicals and Wesleyans placed on private Bible-reading originated in a tradition of great sermonizers, men like Wesley and Jabez Bunting, who articulated a religious culture that revolved around the introspective, affective experience of reading the Bible. We have encountered before this erratic interplay between oral and literacy communication in Protestantism; Edward Irving could be added to the list of great British preachers, even as the apocalyptic speech released from his parishioners was an entirely text-based miracle, a vocal fulfillment of scriptural prophecy. With the advent of the Bible Society (a movement, by the way, that Irving denounced) private Bible-reading begins to preempt the importance of sermons and the integrity of oral transmission: Charles Simeon commented that he never felt closer to God than when he read the Bible (Chadwick 1: 442); and an anonymous frame-maker addressing the Bible Society in 1813 said that "the pure word of God, I read in my Testament, edifies me more than the vain words I hear from the pulpit" ("Ninth Annual Report" 138). Indeed, the "Bible famine" that the Society discovered in Britain at the turn of the century was partly of its own making, since the Evangelical movement was largely responsible for England's recognition that illiteracy among the poor was an unfortunate condition requiring improvement. (Teaching working-class English children to read had been an Evangelical undertaking since the beginning of Sunday schools in the mid-1780s.) Globally, however, faith in the transparency of the printed word could only be sustained by concealing the significant presence of the missionary translator, whose presence intruded at every level—as a sermonizer, an oral reader, and a translator of the text which readers who had been inducted into the new orthographies could read alone. And yet, as the Comaroffs suggest, the Bibles that were thus disseminated were imperfect imitations of both the A.V. and the languages into which they had been translated; they were "hybrid creation[s] born of the colonial encounter itself" (218).

The fact that converting the world to the Bible meant first converting much of it to a Western model of literacy was apparent to Browne and his English readers even if they were inclined to gloss over the time and effort implied by such a massive conversion. With a single-mindedness of purpose befitting an English Sunday-school education, the Bible Society's histories depict African and poor Indian adults eagerly studying the European mediation of their own vernaculars because "all have a desire to read the word of God" (Browne 2: 278). Children on the Gold Coast, the Society's German affiliates relate, teach their parents to read by coming home from the missionary school and writing the alphabet in the sand. Rev. Henry Venn composed an alphabet for the Ga language that was used to produce Bibles for distribution in West Africa, thereby establishing, in Browne's words, "a system of aggressive evangelization, assuredly destined to gain ultimate possession of all the territories of the sons of Ham" (2: 283–84). Venn translates the Bible into Ga and Browne translates Africa into the Bible, justifying "aggressive evangelization" as the fulfillment of a biblical empire where the descendants of Ham are willingly and joyfully converted in the days before the Second Coming.

Similarly, Robert Moffat, a Wesleyan Methodist whose formal education ended at the age of eleven, single-handedly devised a chirographic system for the oral Setswana language, and used it to make a translation of the Bible from the Hebrew and Greek texts—a project that he worked on from 1829 to 1857. In the 1830s he continued to preach sermons in Setswana explicating the Gospels and the Old Testament, and he printed copies of his own spelling books to teach the Tswana to read along with him (Sandilands 1). Describing the conversions that ensued, Moffat proclaimed, "The single reading and study of the Bible alone will convert the world" (Browne 2: 248), thus overlooking his own laborious guidance of the Tswana converts' educations. Elsewhere, however, Moffat lamented the physical and mental anguish of his work, commenting that he had often "felt it to be an awful work to translate the Book of God, and perhaps, this has given to my heart the habit of sometimes beating like the strokes of a hammer" (*Life's Labours* 91). But these personal reflections were reserved for Moffat's final memoirs, published much later in the century. In the Bible Society's histories, his labor and disappointments, like those of other missionaries, are eclipsed by claims of rapid progress and providential success. Such claims had a definite appeal for Protestant readers, who invested in the Bible Society because they believed that the unaccompanied Bible had a wondrous ability to inspire universal consent, as well as gratitude to the Englishmen who brought it.

Despite the outward optimism of the missionaries quoted in Browne's history, it was clear that the Protestant belief in the self-sufficiency of Scriptures for Christian interpretation, a belief fought for and jealously guarded by Dissenters, had met a new challenge in the missionary experience of Asia, Africa, and India. Here the enemy was not the High Church's insistence on the necessity of the Prayer Book and Articles of Faith for a proper regulation of scriptural meaning. It was, rather, the linguistic, cultural, and educational differences that threatened to expose the Protestant Bible as a culturally relative text. The missionaries met this challenge both with direct arguments and (as in Rev. Shaw's correspondence) spectacular anecdotes. Answering the objection that for a "pagan, unacquainted with Jewish antiquities, European history, and Christian doctrine ... there is much in the Bible that he cannot understand," Dr. Morrison, a distinguished Hindu scholar and a translator for the Bible Society, responded with the Pietist argument that understanding really depends on the heart of reader. "The careless, profligate, and proud, in every land, will despise the Bible," Morrison wrote, "but the inquiring mind and the anxious spirit ... will esteem it a 'pearl of great price'" (Browne 2: 205). In a more sensational vein, the Baptist translators at Serampore reported that several Brahmins and members of high caste began to "observe Christian worship on the Lord's day, before they had any intercourse with the Missionaries, *simply by reading the Scriptures*" (Browne 2: 116). And a German missionary related the story of a young Hindu who requested baptism after purchasing a Persian Testament at a fair: "He has had no teacher, the *reading* of the word alone has converted him" (Browne 2: 157).

Without broaching the question of what these Hindus converted to or why, the missionaries' accounts of their conversions verified for English Protestants the clarity, persuasiveness, and self-sufficiency they ascribed to Scriptures. On at least one occasion, a missionary pushed the suspension of disbelief past even the Bible Society's credulity: Robert Yuille, a missionary and translator in Mongolia, was dismissed from service in part because he lied when he wrote to the directors that the chief lama of Khaglan had been reading his translated Scriptures "every morning on his Knees, and with all of the Lamas of the Household with him." Yuille's dismissal was insisted upon by his fellow translators, William Swan and Edward Stallybrass, men of higher standards, who surreptitiously informed the London directors about their colleague's dubious abilities: "Test his skills in *any* language he professes to know—*English*—Latin—Greek—Hebrew—Russ—and the result of such examination may lead to something near the truth of his Mongolian scholarship" (Bawden 294-96). But within Browne's history, neither the credibility of the missionaries nor the relative facility of their work is brought into question. Time and time again, the fantasy of the Bible's reception abroad is the same: missionaries find non-Christians in a state of apprehensive desire for religious enlightenment (Morrison's "anxious spirit"), and once they read or hear the New Testament, they spontaneously endorse an understanding of it sympathetic to Protestant faith.

In contrast to the stories of African and Indian conversions, the stories of evangelization in nations that are already Christian involve a greater dramatic tension, because here the millenarian plot is complete with an Antichrist, the pope. Again, children are crucial to these stories, and they have a commonality with the children in the African stories; both are cast as mediators, guardians, and infallible interpreters of the Bible. For instance, Browne's chronicles of the

Society's activities in the 1830s contain an account of the fate of a certain Belgian Bible, the cherished but outlawed possession of a small group of Protestant villagers. The villagers had managed for some time to outwit the local priests, who knew of the Bible's existence and were on the lookout to confiscate it. One scheme they devised was to leave the Bible buried beneath blankets in a cradle, watched over and rocked by a young girl. Her vigilance eventually became their downfall, however, since a spy for the priests, having noticed her long hours of rocking and watching, guessed that something other than an infant was in the cradle. He gave her away to the priests, who entered the house while the men were out working in the fields and took the Bible, against the girl's protestations (1: 454).

The story is a pastiche of competing iconographies. The substitution of a Bible for an infant is inspired by the dual association of the Bible and the Christ child with the revealed Word of God. And, since the confiscated Bible is presumably a translation into vernacular Flemish or French, it shares with the infant the quality of being an incarnation of the Word into a common human form that only those with corrupt or imperfect faith (i.e., Roman Catholics) consider unworthy of divine habitation. The Madonna figure that guards the cradle is both a child-mother and a mother-child, since she is wrongfully replaced by the Catholic Church's claim to be the only true mother and guardian of the faith. The violence of that replacement, its similarity to a scene of rape or, in biblical terms, to the slaughter of the innocents by Herod, signals the selling into slavery of the true Christian faith to the papal impostor, who is of course not only a false mother but a whore. Interestingly, this competition between two symbolic mothers can occur only in the absence of all real mothers, who have been inexplicably vacated from the scene. The most realistic characters in the narrative (real in the sense that their ontological status is least complicated by symbolic overtones) are the men, who have had to leave home in order to go to work. This necessity does not bind the priests, whose lives are supported by the workingmen's tithes (an unmentioned detail that would not be lost on contemporary readers), and who ironically are thus free to further prey on Protestant families and possessions. This story is typical of the European stories in Browne's and Owen's histories in that it organizes politically and socially complex material into a confrontation where the organizing rubric is religious denomination and literacy.

Like the story of the Belgian Bible, the following story from a missionary in Greece organizes a variety of the Society's conventions (the innate wisdom of children, the superior reliability of private to public reading, the Bible's ability to uproot superstitious beliefs and inculcate pious common sense, and the foreign recipients' gratitude for the Society's work) around an old representative of Catholicism and a young representative of the Bible Society, this time with the victory going to the Bible Society:

> In one of the villages, about four or five hours distant from Canea, a monk (whose name I do not now recollect) was making his visit for the purpose of collecting oil, money, &c.; and for the better furtherance of his designs, he carried with him the relics of some saint, famous for his godliness and piety; these relics he presented to the people to kiss, and make the sign of the cross over them and afterwards to give him whatever they chose. But wherever he went, he was told ... that they had learned better than to worship saints and their relics, since they had the Bible introduced among them, and a school established.... In revenge for his disappointment, he began to cry out against the school, and the distribution of the Bible. And, as if chance had favored his design, he found a copy of the book of Job in the house of the villager where he was, and, opening it, he read the 17th verse of the 4th chapter; but he read it affirmatively, and not interrogatively, as it is. After he had read it, he turned to those present, and began to speak against the Bible printed and distributed by the Bible Society, saying that it contained many blasphemies and sinful things, and frequently referred to this passage. One of the children, who had learned to read in the school, and had listened to him with considerable attention, when he had finished his discourse, said, he did not know that the Scripture anywhere said that man "can be purer than his Maker." ... The boy, taking the book, read the passage interrogatively ... and observed that it only asked the question, if a man shall be "juster than God and purer than his Maker, while he sees

faults even in his angels?" The monk remained silent, and the people drove him out of their village. (Browne 2: 58-59)

What were for English Protestants the controversial relations among oral reading, private reading, and the act of interpreting the Bible find in the story of the Greek monk a polarized and morally differentiated formula: proper reading and interpretation is Protestant in origin, while perversion in reading and interpretation comes from the fountainhead of religious corruption, the Catholic Church. This differentiation represses, however, a similarity that is implied everywhere else in Browne's text: the Bible operates for the Society as the relics do for the monk, as fetishized commodities that are sold for a price incommensurate with their spiritual dividends.

There is a subtext to this dramatic confrontation between the interpretive powers of an old Catholic monk and a young Protestant convert that goes beyond the religious aspects of the Bible Society's enmity toward Catholicism. The Bible Society and what it stands for (the tacit metonymy that links England's promotion of the Bible as a progressive and liberating ideological commodity with the global expansion of its manufacturing and trade economy) is at war with Catholicism and what it stands for. The more explicit metonymy is between the monk and Catholicism's dependence upon ignorance and popular superstition for the maintenance of its ancient clerical and aristocratic privileges. These metonymic associations are elsewhere made more salient by Browne's frequent reiteration of the call for "free circulation of Scriptures"—a slogan that invokes the arguments that English manufacturers and free-trade economists used against trade regulations such as the Corn Laws, which were similarly associated with outmoded aristocratic privilege, and were similarly held accountable for hurting the poor by causing disastrous fluctuations in the availability of vital commodities. Hence, for Browne, the Bible Society signals the beginning of a "true Catholic society" where the "free circulation of Scriptures," a circulation that has been checked "by the Ancient court of Rome," will save "unimagined numbers of families" from "the famine of the Word of God." Phrases such as these engraft traditional English hostility toward the Catholic suppression of the Bible upon the hostility that Britain's manufacturers and merchants felt toward the remnants of dynastic feudalism.

In discourse as well as in practice, the Bible Society merged Protestant ideology with the economic rubric and developing market mechanisms of capitalism. This was true even though in the first three decades of the nineteenth century the East India Company was hostile to missionary intervention in its territories. The Bible Society emulated the structures, policies, and rhetoric of colonial trade even as it was rejected, or at best tolerated, by those agents of colonial trade who continued to abide by the noninterventionist and mercenary attitudes that characterized Warren Hastings's career.[10] In its conviction that cultural intervention in India was absolutely necessary, the Bible Society (like other Evangelical societies for conversion) complemented the direction that the utilitarian influence over colonial policies would take. It was in a sense the quintessential Victorian colonial business, combining commercial organization with moral conviction. By identifying itself as a nonintrusive administrative protectorate, and by building its system of distribution on commercial models, the Bible Society simulated in its organization the advantages that England claimed over other European powers in the battle for a superior trading position overseas. This supremacy was based on commercial and maritime control—on exchange and mobility—and consequently it fostered a rhetoric of maximum liberality and equality between states even as it disguised the fact of English ascendancy. Hence another common feature of Owen's and Browne's rhetoric is their emphasis on "agency" and "instrumentality"—terms that tacitly assert the British Bible Society's ascendancy over its foreign Auxiliaries as the preferred mediator between God and the nations, races, and languages of the earth. Owen calls England the "chosen agent" through which God will globally reveal his truth, and affirms that the Bible Society cannot "desist from its labour" until "through its instrumentality ... the Bible shall accomplish its office" (1: 286). British agency is the link between the Bible as a national trust and a global resource, as in the comment that

"Holy Scriptures are a not a personal benefit, but a trust to be used ... for the benefit of others" (Browne 1: 3). Elsewhere the idea of instrumentality is communicated with greater patriotic zeal: "Let us therefore rejoice, that, under Providence, England has become the honored instrument of [Christianity's] dispensations" (Owen 1: 419). With these formulations the Bible Society conceives both itself and its "parent" nation as agents of a providential source of power: England's claim to global preeminence in the work of Bible distribution is based not on executive authority over its foreign auxiliaries, but on its administrative guardianship over the channels of "free circulation."[11]

In a related fashion, the debate with Catholicism involved both philosophies of language and differing attitudes toward the impact of technology upon sacred writings. The story of the Greek monk selling alms, for example, makes Bible reading into an occasion for exaggerating and refuting the Catholic argument against translations of the Bible into "vulgar tongues."[12] While the Church traditionally argued that the best guard against heresy was to maintain Latin as the privileged language of theological knowledge, the Bible Society believed that the translation of the Bible into spoken idioms was the cornerstone of enlightened societies of self-respecting Christian individuals. Owen includes in his history two letters that praise the Society's translations for their unembellished, simple, and easily accessible style. A striking feature of these letters is that both come from authorities whose own cultures still maintained a distinction between the demotic tongue of common intercourse and an erudite written language reserved for the court and for religious writings. One letter is from the king of Persia, who praises Henry Martyn's Modern Persian Gospel because it is written in "a style most befitting Sacred Books, that is, in an easy and simple diction." A note from the translator of the letter explains that the king has honored the translation by using the word "tilawah" for "read"—"tilawah" usually being reserved for the act of reciting or perusing the Koran (2: 265-67). Thus the Society's desire to treat the Bible as information that must be rendered in every pedestrian dialect finds, in the king of Persia's letter, a word of praise ironically rooted in a tradition that treats sacred writings in an opposite vein, as privileged texts that require protection from common linguistic intercourse.

By adopting empirical and rationalist philosophies of language, the Society symbolically conflated the Bible with another English text of mythical proportions, the Social Contract. When it targeted for Bible translations the languages of Mohawks, Hottentots, and other "neglected little tribes," the Bible Society created an opportunity to relive not only the Christian myth of apostolic origins but also the Enlightenment myth of a consensual passage from natural to rational society. In a speech to the London Missionary Society, a Christian Hottentot reportedly called the Bible "a charter of human liberties" that had taught his tribe to "live like civilized men" and thus had saved them "from the self-destruction of the state of nature" (Browne 2: 246). His language suggests he had been reading at least as much Rousseau as Christian Scriptures. At the Great Exhibition, the Hottentot's words were reiterated by the banner proposed for the Society's booth: "The Charter of human liberty—the Book by which England has become great."[13] Here the Lockean source of consent—the protection of life and property—is replaced with a consensual text, one that merges a religious with a secular tradition, and assimilates images that carry both democratic and imperialistic significance. The multiplicity of languages, like the multiplicity of Bibles, is merely a nominal plurality, for every language has its idiom of unadorned, plain-style prose, free from rhetorical embellishment (the universal idiom of rational, empirical communication). And every Bible translated into these idioms will have the uniform effect of leading its readers to the recognition that God's textual intentions are identical with the intentions of English Protestant culture.

The Society's growing concern that its translators aim for an "easy and simple" diction reflects what I described earlier as the decline of oratory and rhetoric as valid forms of communicating knowledge. This decline is further exemplified by the Bible Society's attitudes toward its own historical textualization. When George Browne updated John Owen's history, he took considerable pains to clarify where he was indebted to Owen and where he departed from Owen's example. The difference between them, as Browne sees it, is the difference between an orator and a historian: Owen had "composed in an ardent strain" and with "eloquent statements" that display "the copiousness of the orator," rather than "the calm recital of the historian." To make his text more credible, Browne has tried to avoid "the warm and glowing character of [Owen's] narrative" and "has purposefully guarded against amplification" (1: vii). These passages suggest that for Browne and his readers the form of prose writing that was most believable, that was least capable of distortion or falsification, was the form of writing associated with the still newly dominant mode of mass communication: the silent reading of print, a silence in which both the reader and the writer participated. Browne's cautious introduction registers the way in which reading itself was changing, becoming more purely a cognitive activity estranged from oral and aural affiliations. And, in turn, it registers the tension he and his readers felt between the impassioned rhetorical embellishments that characterized traditional Evangelical discourse and the empirical diction and objective tone that distinguished the model of subdued and respectable discourse toward which some of them, Browne included, aspired—nonfiction prose. The importance of this change is underscored by the difference between Browne's aspiration to a prose severed from the speaking voice and the models of writing employed in Evangelical tracts from earlier in the century. For example, John Vine Hall's popular tract *The Sinner's Friend* liberally used boldface, capitalizations, multiple exclamation points, and italics so as to emulate in print the rousing modulations of a preacher's voice.

While some of the difficulties of converting the world to print might go unmentioned, there were other and related questions that continued to be raised during the ongoing task of converting the Bible to print. As we saw in the studies of Coleridge and Thomas Arnold, the Bible of the early nineteenth century was an eminently unstable text: the multiplicity, ambiguity, and complex history of the Bible's manuscripts, combined with the problematic relationship between the Old and the New Testament and with Protestantism's valorization of a single, divine text, made for continuing debates about the A.V., debates that were aggravated by new studies of biblical manuscripts. The Bible Society initiated its work believing that innovations in print technology would help resolve some of these debates by making it possible to mass-produce exact reproductions of the A.V. In its first year of operation, the Society sponsored the first edition of the King James Bible using stereotype print, a system that they celebrated as the source of a "correct and standard text" and "a regular and permanent supply" of Bibles (Browne 1: 21). At the same time, the Society began to collect approved editions of the A.V. for comparison so as to continue modifying the stereotyped version and thus proceed toward a definitive text (Browne 1: 31). As members were proud of pointing out, the Bibles were printed "without note or comment," for despite the frequent evidence to the contrary, the Bible Society believed in a categorical distinction between sacred and supplemental writings. Theirs was a large-scale attempt to perfect the archaeological approach to scriptural interpretation, wherein sectarian reconciliation, imagined as global Christian harmony, would be established on the sure support of an original, unmediated text of God's word.

However, as the Society ventured into other languages and other Bibles, the unity of its Protestant coalition was undermined by the inability to separate a fundamental biblical text from the task of translation. Compiling editions of the A.V. that would please all the sects cooperating in the Society was difficult enough, but once they ventured into other languages and other Bibles, agreement began to seem impossible. The conclusion that the Society worked desperately to avoid was that there was no pure, uninterpreted Bible, that in fact every translation was already an interpretation. Their belief exemplifies what Walter Benjamin says of all translations of Holy Writ, that "where a text is identical with truth or dogma, where it is supposed to be 'the true language' in all its literalness and without the mediation of meaning, this text is unconditionally translatable" (82). The first and major challenge to this belief occurred in the mid-

1820s, when a controversy arose over the propriety of issuing Bibles with the Apocrypha for use in European countries; the result, as I mentioned earlier, was that the official ties between the British and the European Auxiliaries were severed. In 1839 a splinter organization, the Trinitarian Bible Society, was formed of ex–Bible Society members who objected to the use of the Latin Vulgate to translate a Bible for European Roman Catholics. In another incident, a group of London patrons insisted on cutting off funds to the Baptist translators at Serampore whom they discovered had translated "baptize" into a Hindustani word for immersion. In the 1820s the two British missionaries in Siberia, Edward Stallybrass and William Swan, worked to complete a Mongolian translation of the New Testament that had been begun in 1807 by Moravian missionaries, one of whom was a celebrated Dutch orientalist, I. J. Schmidt. Stallybrass and Swan found that the Moravians' translation often "did not give the *whole sense* to any particular passage"; for example, their rendering of the creation story in Genesis failed to give sufficient emphasis to the sacred nature of the Sabbath (Bawden 284). In still other instances, the problem was not with translators who manipulated a foreign language to convey a specific doctrinal valence, but rather with the refusal of some non-European languages to conform to the structures of Christian belief. Work on a Chinese Bible was plagued for years by a debate on the best way to render the various biblical names for God. The missionaries wanted a generic term for God that, like the English word, could be used in the plural as well as the singular, thus including false Gods as well as the one Christian God. They limited their choices to "Shin" and "Shangti," but found both inadequate: "Shin" conveyed a rather abstract idea of the nature of the Divine Being, whereas "Shangti," the proper Chinese word for God, was never used to refer to false or evil Gods. After several years of deliberation, the Society sponsored two different versions, one using "Shin" and the other "Shangti." The holy book of empire was beginning to fracture into a number of texts.

The Society's remarkable successes (109 new translations by 1809) and its ostentatious appeals for support were sometimes greeted by

English scholars and High Churchmen with suspicion, and sometimes with outright disdain. Neither Owen nor Browne omits these charges from their histories of the Society, but they use them to the rhetorical end of portraying attacks on the Society as negligible setbacks in an overall picture of dramatic progress. Hence criticisms from High Churchmen (more frequent in the first twenty years of the Society's histories) are interpolated with answers from tracts written by the Society's supporters. As Owen relates, a conservative spokesman for the Society for Promoting Christian Knowledge suggested that in giving the A.V. to the poor, the B.F.B.S. gave too little, since for doctrinal purposes the Bible was only complete when it was circulated with the Prayer Book (1: 164–65). Meanwhile, another Anglican theologian charged that the Bible Society gave too much, because only seven books of the Old Testament and six of the New were "suitable for the study of the unlearned" (Owen 2: 205). Thus the Society's diplomatic policy of printing only the Bible was undermined by the question of which Bible to print, and High Churchmen refused to suffer in silence the dismay they felt for the Society's ideas of what constituted the Bible of Protestant faith.[14]

One attack on the Society that George Browne neglected to mention in his history was an 1827 review of Owen's book written by a frequent contributor to the *Quarterly Review*, Rev. Edward Edwards. Taking up a charge that had been raised in 1812 by Dr. Herbert Marsh, Edwards accuses the Society of rapidly producing poor translations and of claiming responsibility for new translations which, in fact, were merely publications of preexisting and sometimes questionable manuscripts. Edwards cites the example of the Society's Mohawk translator, a convert named Teyoninhokarawen (aka "John Norton"), whose New Testament was suspect not only because it was executed from the English A.V. instead of the original Greek but also because no one except Teyoninhokarawen was capable of judging the fidelity of the translation (9). He incorporates this example into a picture of the Society as a corrupt, lower-middle-class scam for power and money; according to Edwards, every new translation is an advertisement for donations that "increase the coffers of the Society's funds" (6). In 1819, Edwards relates, the Society went so far as to print a Turkish New Testament that was taken from the eighteenth-century manuscript of a "Polish renegado." When the translation was criticized for its "florid style and affectation," the Society responded by printing up new leaves for the most offensive pages and then "having them distributed to those who had bought them in Turkey" (19). No explanation is given, Edwards complains, of how these customers were found, or how they were persuaded to unbind their books and insert the improved pages.

Although Edwards accuses the Society of allowing old translations to masquerade as new ones, what is at stake in his argument has as much to do with dead foreign translators as with living English ones, and with the doctrinal, interpretive, or simply careless alterations of Scriptures that the latter could make. But it is not clear if Edwards is more afraid of the threat posed to Scriptures by these translators or the fact that they signaled a threat to the cultural and political hegemony that traditionally controlled such scholarly labor. The contempt expressed in his essay for the Society's translators seems at once scholarly and social, fueled by the recognition that through the Bible Society a class of "self-educated missionaries" were garnering some degree of worldly influence. None of these men, Edwards complains, has had "the benefit of a regular or learned university education" (23). And, of course, many of them did not have the benefit of an Oxford or Cambridge education, since even if they had the necessary financial resources, as Non-Conformists they were not allowed to matriculate.

Edwards's criticisms suggest that the dismay that England's cultural elite felt when regarding the Bible Society was at once religious (pertinent to the Anglican Church's doctrinal control of the religious literature circulated by English institutions) and political (pertinent to the social and cultural establishment that determined who received a classical education, and who was qualified to represent English interests in the public capacities of a clergyman, a university scholar, or a government official). Although both Owen and Browne omit this information, much of the momentum for the Bible Society's marathon translations came from devoted Dissenters, most of them working class, and only a few of them with extensive university educations. They included the Baptist translators at Serampore, William Carey, who had been apprenticed as a shoemaker, and Joshua Marshman, a weaver; Henry Martyn, the son of a miner who obtained a scholarship to Cambridge, where he was inspired by Simeon to become a missionary, and afterward translated the New Testament and the Psalms into both Hindu and Persian; Robert Morrison, the Presbyterian son of a boot-tree maker who wrote a Chinese translation of the Bible in twenty-one volumes; the Methodist Robert Moffat, who had been apprenticed to a gardener before he went to Africa as a missionary and translated the entire Bible into the Setswana language; and the two translators of the Mongolian Bible, the Congregationalist Edward Stallybrass and the Scottish "freethinking" William Swan, both of whom had studied classics and theology for two years at Homerton College. All these men, to varying degrees, were politically and socially unempowered at home. And all of them went to their foreign missions with the belief that their right to influence the course of empire came from God. Undeterred by continual difficulties (lack of supplies, censorship, interference from the English colonial governments, and their own limited abilities in the languages they were translating), these men spent years writing the books that they believed with all sincerity would contribute to England's millenarian enlightenment of the human population of the earth.

This motive might account not only for the missionary translators but also for the middle-class men, Dissenters or Evangelicals, who contributed to the Society at home and for the women who worked in or ran the Associations. Edwards thought he could persuade people to stop subscribing to the B.F.B.S. by demonstrating that its historian, John Owen, did not describe how the translations were executed but rather reduced them to sensational statistics. He was mistaken, however, because for many of the subscribers these numbers were persuasive in themselves; they were symbolic registers of the donor's role in the progress toward a Christian fulfillment of history. Each Bible, Testament, and Psalter that Owen records equals one more soul won for God, one more soul bought with subscriber's donations: 4,210 Bibles and Testaments are distributed in and round Bristol in 1810; 500 Bibles are distributed in Mauritius in 1812; 73,000 rupees are raised in British India in 1811; 3,000 Testaments are sold in Germany in the same year; 2,000 copies of the Chinese Gospel of Luke are printed in January 1814. In this ideological economy, numbers are abstract signifiers that erase the distinction between poor Englishmen, rich Englishmen, Europeans, non-Europeans, donations, and Bibles—all are quantitatively assessed as incremental contributions to a Protestant British and foreign totality. Far from arousing suspicion, Owen's and later Browne's numerical pyrotechnics worked to attract contributors by implicitly expressing Protestant imperial power as a formulaic equivalency between English donators, translated Bibles, and converted citizens of the world.

What made this equation persuasive was the Bible Society's ability to extrapolate from Evangelical faith affective associations with the Bible that were autonomous with regard to its nature as a text. Consequently, rather than reflecting a textual orientation toward Scriptures, Owen's and Browne's histories reflect a belief that the interpretation of the Bible has already been absorbed into its psychological and social itinerary, and that the Bible universally affects its readers in a predictable and univocal fashion. In this way, the cornerstone of English faith—you are what you read—became the fallacy of Evangelical philanthropy's presumption that it knew what its foreign beneficiaries were reading. And although in England, seditious or extravagant interpretations of the Bible were inescapably apparent (one need only think of Blake, Joanna Southcott, Zion Ward, or the anti-Christian pamphleteer Richard Carlile), upon the unseen narrative space of the colonies and Catholic Europe the Bible Society could project its utopic dream of societies transformed by Bible reading into paragons of Protestant middle-class culture without too much cognitive dissonance, and what dissonance there was could barely be distinguished beneath the fictional vignettes that are continually replayed in Browne's history. Put a translated New Testament into the hands of a non-Christian who knows nothing about the Old Testament or European history, or of a Catholic who has never read the Bible in his or her native dialect, and the result will be a grateful Protestant.

Despite the repetitive simplicity of these plots, many of them condense, as we have seen, a variety of anxieties—linguistic, doctrinal, political, and economic—into symbolic forms. The primary argument that I wish to advance, based on the suggestion with which this section began, is that the child is the crucial figural motif in this condensation, not only because the child is a conventional vehicle for evoking religious sentimentality in Victorian and Evangelical literature, but also because the child eclipses the exchanges of power that are implicit on several levels in the missionary encounters contained in Browne's history. The fictional substitution of a child for the missionary, for the Bible Society, or, in the largest sense, for Christian imperial England, acquits all these purported agents of divine will of being charged with self-interest, undue cultural interference, exploitation, or perverting the meaning of the Book whose Evangelical interpretation bestowed divine agency on these entities in the first place. Children always speak the truth; they never distort, even when, as in the case of the San, their elders make them stay up all night to read to them. Children have a special insight into the spirit of Protestant Scripture, as in the case of the Greek boy who corrected the monk on the proper reading of Job 4.17. And children are the trusted guardians of the Bible, even when they are robbed of their holy commission—as was the Belgian girl, whose vigilance makes her the symbol of embattled Protestantism, under siege by the Antichrist. In all these instances, children vicariously validate the divine agency of the Bible Society because their incorruptible literacy and good intentions prove that the missionary impulse comes from God.

But most important, the displacement of the English missionaries' mediative function onto children does not negate the fact that these children are all foreigners. And, since the majority of these proselytizing children in Browne's text are girls, the identities of missionaries and foreigners are blurred along the lines of gender. The female child hides the fact that the relationship between England and its colonies is a patriarchal one, while her proselytizing actions (she is never represented talking to missionaries; she speaks only to other or potential converts) confirm the belief that English authority asserts itself not through the exchanges of lordship and bondage, but through a linear, steadily expanding transmission of Protestant enlightenment. The female children of the missionaries' stories, all of them sympathizers with the missionary cause, allow the English readers of the histories to identify simultaneously with the providential privilege of their country and with the special power of powerlessness that symbolically belongs to women and children—those who come first in the Bible precisely because they come last in patriarchal society.

There is one last child, again a female, that is particularly important to the Bible Society's tradition. This child was purportedly present at the initial scene that inspired Rev. Thomas Charles to suggest a Bible Society, although she does not make a textual appearance until 1904, when the third of the Bible Society's histories was published. As the story goes, there was a sixteen-year-old named Mary Jones who, at the beginning of the nineteenth century, lived near Charles's parish in Bala, Wales. Following her conversion, Mary Jones began to "so thirst for the Water of Life" that she walked twenty-eight miles across the Welsh countryside to Mr. Charles's parsonage to see if she could purchase a Bible. When he told her that there were no Bibles to be had, she began to cry, and Charles was so moved by this display of her disappointed hopes that he sold her a Bible from his own bookshelf, vowing never to forget the incident in his quest to relieve the Bible famine of Wales (Canton 1: 465).

It is not an exchange of power or knowledge that is at issue in this transaction but rather an exchange of innocent desire. The story confirms the necessary desire or spiritual hunger that the Bible Society had, in 1904, been assuming for years in all the designated recipients of its philanthropy. But at the same time, the true desire that moved the Society and its missionaries is displaced onto the one child that is only a beneficiary and does not partially stand in for a missionary, the one child that does not deliver, read, interpret, or guard a Bible; she requests one. And because Mary Jones pays for her Bible, she proves herself in middle-class terms to be one of the deserving poor. Her fictional treatment reveals the thoroughness with which commodification and religious sentimentality were integrated in the Bible Society, because the moment of her initiation into Evangelical citizenship is a marked by both tears and a purchase. From this mythical moment of origin, the Bibles that change hands in the Society's histories do not represent the text of Christian faith (indeed, it is irrelevant whether they are opened or closed) so much as the ambivalent motives and signifying functions that comprise imperial-Evangelical ideology and that are fictionally distributed between the various parties handling these books. In this story of origins, for instance, the roles that typify the histories' conversion narratives are at once simplified and reversed, and the child-missionary becomes the child-convert, the female subject whose pure and suppliant desire starts (and ends) this signifying chain, Mary Jones coming to Rev. Thomas Charles of Bala, Wales, looking for a Bible.

Reading the Bible and Writing the Empire

When Thomas Charles called upon a group of Dissenters and Evangelicals in London to help him relieve the "Bible famine" in Wales, he helped initiate a movement that brought together two of the most powerful motivations in early Victorian middle-class culture: Protestant bibliolatry and philanthropic concern with the working poor. Slogans such as "the Bible famine," "the destitution of Scriptures," and "starvation for the word of God" affixed a metaphorical hunger to the physical hunger that the poor were suffering, more often than not, in the first four decades of the Society's operation. By a generous interpretation, the energies that Society members expended on ministering to a metaphorical hunger for Bibles reflected their belief that in the face of helpless conditions, spirituality and inspiration are as fundamental to human survival as material goods. In 1831 the Bible Society's Auxiliaries distributed 19,600 Testaments and Psalters to working-class families in anticipation of a cholera epidemic, and in Paisley in 1837 the starving unemployed were assiduously supplied with Bibles. But such efforts often only aggravated the anger of working-class individuals who saw themselves victimized by Evangelical hypocrisy. Louis James states that novelists who wrote about the working class were quick to point out the vicious folly of giving poor people Bibles and tracts instead of food, clothing, and sanitation. He cites as an example J. M. Rymer, the popular writer of penny-issue novels, who "can think of no better way of illustrating Sweeney Todd's demonic hypocrisy than having him distribute tracts to the orphan of the man he had murdered" (115). That Rymer would attach Evangelical hypocrisy to a stock villain suggests the depth of resentment that separated missionary evangelism from many of its would-be beneficiaries. Philanthropy and bibliolatry were colleagues in the Bible Society, but it was debatable whose sense of well-being they best served.

To a large extent, those who participated in the B.F.B.S.—as members, donors, colporteurs, translators, or local organizers—found in their work a sense of empowerment, opportunity, and patriotic participation in the growth of a religious empire. Many of these rank-and-file members were disadvantaged elsewhere in English society, because of their class, their education, or (in the case of the many women who directed the Society's Associations) their gender. And yet, the fictive conversions that the Society's historians produced reflect not so much a celebration as an ambivalence toward religious might and influence, for repeatedly the deliverers of the Word retreat from their own authority. The children who replace them are drawn from a variety of nations and circumstances, but they share with each other a supernatural power—a power that is efficacious, incontestable, and nonthreatening. None of these children will grow up to challenge their religious or colonial guardians; none of them will ever regard English missionaries or merchants as adults of equal stature. In this way, the children of the Bible Society's narratives perform a miraculous dual function: they affirm that the missionary influence does not claim patriarchal power, and they confirm that England does.

Whereas domestically, the Bible Society's chief nemesis was a growing working-class disinterest in religion, internationally one of its chief opponents was the growing European interest in Eastern cultures and religions. The Society met this challenge by promulgating descriptions of Hinduism as a barbaric religion. Rev. Claudius Buchanan, for instance, whose translating projects in Bengal were cut short in 1807 by the East India Company, wrote a book condemning the company's policy of collecting taxes from pilgrims to maintain the temples of Juggernaut, where the pilgrims engaged in "lascivious" and "obscene" rituals (32–34). Such terms became commonplaces as Society tract writers continued to dwell on images of Hindus "throwing themselves to sharks, hanging children [and] burning widows" (Owen 1: 355). It was senseless and unfair, they argued, to regulate the importation of Christianity into India at a time when European orientalists were exporting Hinduism: "If we acquaint ourselves, through the medium of translation, with their mythical absurdities and amatory trifles," one tract writer claimed, "it is but fair that we should afford them an opportunity of becoming acquainted, through the same medium, with the august mysteries of the Gospel" (Owen 1: 344–45). Throughout the 1830s the Bible Society's interpretation of Hinduism as a Christian moral emergency complemented the utilitarian project to bring Western culture to India. Consequently, the opposition the Bible Society had previously received from the East India Company was dramatically reduced after the company lost its remaining commercial functions in 1833 and become a governing body representing the interests of commerce and utilitarian reform.[15] Under the viceroyalty of Lord William Bentinck, the Bible Society and the colonial government emerged as tacit allies, because despite the ideological differences between them, the utilitarian desire to impart English culture to the Indian colonies accorded with the similar desire of missionary evangelism.[16] The colonial government launched campaigns to more aggressively anglicize Indian custom and law: *sati* was suppressed by the British in 1828; measures were passed protecting the rights of Indian converts to Christianity; English was declared the official language of education; and Thomas Macaulay was assigned the formidable task of reforming the Indian Penal Code. At a later point in the century, the blatant cultural disdain toward Hinduism expressed in the Bible Society's publications would be eclipsed by the growth and popularity of orientalist studies, but in the first decades of its existence the Society maintained an aggressive front against Western intellectual interest in the East. Edward Said has suggested that academic orientalism operated for its practitioners in part as a displaced supernaturalism (*Orientalism* 120–23). Conversely, the Bible Society's apparently religious discourse operated as a displaced secularism. It mediated the East to English Protestants not through a discourse of theology or spiritualism, but through a discourse that reduced both Christianity and Hinduism to cultural conditions that fostered predictable behavior and political preferences.

The Bible Society contributed to nineteenth-century imperial ideology by textualizing the world as a Protestant and British totality. The histories that it produced were books that tried to write an empire inspired by, structured by, and composed of the Bible. Consequently, the problems George Browne met with in structuring his Bible Society history reflect the difficulty of structuring, at midcentury, England's colonization of the world. In his preface, Browne writes that he will replace John Owen's method of chronicling the annual activities of the Society with a broader perspective, "dividing the history into two principal compartments, the home and the foreign." The efficacy of this division is sabotaged, however, by the intricate architecture and overweening growth of the Society's posts, missions, and foreign Auxiliaries. The refusal of these heterogeneous and overlapping details to organize themselves into an organic totality becomes an inescapable fact as Browne continues to describe his plan, noting that "the divisions and sub-divisions" of the Society's various operations cannot keep pace with "the wide field of operations" and "the voluminous records" that he has tried to organize into "a comprehensive impression" (1: v–vi). God, the unrepresentable, has become commensurate with empire, which similarly eludes apprehension.

In this way, the final nemesis that haunts the Society at every turn—the Malthusian proliferation of races, tribes, and societies, the escalating mutations of languages and dialects that forever add to the Bible translator's labor—is internalized in the Society in the form of its own textually uncontrollable details, divisions, records, and operations. While supporters of the Bible Society's work in the 1840s had seen its translations as proof of the Bible's adaptability and power to accommodate itself to foreign cultures, by the early 1850s the beneficent power of adaptation seemed less decisive than the fear of the uncontrollable fecundity of linguistic and cultural differences. Evaluating the Society's progress in its first fifty years of existence, one essayist wrote in the *London Quarterly Review*:

> When we glance at the researches of those ninety-two eminent linguists, geographers, and men of science, who enabled Mr. Balbi to present in so accurate a form his invaluable Atlas of languages, in which it is shown how these languages are constantly breeding new offspring, we fear that if the income of the Bible Society be tenfold, at its second Jubilee, what it is now, there will still be more languages into which it will be the duty of the Christian to translate the Scriptures, and millions of the human race will still be ignorant of the Lord of heaven and earth; unless Providence should, as it has often done before, anticipate human plans, by some overwhelming display of its power to dispense, in whole or in part, with human agency. (387)

Against a singular "Atlas," a singular "Christian" translator, a singular "Providence," and a singular "human agency," the "millions of the human race" deploy themselves like a Satanic coalition of differences designed to defer indefinitely the millennium. The others of the Bible Society's quest, the colonial and foreign objects of conversion that must be brought into the community, not only escape assimilation but counteract with their own form of power—the diabolical opposite of translation—the power of linguistic multiplication. This power returns to English Evangelical culture an inverted image of ameliorative progress, threatening to counteract the spread of biblical-imperial literacy with a chaos of voices that cannot be controlled or understood.

In the 1850s the British Empire was politically still on the rise; the cultural totalitarianism anticipated by its Bible Society contributors, however, was on the decline. Confronted with the fact that several decades had passed without the wholesale conversions they expected, the surviving supporters of the B.F.B.S. lowered their millennial expectations and regrouped behind a philosophy of incremental progress, of ongoing diligent labor against insurmountable odds. Browne's history of the B.F.B.S. was published two years after David Livingstone's best-selling *Missionary Travels and Researches in South Africa*, and it was the latter text, with its subordination of religious to ethnographic interest, its emphatic faith in the necessity of promoting commerce in Africa, and its presentation of an indefatigable Briton at home among the exotic dangers of a distant land, that won the imagination of a broader English audience than the B.F.B.S. had ever commanded. When Livingstone first sailed for the Cape of Good Hope in 1841, he took with him 500 copies of Robert Moffat's Setswana New Testament. When he returned to London in 1856, he brought the massive information that he would spend a year compiling into his memoirs. Of this literary challenge Livingstone remarked that he "would rather cross the African continent again than undertake to write another book" (7). Many more books would be written about the English empire, but after the Bible Society's histories, none would be based on the belief that the book of God could contain the world.

Reference Matter

Notes

Introduction

1. W. H. Oliver notes an ambiguity that "surrounds [Ward's] attitude towards his Southcottian heritage." At a later point in his ministry, Ward altered his early claim to be Joanna's spiritual son, claiming that he had done so only as a way of appealing to the limited understandings of the London Southcottians. The influence of Richard Carlile, the atheist and radical political agitator, seems to have been partly responsible for Ward's reversal on this matter (Oliver 153-59).

2. Hopkins offers a detailed accout of Joanna's supposed and protracted pregnancy, detailing the effects of her announcement on her followers and the several medical evaluations that corroborated the belief that she was with child (199-210). Matthews reports the outrage expressed in several British periodical publications toward Joanna's "blasphemous" attempt to compare her pregnancy to that of Christ's mother (69-70).

3. Boon, Ward, and Wroe were all followers of Southcott. Carlile was a radical atheist and publisher who appropriated a secularized version of the Christ story in his political rhetoric. Courtenay, born John Nichols Tom, was a Cornish publican and wine merchant who in the 1830s, apparently under a pathological delusion, traveled to Canterbury and gathered around himself a largely working-class following. His platform included the redistribution of land to agricultural laborers, and when a group of these took up arms the result was a bloodbath near Bossenden farm, four miles outside of Canterbury. Tom's intriguing life story is recounted in detail by Matthews (127-59).

4. Charles B. Holinsworth of Birmingham, a second-generation Shilohite, was largely responsible for the sizable archival record of Ward's life and teachings. Over the course of several decades, Holinsworth assiduously transcribed Ward's writings and republished his tracts, culminating in the 1899 edition of *Zion's Works: New Light on the Bible*, which ran to ten volumes.

5. Homans explicates her belief in the "cultural myth of women's rela-

tion to and subordination within language" (xiii) in the preface and first chapter of *Bearing the Word*.

6. Oliver likewise notes the "antinomian" implications of Ward's messiahship, describing it as a "universalist doctrine which would dissolve guilt and fear by establishing the unreality of sin and punishment.... Sin, conventionally so called, becomes an impossibility" (164–66).

Chapter 1

1. David G. Riede argues that Coleridge's return to an "essentialist or idealist theory of the self" is a late occurrence, and that it replaces his earlier association of self-annihilation with divine consciousness, a capacity which (following Priestley) he ascribed to the writers of Scriptures (180–85).

2. The primary link between Coleridge and Christian Socialism is Frederick Denison Maurice, who acknowledged his debt to Coleridge even if his colleague in the Christian Socialist movement, Charles Kingsley, did not. Charles Richard Sanders traces the genealogy from Coleridge's religious teachings to the various social projects launched by the first generation of Broad Churchmen. Undeniably, some mutations occurred in the transmission. Sanders claims that the common bonds among the "disciples of Coleridge" consisted of "advocating toleration and greater freedom of the mind and in trying to reconcile knowledge and religion, reason and faith" (103). In his practical applications of these beliefs, Frederick Denison Maurice—despite his sense of debt to Coleridge—undoubtedly undertook some projects that Coleridge would not have approved of, and Christian Socialism is a case in point.

3. Anthony John Harding, in his study of Coleridge's hermeneutic theories, argues that the new Bible of historical scholarship "contributed in a major way to the Romantic poetics of inspiration" (8). From Harding's perspective, the most significant exchanges between religious and secular notions of inspiration concern authorship; hence he argues that secular Romanticists were influenced by the Bible historicists' concern with the personalities of the biblical authors. In contrast, my primary concern is with Coleridge's representation of the readers of Scriptures, and with the beliefs about Christian psychology that these representations convey.

4. Scholars who have explored this concern include Mary Jacobus, David G. Riede, David Simpson, and Jean-Pierre Mileur. Jacobus expresses Wordsworth's distressing suspicion that his identity may be a construct of texts: "[*The Prelude*] ... discloses the unease that underlies much Romantic writing about literacy.... The fear covertly expressed in Book V is that it is

not we that write, but writing that writes us; that the writing of the past, rather than 'the spirit of the past' (XI, 342), determines 'what we may become'; and that the language of books is 'unremittingly and noiselessly at work'" (216). Riede describes Coleridge's more sanguine inversion of this belief; Coleridge's literary theory, he claims, arrives "by a roundabout way at the conclusion that although the poet is born and not made, critics—any persons of wide and deep reading—make their own essential self by internalizing the written manifestations of the poet's genius" (218). Along similar lines, Simpson comments on the Coleridge of *Biographia Literaria*: "Here the author's essential (publishable) subjectivity is declared as the product of definite educational and reading experiences nurturing an original instinct" (*Romanticism* 142). Mileur makes the strongest statement on this topic, for he understands Coleridge's concept of the imagination to be dependent upon literature: "imagination is the self-image that the textualizing consciousness 'discovers' in its object; it is the pretext which is the warrant for the textualization performed by interpretation" (159).

5. De Quincey's essay "The Poetry of Pope" first appeared in the *North British Review* for August 1848. The introductory discussion of the essay, from which this quotation is drawn, is frequently anthologized under the title "The Literature of Knowledge and the Literature of Power."

6. A related passage occurs in an appendix to *The Statesman's Manual*, where Coleridge argues that erroneous interpretations of the Bible can be prevented by an attitude that Christians should adopt in all areas of life: "For all things that surround us, and all things that happen unto us, have (each doubtless its own providential purpose, but) all one common final cause; namely, the increase of Consciousness, in such wise, that whatever part of the *terra incognita* of our nature the increased consciousness discovers, our will may conquer and bring into subjection to itself under the sovereignty of reason" (89). Commenting upon Coleridge's images of the Bible as a force at once expansive and centralizing, Mileur suggests that Coleridge conceives of postbiblical history as "our collective effort, generation by generation, to expand ourselves to fill the creation marked out for us by the Bible" (95). In Mileur's explanation, as in the preceding quotation from *The Statesman's Manual*, mental expansion and territorial expansion are at once conflated and glorified by their assumed enactment of the meanings and the goals included in a still-unfolding sacred narrative. Thus, as Mileur goes on to state, our ongoing and always incomplete acts of meaning are for Coleridge mandated by the divinely instilled desire "to match ourselves to the fullness of being intimated in the Bible" (96).

7. Jerome McGann writes that the idea of a Harmony or Unity of Be-

ing was a philosophical goal of most Romantic theorists, most of whom, like Coleridge, possessed a Germanically influenced passion for systematic knowledge (41).

8. Although Coleridge was himself a High Churchman, his anxiety about the deleterious effects of popular literature was compatible with Evangelical and fundamentalist denouncements of the effects of entertaining reading, especially on women and the working poor. The fundamentalist religious discourse on the relationship between secular literature and character tended to be straightforwardly deterministic—more so, certainly, than it was when treating the relationship between the Bible and spiritual development, which is similarly deterministic but descriptively more varied and colored with some degree of tension in the form of spiritual anxiety and relapse. For Coleridge, the topic is more nuanced, in part because of his concern to preserve a special status for English poetry, an ostensibly secular genre that confuses the divide between secular and sacred literature because it activates the whole man, much in the way that "religion is a total act of soul" (*Statesman's Manual* 90). Coleridge's thoughts on this matter are deeply informed by the work of Herder, an influence that only exacerbated his inability to reach a decisive conclusion, and thus even in his later writings Coleridge wavers between classifying the Scriptures under the rubric of great poetry and maintaining a hierarchy in which the Bible is the ascendant text, that which illuminates and gives purpose to others. Likewise, the spiritual dialectic between Bible reading and faith which unfolds in *Confessions of an Inquiring Spirit* is of the same order of agile complexity as Coleridge's earlier analyses in *Biographia Literaria* of the process of reading poetry. But toward the category of popular literature there is, throughout his career, no ambivalence. Here the distinctions are unequivocal and Manichaean: *Biographia Literaria* claims that books have decayed from the status of "religious oracles" to "degraded ... culprits" (33); *The Friend* states that the sole purpose of novels and bad biographies is to gratify curiosity and gossip (2: 151, 153–58; 1: 148–49, 356–57); and *The Statesman's Manual* derides the reading public as "the misgrowth of our luxuriant activity" (36).

9. "If the empirical self is grounded in error," Knapp observes, "then the truth about the self ... is always purchased at the cost of individual agency" (46).

10. A more detailed exploration of the social and political underpinnings of Coleridge's interpretive models is offered by Klancher (150–70), who argues that Coleridge "sought to construct an audience that was *also* an institution, a body of readers and writers capable of governing the relations between all the emerging audiences of the nineteenth century over

whom, individually, no institution could claim control" (151). The interpretive authority for this diffuse social institution is the clerisy, which Klancher astutely argues (in a manner that goes against the tendency of my analysis) is a classless construct, composed of members drawn from all social classes and alienated into an impartial, metacritical interpretive community. In this way, Coleridge hopes to create a cultural force situated, ideally, "beyond classification and beyond ideology" (169).

11. Hans W. Frei traces the emergence and decline of Pietism in the seventeenth and eighteenth centuries, noting the emphases that the movement placed upon a mystical element in the words of Scriptures and upon the necessity of reading the Bible "devoutly and through the Spirit." Thus, for the Pietists, the Bible is inspired in a double sense; not only are its words "divinely given," but reading it "becomes a means of grace to awaken men's spirits" (158). While most Pietism lacked the philosophical grounding of Coleridge's biblical hermeneutics, it was a dominant thread in a progression that Frei traces through Herder and more generally to "romantic and idealist modes of sensibility." For Frei, the point of commonality is the belief that meaning in the world is shaped by the manner in which an individual self-consciously positions himself or herself toward the world (200–201).

12. Barth describes a similar act of self-duplication from the opposite perspective, where it is God and not man that generates an alter image: "as Will God causes his own reality, while as 'personeity' (the source of personality) he is other-directed.... The next step must be some kind of act or movement, necessarily causative, towards a reality other than the Self" (*Coleridge and Christian Doctrine* 89).

13. Analyzing the hermeneutic narrative within *Biographia Literaria*, Rajan poses the following argument: "Having first assumed the position of an author who needs the right reader to complete his project, Coleridge then becomes a reader in search of the appropriate author to embody his intentions.... If the first part sketches the author's need for a prophetic reader, the second part introduces precisely that reader and raises the question of whether the 'author' is not a construction of the reader" (109).

14. Derrida's analysis of logocentrism is carried out in several of his works, mainly from the 1960s and 1970s. Most relevant to this discussion are the opening chapters in *Of Grammatology*, where Derrida contests the structuralist account of language for the privilege and priority that it assigns to the *phone*, or spoken word. This privilege, he argues, is reflective of an important premise that underscores Western metaphysics—the assumption that when one speaks, one is present to one's self in an absolute and unmediated way. Thus the Western tradition tends to confine writing

to the secondary role of representing speech, where "speech" is understood as a pure presence—a primary reality that precedes all interpretation (7–8).

15. Susan Eilenberg notes the ontological insecurity occasioned by Coleridge's relationship to textuality and suggests that it is ultimately redeemed as a source of the imagination: "What appalls the writer, the sense of being overwhelmed by influence and becoming what he reads, also cheers him: the curse of ventriloquy is also a blessing and a reassurance. That taint of vocal alienation, the othering or uttering of voice from self, is imagination. In Volume II he claims it, this power analogous to the echo of a quotation, not for himself, but for Wordsworth" (167). Mileur also notes a movement in *Biographia Literaria* away from the project of establishing a coherent autobiographical identity, but he does not see this as a source of discomfort: "Coleridge is not so much interested in validating one identity over another as in reconciling the conviction of identity with the diversity of competing, sometimes contradictory voices in which it finds expression" (102).

16. This suggestion is in keeping with the conventional image of an elder Coleridge's distaste for a selfhood he was nonetheless afraid of losing. Jerome McGann glosses the confused pronouns in the late poem "Constancy to an Ideal Object" with the suggestion that "now the object that [Coleridge] is afraid of losing is individual identity.... Constancy to an ideal object places one in a state of 'positive negation' ... an aggressive condition of vagrancy where recognized identities undergo a process of dissolution, disappearance, and fragmentation" (106–7).

17. For an explanation of Evangelical attitudes toward literature, see Jay, 193–97.

18. The account here is drawn from the following sources: Baxter, Pilkington, Norton, Hair (27–36), and Drummond (136–64).

19. Likewise, an anonymous pamphleteer attempting to discredit the tongues in Irving's church returns several times to what he considers the shameful fact that the supposed gifts enable women to assume the roles of preachers and teachers in the church (*Unknown Tongues* 13–18).

20. In her study of the feminist tradition within Owenite socialism, Taylor considers some women chiliasts, including Joanna Southcott, who she believes found in the millenarian tradition resources of belief that enabled her to rise above the circumscribed destiny of a mere working-class woman. However, Taylor also notes that after Joanna's death, Southcottianism lost what radical edge it had and was recuperated as a conservative movement mostly dominated by male clerics (165–66). Valenze relates that Wesley initially opposed female preachers but was eventually won over by his interactions with these women. Even so, around the turn of the nine-

teenth century, as the Wesleyan leadership turned more conservative, women preachers faced growing opposition from church leaders (51–52). However, because many of the female preachers that Valenze studies ignored admonishments from the leaders of their churches, she ascribes the primary cause of their disappearance to changes in working-class life. Among these changes she lists the "new standards of respectability and behavior," defining the public world as male and the domestic world as female, replaced the more flexible ways of earlier years (278).

21. Of the many encapsulations of Irving's thesis, the following is representative: "[Christ] took sinful flesh, or fallen human nature, and upheld it holy against the devil, the world, and the flesh, and the influence of all these upon the mind. He stood immovable, always abounding in the work and will of his Father; and so having met all sin, and all weakness, and all mortality, and all corruption, and all devils, and all creature-oppression, and all creature-rebellion in his flesh, in his body, he strangled them there, he did judgment upon them there, he resisted, he overcame, he captured them" (*The Orthodox and Catholic Doctrine* 8).

22. Barth, however, goes to some lengths to prove Boulter wrong (*Coleridge and Christian Doctrine* 128–35). However, even Barth admits that Coleridge "gives the impression of being uninterested in the details of the life of Christ" (135). Wilson attributes Coleridge's ambivalence toward the "personeity" of God to his theological debt to Spinoza: "Only in Spinoza could he find a rational proof for the existence of God, but even there was denied the ability to attribute personhood to God"; as Coleridge lamented: "I could not reconcile personality with infinity; and my head was with Spinoza, though my whole heart was with Paul and John" (453).

23. Because of his heretical view of Christ's nature, Irving has in recent years attracted the attention of the historian Boyd Hilton. Hilton's larger argument is that the shift in emphasis in Victorian Christianity from the atonement to the incarnation had important economic and social repercussions. Because of Irving's concern with Christ's very human experience of temptation, he marks an important point of transition in Hilton's overall picture between an early Evangelicalism's "obsession with sinfulness" and the pervasiveness later in the century of a Broad Church emphasis on "Christ as a noble exemplar rather than primarily as a savior" (298–99).

24. For example, one of Irving's sermons on the incarnation exhorts its Christian readers to emulate Christ's strength in their own internal struggles with Satan. By doing so, they will not only grow into his image but also be "led into the deep things of God" and made "perfect in every good work" (1: 210–11). In his copy of Irving's sermons, Coleridge expressed his chagrin with these statements in extensive marginal notes.

25. As de Man writes, glossing Coleridge's well-known analysis of the symbol in *The Statesman's Manual*, "In truth, the spiritualization of the symbol has been carried so far that the moment of material existence by which it was originally defined has now become altogether insignificant; symbol and allegory alike now have a common origin beyond the world of matter. The reference, in both cases, to a transcendental source, is now more important than the kind of relationship that exists between the reflection and its source.... Starting out from the assumed superiority of the symbol in terms of organic substantiality, we end up with a description of figural language as translucence, a description in which the distinction between allegory and symbol has become of secondary importance" (192–93).

26. McGann suggests that the shift of concern in Coleridge's thought from poets to the clerisy reveals two aspects of his intellectual beliefs. One, that "Coleridge never ceased to believe that ideas shaped historical events—that thought always preceded and determined action rather than the other way around," and two, that "even as Coleridge, like Hegel, saw real human history flow unselfconsciously out of the precedent Idea, he lost his conviction that this pattern could be surely grasped, even unselfconsciously, in the single inspired individual ... the determining primacy of the creative person, collapsed under the pressures which Coleridge's own mental pursuits placed upon it" (104).

27. A similar observation begins J. Hillis Miller's *The Disappearance of God*: "Everywhere the world mirrors back to man his own image, and nowhere can he make vivifying contact with what is not human" (5). In Miller's estimation, these anthropocentric tendencies are inherently secular, and as a consequence, he believes that the imaginative appeal of incarnational doctrine falls into abeyance throughout much of the nineteenth century (only to be resurrected in Hopkins's poetry). His depiction runs contrary to my emphasis on the increasing ideological significance of the incarnation in Victorian culture.

Chapter 2

1. Herbert Marsh translated J. D. Michaelis's *Introduction to the New Testament* into English and supplied a lengthy commentary that was well respected in Germany and was denounced by conservative theologians in England. Marsh was later elected to the Lady Margaret professorship at Cambridge, and in his lectures he presented a newly liberal and scientific form of biblical criticism. Pusey's reputation for German scholarship was notorious among the Oriel group, at first arousing Newman's suspicion (Mozley 2: 256). Pusey, however, maintained his conservative beliefs, unlike Connop Thirlwall, who came to hold the opinion that plenary inspi-

ration was untenable. Among the handful of scholars in England with an extensive knowledge of the Higher Criticism was an Irish Presbyterian, Samuel Davidson, who gained a significant reputation in Germany for his biblical scholarhip. Davidson outlined the findings of "Rationalists" such as Eichhorn and De Wette in his *Lectures on Biblical Criticism* (1839). For such research Davidson eventually paid a price, because like Coleridge's and Thirlwall's, his Protestant faith in plenary inspiration did not survive his rationalist encounters, and in 1857 he was dismissed from his professorship at Lancashire Independent College for alleged heresies committed in his revisions of Thomas Hartwell Horne's Old Testament commentary. Against these charges, Davidson defended himself with the self-incriminating charge that Horne had not been sufficiently acquainted with German writers on biblical criticism (vii).

2. The generic English term for skeptically inclined German biblical scholars (i.e., those who contested the chronology of the Bible's books, or who questioned the identity of its purported authors, or who qualified its plenary inspiration) was "neologist." Originally a term used to denote the introduction into English parlance of "barbarous" or "corrupting" words, it was not until the late 1820s that "neology" developed specifically theological connotations. "Neologism" was, however, almost always used as a reference to German words. From early on, commentators who censured the importation of Germanic words imputed lack of patriotism to that activity, a slight on the capacities of the English language. In 1830, for example, Jeremy Bentham was reviled for "thinking his native English too barbarous and uncultivated to express his philosophical thoughts," and coining "neologisms like 'codification', which he never sufficiently defines" (Lewis 78). The shift to using "neology" as a pejorative for German theological ideas is exemplified by an 1838 review of Strauss's still untranslated *Das Leben Jesu*. For Strauss as for all German exegetes, the reviewer charged, "Neology not Theology—Variation not Fixity is their united pursuit" ("Strauss" 140).

David Simpson (*Romanticism*, 64–103) and Marilyn Butler (115, 121) discuss the turn-of-the-century ideological ramifications of British images of France and Germany. Simpson argues that "by about 1800 ... the image of Germany was sufficiently manifold to include the traditional French proclivities towards both system and theory and libertine self-indulgence.... For the *Anti-Jacobin*, theoretical, political, and sexual liberation came together.... Now it was sex as well as systems that threatened English common sense and social life, for 'to immoralize a Nation is the surest way to *revolutionize* it'" (100).

3. Duncan Forbes traces several of the late-eighteenth- and early-

nineteenth-century instances of the developmental model of history in Scotland and England, focusing on the modern sources with which Arnold and other liberal Anglicans would have been familiar. Niebuhr is chief among them, although Forbes notes that Arnold had read Vico and hence had something more than a derivative knowledge of historical *ricurso*. Ruth apRoberts qualifies Forbes's account, demonstrating the crucial influence of Herder, who altered the Viconian *ricurso* to account for a perception of linear progress; Herder's historiography, apRoberts suggests, "takes on a spiralling movement, implying a slow, eddying progress" (25–26). Hence, for apRoberts, Vico reaches Arnold only after an elaborate and transformative mediation: "what appears to be Vico in Thomas Arnold is often Herder ... by way of Niebuhr" (63n).

4. Thirlwall had translated Schleiermacher's *Critical Essay on the Gospel of Saint Luke*, which appeared in 1825. Like other liberal theologians in Britain, he paid a price for his views in his career, most of which was spent in the isolated and impoverished Welsh see of St. David's, where he had gained preferment as bishop in 1840.

5. Ironically, the study of the Bible as literature had begun in England in the eighteenth century with Robert Lowth. (Thomas Preston pushes the date back even farther, noting that the seventeenth-century English exegetes Henry Lukin and John Edwards also dwelt on the literary value of the Bible [112–13].) Lowth's study of literary genres and "oriental" strains in the Old Testament was better known in Germany than in England, and was a profound influence on Herder's *Vom Geiste der Hebräischen Poesie*.

6. In fact, as de S. Honey observes, the Arnoldian public-school pedagogy was in more ways than one analogical with the Arnoldian Bible, for the developmental model of history was at Rugby translated into a developmental model of individual male growth (19). Thus the sixth-form boys—those who survived the first years to achieve a reliable level of moral maturity—oversaw the character development of the boys beneath them, the juvenile "slaves of custom" whose worship of brute strength made them akin to morally undeveloped Old Testament Jews. Behind Arnold's classification of ancient Israel as morally undeveloped is a vast discourse of Christian Victorian attitudes toward Judaism, a mixture of an anti-Semitism often rooted in classical training and of religious superstitions that inspired extravagant plans to convert the Jews.

7. The widespread attachment to the A.V., however, was not an absolute hegemony. Alternative translations of the Bible—"improvements" on the A.V. in the sense that they reflected either doctrinal differences or newly available information—were published without the Church's approval in the eighteenth and nineteenth centuries. Many of these, such as

Samuel Sharpe's 1840 and 1865 biblical translations, were Unitarian projects. In addition, British men and women who knew some Hebrew (among the working and lower middle classes, such people were almost always Non-Conformists) were able to compare the A.V. with Hebrew versions made available by printers such as Benjamin Boathroyd, an Independent who published a Hebrew Bible in 1810-13 at his own printing press in Pontefract. Robert Young's 1862 translation of the Hebrew Bible was among the most literal ever; like Boathroyd, he was a bookseller who studied Hebrew (see H. Pope 539-44). Such widespread inquiry into questions of scriptural translation is evidence of a complex social antagonism loosely constructed along the axes of class/religious affiliation/educational background. Newman spoke from within a tenuous hegemony of Anglican belief in the social and ideological cohesiveness of the A.V. when he commented that he would rather have "every fault in the A.V. implicitly swallowed than to have it made the sport of scholarship, such as scholarship was in those days" (Mozley 1: 178).

8. As many scholars have noted, the need to balance physical and mental exertion drives the narrative of *Tom Brown's Schooldays*, Thomas Hughes's fictional account of Rugby life. Tom Brown, the paragon of the athletic and mischievous English boy, befriends the effeminate George Arthur, an excellent student of Latin. Tom eventually learns not to crib George's homework, and George develops into a fairly good football player. The nostalgia Brown feels at the last cricket match of his Rugby career suggests the power of communal identification that was imbibed by the ideal graduates of Rugby and lingered in their memories to guard the integrity of their adult lives. Regenia Gagnier explores the importance of hegemony both within public-school life and afterwards, noting that the moment of Arnoldian reform is a crucial one in the transformation of the public schools from "a symbolic bastion of an aestheticized childhood" to "an ideological state apparatus, an institution for the formation of national character" (174). For Gagnier, the process of socialization and the inscribing of a communal identity is a distinctive feature of this transformation; hence the denouement of Hughes's narrative is a psychological and ideological victory, one that leaves "no room for an antagonistic alterity ... 'there wasn't a corner of [Tom] left which didn't believe in the Doctor'" (226).

9. J. R. de S. Honey argues that the emphasis on athleticism in public-school education arose in the mid-Victorian period, after Arnold's death. He further argues that, like other characteristic aspects of Victorian public-school education, the emphasis on athleticism was not so much a feature of Arnold's actual (and somewhat inchoate) agenda as it was a part of the Arnold legend (46 ff.). C. L. R. James puts the case in more polemical terms:

"The English ruling classes accepted Arnold's aims and accepted also his methods in general. But with an unerring instinct they separated from it the cultivation of the intellect and substituted for it organized games, with cricket at the head of the curriculum.... Arnold would have repudiated this" (162).

10. The question of whether or not the publicly displayed gender traits which Victorians classified as feminine or masculine connoted sexual preference has been the subject of much debate in the past decade of cultural studies. Oliver Buckton's essay summarizes some of these critical opinions as they pertain to Victorian perceptions of Newman's sexuality. Citing Dellamora and Hilliard, Buckton argues that charges of male effeminacy were implicitly aligned with charges of homosexuality (both being terms of disparagement), and thus Newman's imputed homosexuality was an integral and indeed inseparable part of the complex ideological conflation of religious faith and sexual identity in mid-Victorian England (372, 375). Buckton further notes the solicitude with which public-school memoirs differentiated close male friendship from homosexual relationships (368)—a point corroborated by Vance (149) and Dellamora (74). In contrast, John Addington Symonds's memoirs emphatically make no such distinction. Describing the routinely homosexual activity among schoolboys at Harrow, Symonds writes, "Every good boy of looks had a female name, and was recognized as a public prostitute or some bigger boy's bitch. Bitch was the word in common usage to indicate a boy who yielded his person to a lover.... Here and there one could not avoid seeing acts of onanism, mutual masturbation, and the sports of naked boys in bed together" (94).

11. The 1838 sermons on prophecy were set in a context of widespread preoccupation with prophetic keys to an imminent Second Coming. For his many contemporaries who engaged in prophetical practices, Arnold had ambivalent feelings, despite his own periodic displays of apocalyptic foreboding. Whereas in his lectures on history Arnold gave rein to millennial beliefs, in his role as an Anglican minister he was quick to discredit the particular millenarianism of zealous preachers. At issue here was the social and psychological volatility of prophecy—a volatility which could yield embarrassing sensations, such as we saw in the previous chapter. Of the initial reports of glossolalia in Edward Irving's Regent Square church, Arnold agreed that "if the thing be real" it could only portend "the day of the Lord" (Stanley 174). Several years later, however, long after the spurious reality of the tongues had been recognized, Arnold delivered the two sermons on prophecy which, like his sermons on accommodation, deflected attention away from divine intervention and apocalyptic excitement and toward ethical principles and practice.

12. The specific passage in the sermons on prophecy which defines biblical prophecy as a moral corrective to history reads as follows: "Common history, amid a vast number of particular facts and persons can hardly trace the general principles of the characters which are to be deduced from them.... Now what History does not and cannot do, that Prophecy does ... [it] fixes our attention on principles, on good and evil, on truth and falsehood, on God and his Enemy. Here, there is no division of feeling, no qualified sympathy; the one are deserving of our entire devotion and love, the other of our unmixed abhorrence" ("Two Sermons" 93). However, the stable reference point which the Scriptures seem to provide is, a few moments later, called into question. When Arnold turns his attention to the Judaic Scriptures, illumination is described as a light shed not by prophecy onto history but rather by history onto prophecy: "The people of Israel ... stand forth in the History and the Prophecy of Scriptures as the representatives, so to speak, of the cause of God and goodness. But the History shows that they were very imperfect representatives of it, and therefore can only be imperfectly the subject of the promises of Prophecy.... They are ... [the] signs of ideas, which Prophecy uses, as revelation avails itself of human language; a shadow of reality, but not its substance" (94–95).

13. I refer here to the now-canonical description of the symbolic which Coleridge offers in contrast to the allegorical: "A Symbol is characterized by a translucence of the Special in the Individual or of the General in the Especial or of the Universal in the General. Above all by the translucence of the Eternal through and in the Temporal. It always partakes of the Reality which it renders intelligible; and while it enunciates the whole, abides itself as a living part of the Unity, of which it is representative" (*Statesman's Manual* 30).

14. Along these lines, Duncan Forbes comments that "impartiality, for Liberal Anglicans, did not mean the absence of a standpoint ... it meant having the best standpoint ... and this Christianity alone could provide" (124). Likewise, Rosemary Jann states that Arnold "found it hard to distinguish between intellectual error and moral wickedness in the Tractarian position" (3). Frances J. Woodward locates an abandonment of this biased form of impartiality among Arnold's own children. She observes that Arnold's son William embraced a more literal definition of "impartiality" by opposing a proposal which would bring the Bible into Indian government schools but prohibit Indian religious texts. "Steeped through though he was in his father's writings," Woodward states, "William Arnold had deliberately adopted the impartiality that is profaneness" (15).

15. Another Victorian relevant to this discussion is Frederic W. Farrar, who served as headmaster at Marlborough School before rising to the post

of Dean of Canterbury. Like Hughes, Farrar attempted the genres of both schoolboy epic and life of Christ: he was best known for his *Life of Christ* (1874), although his public-school novel, *Eric or, Little by Little* (1858), was also quite successful. Not only in his choice of subject matter but also in his rhetoric Farrar expresses certain Arnoldian values: while on the one hand insistent that Christic imitation was the cornerstone of modern religious life, Farrar also warned his late Victorian audience away from potential hazards of the Thomas à Kempis's *De Imitatione Christi* by noting its excessive self-absorption, its tendency to dwell on the self to the exclusion of a properly Christian emphasis on social involvement (*Companions* 21–22). Along similar lines, the Christ of his *Life of Christ* avoids mental "excess" by living a healthy physical life: "[Christ's] life and death shows exceptional powers of physical endurance.... He seems to have possessed that blessing of ready sleep which is the best natural antidote to fatigue, and the best influence to calm the over-wearied mind.... Even on the wave-lashed deck of the little fishing boat as it was tossed on the stormy sea, He could sleep" (240)

Chapter 3

1. Elinor S. Shaffer exemplifies the renewed interest in Christ in the early nineteenth century with observations on Hegel, Coleridge, Goethe, and finally Jean Paul's dramatic *Rede des toten Christus*, a portion of which Carlyle translated in "Jean Paul Richter Again" (1829). As Shaffer comments, "the more the theology of the age came to stress Christ as the link between man and a distant God, or like Schleiermacher himself, Christ himself as man, the more He too became cut off from God" (61).

2. These more or less canonical representations of Christ emerged against the backdrop of a religious publishing industry that produced Gospel harmonies, New Testament commentaries, New Testament stories for children, and prophetic analyses of Revelation. A sampling of such works that were available at mid-century to pious readers of several denominations includes the following titles: *The Parables of Our Lord*, by the Wife of an Irish Clergyman (1837); *Gospel Stories, illustrative of the incidents in the History of Our Saviour* (1845); *Lectures Explanatory of the Diatessoran, or History of Our Lord Jesus Christ*, by J. D. MacBride (1835); *An Evangelical Life of Our Saviour* (1820); *The Words of Lord Jesus*, by John Reed (1823); *The Life, Doctrine and Sufferings of Our Blessed Lord*, by Rev. Henry Rutter (1830); *Christ an Example for the Young*, by Robert Mimpriss (1854); *Reflections on the Genealogy of Jesus Christ* (1836); and *Gershem, or, the 33,000 Words of Jesus Christ* (1847). Denominational treatments of Christ differed from one another not so much in content (there being little room for in-

novation here) as in tone and genre. Even these distinctions, however, were not clear-cut; moreover, religious authors frequently employed the fictional and lyrical modes that were, strictly speaking, considered profane by Evangelical and conservative Non-Conformists. One example is the work of Robert Montgomery, a clown at the Bath theater who also wrote religious lyrics. In 1832 he published a long poem titled *The Messiah*. Despite negative reviews from both secular and religious journals, *The Messiah* passed through eight editions by 1842. The modest popularity of *The Messiah*, attests to the presence of a theologically flexible lower-class readership with some influence in the literary marketplace.

3. While my primary focus in the following two chapters will be on the manner in which nineteenth-century Christology interacted with the politics of gender in England, a more explicit and more extensive dialogue between Christology and political issues was occurring at roughly the same time in Germany. Marilyn Chapin Massey has traced the political subtext to the several editions of Strauss's *Das Leben Jesu*, arguing that the "genius" Christ of the third edition of 1838 was ensconced in a complex philosophical discourse, employed primarily by Left and Right Hegelians, wherein a masculine or politically active type of genius was opposed to a feminine and inwardly directed type of genius. These metonymic chains also extended into class, as evidenced by the left-wing Hegelian Arnold Ruge's denunciation of the modified Christ of Strauss's third edition as an "aristocratic" portrayal (Massey 114). By juxtaposing this Christ to that of the earlier 1835 edition, Massey finds in the history of Strauss's book an analogue for German political history of the same decade: while "the 1835 *Life of Christ* caught up and changed the idioms of German culture to present an image of people struggling collectively for their freedom," the altered edition of 1838 "offered the palliative of an aristocratic Christ, a genius Christ, who was the epitome of the perfection of the inner life" (149).

4. If nothing else, the Evangelical movement strengthened the associations between women and religion by virtue of the fact that so many women were active in Evangelical philanthropic and missionary societies and often assumed leadership roles. However, Vance argues that Kingsley's reasons for objecting to Evangelicalism had less to do with its feminization of religion than with its residual Calvinist disdain for the body. Thus Kingsley lumped Evangelicalism in with Tractarianism as "Manichee" religious beliefs, movements whose "rejection of the physical world ... ran counter to his insistence on a healthy body and a healthy mind" (30–35). But Vance also notes that at the popular level the muscular Christian notion of manliness was a less sophisticated rejoinder to the notion that, as the Baptist preacher C. H. Spurgeon summarized, "if you become a Christian you

must sink your manliness and turn milksop" (quoted in Vance, 26). The writings of Sarah Stickney Ellis exemplify how practical associations between women and religion were verified by an essentialist discourse; among the qualities that Ellis attaches to both women and Christ were self-sacrifice, devotional purity, and "the capacity for ... intense enjoyment" (156-214). Florence Nightingale seemed to take such advice to heart; as we shall consider in Chapter 5, Nightingale concludes her feminist tract *Cassandra* with the prophecy of a female savior.

5. As Jeremy Maas explains, for the figure of Christ Hunt used a variety of models: Elizabeth Siddal for the hair, Christina Rossetti for the face. Additionally, Maas has uncovered evidence that Hunt might also have employed a third model, Henry Clark, who would have sat, as Maas determines, "primarily for the figure, rather than the features, of Christ" (39-42).

6. Kingsley's characterization of Jameson's religious upbringing is misleading: she was born in Dublin of an Irish father and an English mother, and Jameson claimed that efforts to indoctrinate her in childhood were undercut by her "confused and heterodox" understanding of the Bible (Jameson, *Commonplace Book* 127). Moreover, Jameson later became active in the cause of Catholic and Protestant religious orders for women—a movement that Kingsley did not believe to be consistent with Protestant belief.

7. For Maynard's discussion of Kingsley's views of femininity and female sexuality, see pp. 120-21.

8. Reconstructing events more than fifty years past, Hunt traces the Brotherhood's origins to conversations he had with John Everett Millais in late 1847 and early 1848. One crucial conversation takes place over Hunt's painting *Christ and the Two Maries*. In response to Millais's suggestion that he refer to the prints of the old masters, Hunt is moved to eloquence: with the principles of the old masters he won't be satisfied, for after much cogitation Hunt has developed "scruples" that are "nothing less than irreverent, heretical, and revolutionary." Against the "paralyzing content" of the Reynolds school—its complacency with "settled laws" that have "no living power"—Hunt opposes the preferability of a long apprenticeship to nature, because "dogma," Hunt affirms, "does not transmit genius." As impertinent toward the authority of the Royal Academy as he would be humble toward that of nature, Hunt concludes on a note that seems to sentence the Pre-Raphaelites to a protracted adolescence: "Children should begin as children," he tells Millais, "and wait for the years to bring them to maturity" (1: 82-86).

9. Comte's late philosophy relinquished the more scientific diction of

its earlier phases and established women as the objects of worship in his new "religion of humanity." This form of worship, he insisted, was entirely consistent with the tenets of his positivism: "Positivism ... encourages, on intellectual as well as moral grounds, full and systematic expression of the feeling of veneration for women." The truly mystified nature of this veneration becomes inescapably apparent in the following paragraph, in which, as in other instances cited in this chapter, women are sources of improvement for male worshipers whose inferiority and dependence are oddly canceled out by their explicit monopoly on power: in the Positivist future, Comte prophesies, "the enervating influence of chimerical beliefs will have passed away; and men in all the vigour of their energies, feeling themselves the masters of the known world, will feel it their highest happiness to submit to the beneficent power of womanly sympathy. In a word, Man will in those days kneel to Woman, and to Woman only" (287–88).

10. The thesis that, within the discourse that Ruskin participates in, normative subjectivity is aligned with human imperfection and is gendered masculine is reinforced by Sawyer's later description of Ruskin's distinction between sublime and visionary art: "For Ruskin, sublime art induces identification with masculine energy, visionary art contemplation of the beautiful as an object; in religious terms one form is 'taken in' like the eucharist, the other beheld as an icon or memorial" (83).

11. In fact, as Gary Wihl observes, the second section of *Modern Painters II* was added to the manuscript during one of its revisions (43).

12. In a similar vein, Sussman suggests that Millais's *Christ in the House of His Parents* demonstrates a concern with picturing the family as "a center of bourgeois value, as the source of economic support and emotional nurturance," but at the same time registers anxieties "about manliness and particularly male sexuality" (121).

Chapter 4

1. The discussions of Dickens's attitudes toward childhood in this chapter are generally informed by Kincaid's book, most particularly Chapter 6, "The Gentle Child" (217–43), and Chapter 8, "The Wonder Child in Neverland" (275–98). As Kincaid notes, it is important to recognize the historical conditions which accompanied the emergence of Victorian discourses of domesticity and sentimentality. Philippe Ariès has given a thorough account of the role that changing attitudes toward childhood played in the emergence of the modern family. For our purposes, two of his findings are of note. First, Ariès suggests that the perception of a qualitative difference between childhood and adulthood occurred in European culture alongside

the demarcation of differences between home and public life. In the seventeenth and eighteenth centuries "the family organized itself around the child," Ariès writes, "and erected the wall of private life between family and society" (413). Second, Ariès observes that the modern concept of childhood embodied the paradoxical notion that children had both an innocence to be preserved and a weakness to be modified. Thus the ritual of a child's first communion in seventeenth-century France placed weight on both the innocence and the rational capacities of children, who were presumably capable of comprehending the doctrinal significance of the sacrament even while they were intellectually incapable of grievous sins (122, 127). In their symbolic dimensions, the children of Dickens's early novels reflect this historical genealogy. Characters such as Nell, Oliver, Tiny-Tim, and Paul Dombey are central to their respective families and to the constitution of their families as private spaces which are set off from, and to an extent hostile to, the public activities of work, trade, and money. Moreover, all these children differ from adults by virtue of a wise innocence. In this latter capacity, the Dickensian child must be understood more specifically as a Victorian rendering of a Wordsworthian inheritance, where the child is closest to the divine only as long as its qualitative difference from the adult is preserved. Given wide social currency, this attitude toward childhood became a source of comfort for infant mortality; it also became a source of maudlin excess in literature, as evidenced by the theatrical deaths of Paul and little Nell, or (to cite a non-Dickensian example) by *The Dairyman's Daughter*. In these ways, the cultural ramifications of childhood in the early nineteenth century provided Dickens with a powerful and untapped topos. As Kathleen Tillotson observes, Dickens was the first British novelist to put a child at the center of novels written for adults (50).

2. Throughout this chapter I type Dickens's style as "sentimental," although the complex history of the term makes it difficult to invoke unreflectively. By "sentimental," I refer to a loosely categorizable genre of fiction in the later eighteenth and early nineteenth centuries which centered moral and religious judgment in the emotions; identified the cultivation of these emotions with the family, nature, and femininity; and presented this alliance of morality and feeling, of domesticated nature and domestic proclivities, as a barrier against the perceived hostility of materialist psychology and rational empiricism. Sentimentality was typically identified with idealism in Romantic and Victorian criticism; as Fred Kaplan notes, writers of the period emphasized the "idealist" tendencies of sentimentality so as to underscore its opposition to philosophical and literary realism (5–7). Consequently, literary reviewers such as David Masson, Walter Bagehot, and George Stott described Dickens as an idealist more frequently and more

In Christ's estimation, the cultural forces which assigned women a special moral talent and assigned popular novels responsibility for social edification worked both to enhance the success of women novelists and to fuel a backlash against them. This backlash echoed the predicament as well as the rhetoric of Muscular Christianity: it "added a valence of heroic masculinity" to the efforts of Victorian men of letters (30). Christ's comments are made in the context of a discussion of Victorian "sage" literary figures. There is some disagreement, however, whether novelists can properly be classified with Victorian prose "sages" such as Carlyle and Ruskin. While John Holloway defines sage writing as both fiction and nonfiction prose, George Landow more strictly defines it as nonfiction prose which is typologically structured after the model of biblical prophecy. In either case, as a measure of the power which Victorians assigned the celebrities of their print culture, the phenomenon of the Victorian "sage" underscores the kinds of pressures and expectations placed upon Dickens, and consequently helps us identify and understand the instances of self-reflexive narrators in his novels.

8. Margaret Oliphant argues that the greatest strength of mid-century Dickens lies in his ability to portray idealized domestic scenes: "Nowhere does the household hearth burn brighter—nowhere is the family love so warm—the natural bonds so strong; and this is the ground which Mr. Dickens occupies *par excellence*" (452). Oliphant goes on to identify the stylistic strengths of Dickens's writing with the moralized values celebrated by his writing. She suggests that the particular moralism of Dickens's novels necessitates the emasculation of their male protagonists. Thus Dickens's heroes are "all young by necessity"—they are "not the young men of clubs and colleges," but rather characters who are "homebred and sensitive, much impressed by feminine influences, swayed by ... the laws which were absolute to their childhood" (451). An infantilized author, Dickens now seems qualified to pronounce with authority what Oliphant calls "the law of kindness sublimated into charity, Love, [which] is the pervading spirit of the Gospel" (465). Along similar lines, David Masson describes Dickens as a "feminine sensibility" which assumes a "looser, richer, and freer texture" than that of a more "masculine" stylist such as Thackeray (9). Although troubled by the "careless and languid" tendencies of this "weak" style, at the end of his essay Masson makes what appears to be an automatic association between a feminized writing and a sentimental moral philosophy, for "kindliness," Masson affirms, "is the first principle of Mr. Dickens's philosophy, and the sum and substance of his moral system" (82). Likewise, an anonymous reviewer in *Fraser's* celebrates Dickens's "deep reverence for the household sanctities, his enthusiastic worship of the household gods"

(698). This reviewer sees in Dickens the power to "humanize the world," and he personifies Dickens's authorial power in what is now a familiar fashion: France, the reviewer notes, "has condescended to pronounce Boz *un gentil enfant*" ("Charles Dickens and *David Copperfield*," 700).

Walter Bagehot employs similar conventions, but to pejorative ends, by objecting that Dickens's "sentimental confusion" is "utterly deficient in the faculty of reasoning" (83–84). In case we miss the implicit connections of femininity, childhood, and irrationality, Bagehot renders them explicit in his ensuing analogy: Dickens, he remarks, is like the small girl who asks her mother, "What shall I think about?" The only answer to this question—coming as it does from a source wherein credulous naiveté is wedded to creative genius—is "My dear, don't think" (83). George Stott, pursuing an argument similar to Bagehot's, berates Dickens for his "feminine incapacity to think abstractly" (222) and concludes that this fault manifests itself in the disregard for "learning, culture, and sagacity" which is an article of faith in the Dickensian "gospel of geniality" (224). The social innuendos of Stott's argument are evidenced not only in the journal for which he writes (the *Contemporary Review*), but more suggestively by an example he offers: "For good breeding and refinement [Dickens] exhibits a very decided contempt," Stott claims, a fault evidenced by the fact that Dickens "seems incapable of creating a gentleman" (223). With no characters who are happy embodiments of gentlemanly masculinity, he complains, we must accept such social aberrations as Florence Dombey keeping company with Captain Cuttle. Like the other reviewers, Stott draws an analogy between the Dickensian style and Dickens himself, but he adds an element of class distinctions to the argument; Dickens writes in a feminine and irrational style, Stott suggests, because he lacks the education and social breeding that would have properly masculinized him.

9. For other discussions of Dickens's treatment of "fallen women," see Laurie Langbauer, Amanda Anderson, and Patricia Ingham. Anderson offers a brief overview of other criticism which addresses Dickens's interest in prostitution (67n). Her own work argues that in his treatment of prostitution, Dickens combined "competing versions of character and selfhood" in such a way as to endow his fallen women "with a peculiarly modern form of self-consciousness" (79). Along comparable lines, Ingham assesses Dickens's "fallen girls" as characters who achieve a higher degree of agency and individuality than the other, often homogeneous female characters of his novels (61). In contrast, Langbauer's essay pursues a more formalist line of argument. She explores the possibility of a "collusion" between the "waywardness" displayed by many of Dickens's female characters and his innovations in the genre of the romance novel (428).

10. Among the novels in which Walder identifies Evangelical tropes are *Pickwick Papers*, *The Old Curiosity Shop*, *David Copperfield*, and *Bleak House*—novels that span roughly the first two decades of Dickens's career. For my purposes, Walder's recognition of the salience of conversion narratives in the novels of the 1840s is particularly telling—*Martin Chuzzlewit* (1843–44), *A Christmas Carol* (1843), and *Dombey and Son* (1846–48) are all examples, according to Walder, of Dickens's vexed relationship with the Evangelical emphasis on personal regeneration (114–16). Norris Pope also explores at length the importance of Evangelicalism and especially Methodism for Dickens's literary imagination and ethical beliefs, concluding that his hostility toward them "was shaped as much by literary, social, and ethical considerations as it was by theological scruples or first-hand experience of the evangelical world" (41).

Chapter 5

1. As Mary Poovey has explained, Nightingale circumnavigated her culture's stereotypes of gender, in turn enlisting and combating them to suit her own purposes. Poovey identifies two seemingly inhospitable narratives, "a domestic narrative of maternal nurturing and self-sacrifice and a military narrative of individual assertion and will," that operate simultaneously in Victorian images of Nightingale and in Nightingale's rhetorical manipulation of these images (*Uneven Developments* 169). Elaine Showalter has made a similar case for Nightingale's anomalous religious convictions, arguing that faith at once fueled her enormous productivity and set her at odds with prevailing Protestant sentiments concerning women's mission. She notes that Nightingale "translated intellectual and vocational drives into the language of religion, the only system that could justify them" ("Florence" 397). And yet her use of religious language, despite the reinforcement it gave her from a traditional body of authority, was entirely heretical; Nightingale "subvert[ed]," Showalter writes, "the Protestant ideology of humility and submission, especially as applied to women" (408). Showalter's account is largely biographical, while Poovey focuses on representations of Nightingale. But for both critics, Nightingale is an ambivalent feminist ancestor, one who negotiated her way between traditional images of femininity and suffragist attempts to shatter those images, conforming to neither school.

2. Three different textual sources of *Suggestions for Thought to Searchers After Religious Truth* will be cited in this chapter. The original three-volume work will subsequently be cited as Nightingale, *Suggestions* 1860. But because the original version is only available in a few libraries, I have, where possible, cited the more readily available edition of excerpts from

Suggestions for Thought compiled by Michael D. Calabria and Janet A. Macrae in 1994, subsequently cited as Nightingale, *Suggestions* 1994. A disorderly work, *Suggestions for Thought* provides a challenge to the editor who wishes to present a coherent and representative arrangement of excerpts. Calabria and Macrae's remedy is to compile representative passages under topical headings; consequently, they do not include the *Cassandra* section of *Suggestions for Thought* in its entirety. For this reason, when quoting passages from *Cassandra*, I refer to yet another edition, "Cassandra" and Other Selections from "Suggestions for Thought," edited by Mary Poovey, and cited as Nightingale, *Cassandra*.

3. See Chapter 2, note 15.

4. Comte and Schleiermacher are especially salient influences on *Suggestions for Thought*. Discussing her attitude toward Comtism, Cook notes that Nightingale sympathized with the belief that nature and culture operate according to scientific laws. But he also cites her objections to the impersonal nature of agency in the Comtian system. For Comte, the laws which ordered natural and historical phenomena were intrinsic to the phenomena, and not, as Nightingale believed, the directives of a conscious God, of a personalized "Law-Giver" (Cook 2: 218–19). The familiarity with Comte that Nightingale demonstrates in *Suggestions for Thought* is not only timely but, in terms of his British reception, slightly ahead of the times. Comte's major works had been completed in French by 1854; Harriet Martineau's popular abridged translation of *Cours de philosophie positive* appeared in 1853, as did George Henry Lewes's summary of Comtian philosophy. Mill's more comprehensive and interrogative *Auguste Comte and Positivism* did not appear until 1865. Since *Suggestions for Thought* was drafted first in the early 1850s and then again in 1860, it seems that Nightingale was in the vanguard of English thinkers who in the 1850s were assimilating into their own ideas Comte's belief in the metaphysical importance of scientific laws. It is often difficult to separate the philosophical from the theological components in Comtism, and Nightingale's work is no exception. Arguably, philosophy and theology were always implicitly interconnected in Comte's writings, but it was not until his later work that the two achieved an explicit, albeit occult merger, much to the embarrassment of some of his defenders. Cashdollar suggests that when Victorian Christians overcame their fear of Comte, one thing they found agreeable in his works was the "way [he] fused the divine with the human" (15). Incarnational theology, such as that adopted by Nightingale, was hospitable to this emphasis in his thought.

Nightingale's exposure to German thought, at least initially, was due to the influence of Christian Baron von Bunsen, the well-known diplomat, linguist, and orientalist who was a family friend of the Nightingales' and an important conduit for German philosophy into England. In the 1840s, when Florence was in her twenties, Bunsen introduced her to works by Schopenhauer, Schleiermacher, and Niebuhr (Calabria and Macrae xxiv). Schleiermacher's effect on Nightingale can be traced in her belief that the function of Christ in Western religious development is to introduce the notion of divine perfection to human consciousness. However, judging from *Suggestions for Thought*, Nightingale does not seem to think that a historical Jesus is necessary for this metaphysical result, and in this regard she differs from Schleiermacher, who held Christ to be the highest exemplar of god-consciousness and the pivotal moment in salvation history. Surprisingly, given her aversion to Strauss, *Suggestions for Thought* recalls the conclusion of *Das Leben Jesu* in this matter. Like Strauss, Nightingale seems to think that the symbolic significance of the incarnation is not dependent on Christ's status as the literal son of God or even as an infallible genius. However, Nightingale did not read Strauss until 1865, at which time, judging from Jowett's responses to her comments, she found his theories objectionable (see Jowett 76, 81–82, and 90). Most likely, Nightingale objected to Strauss for much the same reasons that everyone did; his mythical decipherment of the Gospel story was by popular consensus felt to be the most horrific assault on Christian faith outside of Darwinism. Had she given more careful consideration to *Das Leben Jesu*, she might have found another, albeit comparatively less significant ground of dispute. The conclusion of *Das Leben Jesu* sounds a Calvinist note of bodily disdain; man's natural existence, Strauss comments, is a condition to be overcome by, in symbolic terms, "crucifying his sensible existence" (778). Nightingale, in contrast, held sensible existence in high esteem and chastised the tradition that preached the shame of human nature; such humility, she opined, is wrongheaded and offensive to God (*Suggestions* 1860, 3: 82). One can see the attraction this empirical epistemology of religion had for her. The holistic conception of human nature balanced the claims of the body with those of the mind in a way that lent dignity to the healing profession and its methodology of empirical observation.

5. Cook describes Mill's response to *Suggestions for Thought* and an allusion to *Cassandra* that appears in *Subjection of Women* (1: 471n); Evelyn Pugh further documents Mill's debt to *Cassandra* (136).

6. Several scholars have documented and analyzed Nightingale's attitudes toward the women's rights movements of her day. A detailed account is provided by Pugh, who in focusing on Nightingale's correspondence with J. S. Mill clarifies Nightingale's dislike of suffragist writing and of women's collective action. Whereas Mill believed it necessary for

women to form partnerships aimed at systematic political reform, Nightingale refrained from social coalitions, Pugh concludes, preferring to rely upon "individual action," the belief that "women could solve their problems by perseverance and hard work" (137).

7. I am using "latitudinarian" not in its specific historical sense but rather in the generic and usually disparaging sense in which it was commonly used in Victorian theological discourse, where it is associated with indifference to points of doctrine. As Poovey explains, Nightingale also associated theological relativism with the Evangelical movement, whose influence she came under in the 1840s, but soon rejected ("Introduction" xvi). This experience Poovey understands to inform the following pronouncement in *Suggestions for Thought*: "It is a mistake to refer to 'private judgment'—those words are dangerous, because they seem to imply that one person may judge one way, and another, according to their 'private' views of things ... whereas it is the truth, as it were, which *judges* for us. The principle of 'private judgment' ought to mean (if it means anything) that we are to search earnestly with all our mights for the truth" (1860, 2: 294).

8. As Philip Rosenberg observes, Carlyle's early writings invoke the concept of work in a frustratingly unspecified fashion. However, Rosenberg goes on to argue that in *Sartor Resartus* Carlyle did sketch out a more refined analysis of work, and in Rosenberg's opinion, this analysis has much in common with Hannah Arendt's neo-Hegelian model of three levels of action—work, labor, and action—each of which entails a different conception of the relationship of the subject, the social, and the political (28, 57). Rosenberg's observations are relevant to the discussion of Nightingale because they underscore the fact that her concept of work represents a complex matrix of Hegelian metaphysics, Protestant morality, and the emerging political philosophies of industrialized Europe.

9. Marx's most concise critique of Feuerbach on this score occurs in the brief text "Concerning Feuerbach" (widely known as the "Thesis on Feuerbach"): "Feuerbach resolves the religious essence into the *human* essence. But the human essence is no abstraction inherent in each single individual. In its reality it is the ensemble of social relations. Feuerbach, who does not enter upon a criticism of this real essence, is consequently compelled: 1. To abstract from the historical process and to fix the religious sentiment as something by itself and to presuppose an abstract—*isolated*—human individual. 2. Essence, therefore, can be comprehended only as 'genus', as an internal, dumb generality which *naturally* unites the many individuals" (423).

10. Showalter states at the introduction of her 1991 essay on Nightin-

gale and Margaret Fuller: "The histories of Nightingale and Fuller are part of that secret archive of feminist intellectuals attempting to work within a discourse and an institution that has been shaped and controlled by men" ("Miranda and Cassandra" 313). Showalter concludes that the attempt, in Nightingale's case, was at best a mixed success; the revisions that Jowett encouraged, Showalter believes, disciplined and deformed *Cassandra* into "a patriarchal epistemology" (320). Landow places *Cassandra* specifically in the Victorian tradition of "sage writing" and, like Showalter, is interested in the textual consequences of Nightingale's forced entry into this predominantly male genre. However, he attributes greater success to Nightingale in this regard, arguing that she adopts the sage's "aggressive style of [biblical and classical] reinterpretation" in a manner that at once curries favor with her reader and effectively communicates a woman's perspective ("Aggressive (Re)interpretations" 42–43).

Chapter 6

1. A thorough history of the British and Foreign Bible Society is provided in Leslie Howsam's *Cheap Bibles: Nineteenth-Century Publishing and the British and Foreign Bible Society*. Howsam analyzes the publication history of the Bible Society as a phenomenon with broad-ranging social and economic dimensions. She characterizes this phenomenon as "'a Bible transaction,' a complex set of relations that were commercial, personal, philanthropic and cultural" (2).

2. In the early 1800s the Board of Control of the East India Company was divided over the advisability of evangelicization, and in effect a war was waged between missionaries who favored aggressive cultural and religious intervention and company agents who preferred either no religious interference or the reserved demeanor of the Anglican missionary tradition. The first victory went to the conservatives in 1807, when missionary operations at the College of Fort William in Bengal were greatly curtailed, and its department for translating the Bible was abolished. Dr. Claudius Buchanan, the Evangelical vice-provost of the college, was dismissed, and afterwards he launched a polemical campaign against the East India Company. In the same year that Buchanan was dismissed, Thomas Twining, an agent of the company, lost his bid to prohibit the B.F.B.S. from operating in the company's territories. Twining's arguments exemplify the combination of religious tolerance and business rationale that informed most of the company's policies: Twining said he could not be "a mere spectator in the attempt to wound the tenderest feelings of the natives of India"; moreover, he feared such a disturbance "would drive us from the portion of the globe with as much ease as the sands of the desert are scattered by the wind" (28–

29). The Board of Proprietors decided against Twining's resolution. Missionaries tended to claim that their efforts were seriously impeded by the company—John Clark Marshman, for example, complained that at no time in his 60-year experience did the Parliament, the press, or the Board of Control take the side of the missionary cause (2: 470–72). But in the early nineteenth century, Parliament and the Board of Control passed several actions protecting and at times supporting the rights of missionaries in India. And in 1813, after the company was deprived of its commercial monopoly, Dr. Buchanan attained his longstanding desire to see the establishment of an Indian episcopacy.

3. Initially, the B.F.B.S. was patronized almost exclusively by Evangelical clergy, Dissenting ministers, and upper-middle-class laity. As it developed, however, it became a more middle- and lower-middle-class organization. Among the Society's first members were Rev. Charles Simeon, the popular Cambridge theologian, and several members of the wealthy Evangelical Clapham sect, including William Wilberforce. After Lord Teignmouth, a former governor-general of Bengal, accepted the post of president, the bishops of London, Durham, Exeter, and St. David's sent in their names as subscribers. The original costs of subscription, ranging from one guinea to fifty pounds, were prohibitive for lower-middle-class incomes, but as early as 1805 an Auxiliary Bible Society was formed in London offering memberships ranging from two to seven shillings. In 1854 the British and Foreign Bible Society reported 3,315 domestic Auxiliaries, Branches, and Associations. The Auxiliaries operated in much the same fashion as the parent institution in London, while the Associations, which made only group contributions to the Society's general funds, did not give official memberships and were primarily distribution centers for the Society's Bibles. In theory, the Auxiliaries were independent organizations, but Howsam reports that "there was a constant tension between the autonomy of Auxiliaries and the authority of the central office" (47). While the members of the Auxiliaries were most often clergymen and affluent middle-class Evangelicals and Dissenters, the majority of the participants in the Associations came from the lower middle class. Women were most active at the level of the Associations, probably because there they could serve in a higher capacity—of the 2,482 Associations reported in 1854, more than half were conducted by women.

4. It is frequently pointed out that missionaries to India and Africa seemed equally concerned with inculcating European manners as with Christian theology. As one missionary from Tanjore wrote the Society, "The moral conduct, upright dealing, and decent dress, of the native Protestants of Tanjore, demonstrate the powerful influence and peculiar excel-

lence of the Christian religion. It ought, however, to be observed, that the Bible, when the reading of it becomes general, has nearly the same effect on the poor of every place" (Owen 1: 323). From South Africa, Robert Moffat wrote of the civilizing effect that his translation of Luke had on the Tswanas, concluding "thus, by the slow but certain progress of Gospel principles, whole families become clothed and in their right mind" (*Missionary Labours* 505).

5. Both Owen's and Browne's histories reflect early Victorian preoccupations with prophecy and specifically with the spirit of postmillennialist optimism that fueled the activities of Evangelical reform. W. H. Oliver offers a useful description of the differences between pre- and postmillennial thought: postmillennialists stressed that Christians themselves were responsible for achieving the massive global conversions which would precede Christ's return to earth; premillennialists, in contrast, expected that Christ's sudden and dramatic return in glory would vindicate their disdain for the self-congratulatory optimism of those who celebrated progress, embraced democracy, and overlooked the sinfulness of the English nation. Postmillennialists were embarrassed by such prophetic excesses, and identified wholeheartedly with England's providential role as a global disseminator of Christian enlightenment. It was this component of postmillennial rhetoric—a combination of avowed faith in Christian teleology and certain faith in English cultural superiority—that gave the middle- and lower-middle-class reforming societies their distinctive character, separating them from both the more politically inclined chiliasm of working-class prophetic thought and from the similarly reform-minded but secular attitudes of the utilitarians (Oliver 20–24).

6. There is also a historical reason for the prevalence of images of literate children teaching their elders: as David Vincent documents, from the 1830s through the end of the nineteenth century, children in Britain tended to be more literate than their parents by about twenty points (26).

7. Although the missionaries were fairly candid about their experiences in their memoirs, they often only expressed their doubts retrospectively, after they began to enjoy some success. Robert Moffat, in one of his published memoirs, noted after the end of his first ten years among "indifferent" Tswanas that "the moral wilderness was now about to blossom.... The simple Gospel now melted their flinty hearts; and eyes wept, which never before had shed the tear of hallowed sorrow" (*Missionary Labours* 496). In a gesture that typifies missionaries' writings, Moffat reads the otherness of the Africans as Evangelical allegory—the cold heart of the inaccessible heathen needs the emotional stimulation of the Gospels to acquire the sentimentality that makes him recognizable in Western eyes. Evi-

dence that the Bible was not taking root in an area was often viewed through the screens of nationalism. Claudius Buchanan observed that in India, Christian missions flourished more where there were few French inhabitants, since French Christians set such an unfavorable example (54–55). In fifty years of "sporadic campaigning" in Mongolia, Moravian missionaries only attracted "a few unfortunates" into the church, but a lot of hostility from the Kalmucks—failures that the Bible Society attributed in part to the laziness of the Moravians (Bawden 45–46). In contrast to Moffat's and Buchanan's nationalistic processing of frustration, Mrs. Anne Hodgson, who spent several years in Africa as the wife of a Wesleyan missionary, concluded that there was something insidiously disingenuous about the way the missionary societies in England depicted missionary life in Africa: "Our eyes are not gladdened with seeing multitudes flock to the standard of the cross, nor our ears with the interrogatory 'What must I do to be saved?' A very difficult language is to be acquired, with a poor interpreter, who is of a dreadfully bad temper; sometimes he will answer a question, and sometimes he will not" (W. Shaw 171). The difference between domestic fictions and foreign realities in the missionary experience was aided by the fact that missionaries seldom returned to England to speak in person about their adventures, and if they had, Elisabeth Jay conjectures, they "would have found scant welcome from crowds accustomed to hearing of the Society's achievements from noble and famous rather than the labourers in the field" (169).

8. James Clifford cites Derrida as the catalyst for a debate that has unsettled "the sharp distinction of the world's culture into literate and preliterate; the notion that ethnographic textualization is a process that enacts a fundamental transition from oral experience to written representation" (118). Hence Clifford argues that there is less of a distinction between literate and nonliterate societies than anthropologists traditionally presume, because "non-literate cultures are already textualized; there are few, if any, 'virgin' lifeways to be violated and preserved by writing" (117). The other side of this argument is perhaps best represented by Walter Ong, who emphasizes essential differences between oral and literate cultures, and notes that, among other things, oral cultures rely solely on memory, do not conceive of language in visual terms, and tend to use concepts in a situational as opposed to an abstract frame of reference. However, these considerations have led Ong to a conclusion that Clifford might find sympathetic, insofar as it expresses orality and literacy as interactive rather than polarized conditions: "Without textualism, orality cannot even be identified; without orality, textualism is rather opaque and playing with it can be a

form of occultism, elaborate obfuscation—which can be endlessly titillating, even at those times when it is not especially informative" (169-70).

9. The Bible Society's attitude toward translation straddles the two poles that George Steiner identifies in linguistic theory as the "relativist" and the "universalist." On the one hand, insofar as the Society's translators sought analogies between Scriptures and the target languages, their translations reflect the emphasis placed by contemporary linguists and cultural historians (Herder, Mme de Staël, Humboldt) on the reciprocities between language and national character and habits of belief (see Steiner 73-85). On the other hand, the unique universality that Society translators attributed to the Bible overrode these relative conditions of language. In the mid-century writings of the Society, this mixture of relativist and universalist views was harmonized through quasi-evolutionary terminology, where the Bible was frequently described as an ideal type that entered into various linguistic species with more or less representational success. As Henry Rogers wrote in the *Edinburgh Review*, "It has not been given to any other book of religion, thus to triumph over national prejudices ... varying by every conceivable diversity of language.... The Bible adapts itself with facility to the revolutions of thought and feeling ... and flexibly accommodates itself to the progress of society" (316-17). Although the Bible Society's concern with the relativity of languages was informed by contemporary trends in linguistic and cultural theory, their belief that the Bible was still absolutely translatable was not unique either to that period or to Christianity. Even though there was no single Bible in early Victorian England—the discovery of new manuscripts and the debates over textual variations were constantly challenging the integrity of both the King James version and the Hebrew and Greek texts—Protestants still maintained faith in an ideally authoritative text, wherein, as Benjamin says of all holy writings, "language and revelation are one" (82).

10. Throughout the nineteenth century, Victorians posited a radical shift toward philanthropic improvement in England's rule of India after Hastings's trial revealed the abuses that were performed under the mandate of turning profits. John Seeley, the Cambridge professor of history who was cynical enough to proclaim that "we seem ... to have conquered and peopled half the world in a fit of absence of mind" (12), still held in 1881 to the interpretation that in dissolving the East India Company, the English government had effectively subordinated its commercial to its philanthropic interest in India: "[In the eighteenth century] it was no affair of ours whether the Hindus had a bad Government, or had no Government at all and were merely the prey of armed plunderers.... But since 1851 it has

been removed. The very appearance of a selfish object is gone. The Government is now as sincerely paternal as any can be, and, as I explained, it has abandoned the affectation of not imparting the superior enlightenment we know ourselves to possess on the ground that the Hindus do not want it" (205).

11. The B.F.B.S. was always fundamentally a British institution, even though by 1854 there were 64 foreign Bible Societies that contributed a large amount of effort and independent initiative. After the Apocrypha controversy of 1825, the connection between London and the European societies was officially severed, but the B.F.B.S. eventually reestablished staffs of Continental agents in major European cities, as Howsam explains in some detail (160–61). Toward most of the remaining home operations the B.F.B.S. maintained an attitude that was partially fraternal and partially condescending: in its annual reports, the Bible Society's secretaries diligently chronicle the operations of foreign Societies, but also relegate those operations to the role of channels of circulation that flow outward from the Society's center in London. The rhetorical conventions that typify these reports reflect the patriarchal character of the Bible Society's structure. Most commonly, the Society is described as a fountain with tributaries or as a sun dispersing darkness. Such metaphors could be used to the Society's disadvantage by members of foreign auxiliaries who felt that their British brethren exaggerated their importance. In 1813 a Soldier of the American Revolution published a letter accusing the Society of falsely projecting itself as "the sole proprietor of God's light to the world" (6). There were other "British lights," he remembers, of which Christians should be less proud—the lights of American churches burned by British soldiers during the recent war (18). Although the soldier's letter begins on a conciliatory note, by the end of it he seems to want the American Bible Society to wage another war of independence against the patronage of its British parent, arguing (in a phrase that perverts the British secretaries' other favorite metaphor) that "the vile mother and monster Britain has been the source and fountain of all the wars in Europe" (22). Not surprisingly, such inflammatory accusations from within the ranks of affiliated Bible Societies did not find their way into the Bible Society's official histories.

12. Other stories illustrate this point more graphically. A few pages earlier, Browne cites the example of an old Greek priest who went to observe a missionary school where young girls were learning to read the Bible. At the end of his visit, the monk is quoted as saying: "I only learned to read a little and became a priest, and although I read at Church prayers and portions of the Bible, they are in Ancient Greek, and I cannot understand them.... I, who have grey hairs upon my head, have been receiving lessons

from children. How I would like to sit down with these children, and learn the Scriptures!" (2: 45–46). Still other stories assume a tone more polemical than sentimental: "A zealous Roman Catholic priest, afterwards a no less zealous Protestant, was brought to examine one of our Flemish Testaments, in the following singular manner. A colporteur had sold a copy to one of his parishioners. The poor man, frightened by a violent sermon preached by another priest, hastened home, took his Testament, and carried it to his own priest (the one in question) and begged him to burn it.... The priest, it appears, was afterwards induced to read the Testament left with him. Afterwards ... he became a Protestant minister" (Browne 1: 456).

13. At first, the Bible Society's application for a booth at the Great Exhibition was refused by Prince Albert, who objected to the implied association of the Bible with the proclaimed subject of the exhibition, modern industry. A long correspondence ensued, and the booth was approved (Chadwick 2: 461–62).

14. Perhaps the most energetic of the Society's critics was the High Churchman Rev. Herbert Marsh, the Lady Margaret professor of divinity at Cambridge, who between 1811 and 1812 produced one speech and three pamphlets condemning its existence. In his third and most extensive pamphlet, Marsh leveled the scathing charges that the Bible Society sponsored unqualified translators, produced translations that were detrimental to faith, and, moreover, made spurious claims to translations for which it was not responsible. In December 1811, Marsh addressed a public meeting in the Cambridge Town Hall to argue against the establishment of a Cambridge Auxiliary Bible Society. Marsh's "violent language" had the detrimental effect of arousing "a strong feeling in favour of the Bible Society, and after an enthusiastic town-hall meeting, the auxiliary was established against his wishes." In the following month Marsh continued his campaign against the Society with two pamphlets. Among the respondents to these pamphlets was Rev. Simeon, whose considerable influence at Cambridge was responsible for the Auxiliary in the first place. Owen summarizes Marsh's arguments, along with lengthy excerpts from the rebuttals of the Society's spokesmen, in 2: 143–211.

15. Seeley argued that English trade in India did not begin to prosper until after the East India Company was deprived of its monopoly in 1813, and that great trade with India only began after 1833. In his lectures at Cambridge, he used this point to demonstrate the superior efficacy of a colonial system that did not engage in "sordid rapacity," but rather maintained separate channels for governmental and commercial activities (209–15).

16. Patrick Brantlinger describes the relationship between missionary

Evangelicals and utilitarian colonialism as one with more important similarities than differences: "The Evangelicals and utilitarians insisted that the chief objects of British imperialism were the conversion and civilization of India.... The utilitarian project of social reform often conflicted with the Christian conversion advocated by the evangelicals, but both goals involved a belief that ran counter to the most extreme forms of racism: no matter how benighted or tyrannized by custom and false religion, Indians were capable of education, improvement, progress" (106). Along similar lines, Eric Stokes has argued that utilitarians assimilated aspects of the evangelical missionary tradition to produce a philosophy of government that coupled an elaborate legislative system with a centralizing commitment to the necessity of supervision.

Works Cited

Altick, Richard D. *Writers, Readers, and Occasions*. Columbus: Ohio State University Press, 1989.
Anderson, Amanda. *Tainted Souls and Painted Faces: The Rhetoric of Fallenness in Victorian Culture*. Ithaca: Cornell University Press, 1993.
apRoberts, Ruth. *Arnold and God*. Berkeley: University of California Press, 1983.
Ariès, Philippe. *Centuries of Childhood*. Trans. Robert Baldick. New York: Alfred A. Knopf, 1962.
Armstrong, Nancy. *Desire and Domestic Fiction: A Political History of the Novel*. Oxford: Oxford University Press, 1987.
Arnold, Matthew. "Rugby Chapel." In *Collected Works of Matthew Arnold: Poetry and Prose*, vol. 1, ed. John Bryson. Cambridge, Mass.: Harvard University Press, 1954.
Arnold, Thomas. "The Bible." In *Miscellaneous Works of Thomas Arnold*, 146–59. New York: D. Appleton & Co., 1845.
———. "The Church." In *Miscellaneous Works of Thomas Arnold*, 1–72. New York: D. Appleton & Co., 1845.
———. "Early Roman History" (1825). In *Miscellaneous Works of Thomas Arnold*, 378–403. New York: D. Appleton & Co., 1845.
———. "The effects of distant Colonization on the Parent State; a prize essay, recited in the theatre at Oxford, June 7, 1815." The Collection of the British Library.
———. "Essay on the Right Interpretation of Scripture." In *Sermons*, 2nd ed., vol. II, 427–78. London: B. Fellowes, 1832–34.
———. *History of Rome* (1838). 2 vols. New York: D. Appleton & Co., 1872.
———. *Introductory Lectures on Modern History* (1842). New York: D. Appleton and Co., 1880.
———. *Principles of Church Reform* (1833). In *Miscellaneous Works of Thomas Arnold*, 73–130. New York: D. Appleton & Co., 1845.
———. *Tracts for the Times*. In *Miscellaneous Works of Thomas Arnold*, 236–89. New York: D. Appleton & Co., 1845.

———. "Two Sermons on the Interpretation of Prophecy" (1838). In *Religious Controversies of the Nineteenth Century*, ed. A. O. J. Cockshut, 93–103. Lincoln: University of Nebraska Press, 1966.

Auerbach, Nina. *Romantic Imprisonment: Women and Other Glorified Outcasts*. New York: Columbia University Press, 1985.

Bagehot, Walter. "Charles Dickens." *National Review* 7 (1858): 458–86.

Barrell, John. "Death on the Nile: Fantasy and the Literature of Tourism 1840–60." *Essays in Criticism* 41 (Apr. 1991): 97–127.

Barth, J. Robert, S.J. *Coleridge and Christian Doctrine*. Cambridge, Mass.: Harvard University Press, 1969.

———. "Coleridge's Scriptural Imagination." In *Coleridge, Keats, and the Imagination: Romanticism and Adam's Dream*, 135–42. Columbia: University of Missouri Press, 1990.

Bawden, C. R. *Shamans, Lamas, and Evangelicals*. London: Routledge and Kegan Paul, 1985.

Baxter, Robert. *Narrative of facts characterizing the supernatural manifestations, in members of Mr. Irving's congregation, and other individuals, in England and Scotland, and formerly in the writer himself*. London: James Nisbet, 1833.

[Bayley, Robert Slater.] "The British and Foreign Bible Society." *London Quarterly Review* 1 (Dec. 1852): 353–93.

Benjamin, Walter. "The Task of the Translator." In *Illuminations*, trans. Harry Zohn. New York: Schocken Books, 1969.

Bernal, Martin. *Black Athena*. Vol. 1, *The Fabrication of Ancient Greece (1785–1985)*. New Brunswick, N.J.: Rutgers University Press, 1987.

Bhaba, Homi K. *The Location of Culture*. London: Routledge, 1994.

[Blackett, J. B.] "Dr. Arnold's *Lectures*: The Church and State." *British and Foreign Review* 16 (Jan. 1844): 363–97.

Boone, Elizabeth Hill, and Walter D. Mignolo, eds. *Writing Without Words: Alternative Literacies in Mesoamerica and the Andes*. Durham, N.C.: Duke University Press, 1994.

Boulger, James D. *Coleridge as Religious Thinker*. New Haven: Yale University Press, 1961.

Brantlinger, Patrick. *Rule of Darkness: British Literature and Imperialism, 1830–1914*. Ithaca: Cornell University Press, 1988.

Brontë, Charlotte. *Jane Eyre* (1847). The Clarendon Edition of the Novels of the Brontës. Ed. Jane Jack and Margaret Smith. Oxford: Oxford University Press, 1969.

Browne, Rev. George. *The History of the British and Foreign Bible Society, from its Institution in 1804, to the Close of its Jubilee in 1854*. 2 vols. London: Bagster and Sons, 1859.

Buchanan, Rev. Claudius. *Christian Researches in Asia* (1811). Boston: Samuel T. Armstrong, 1812.
Buckton, Oliver. "'An Unnatural State': Gender, 'Perversion,' and Newman's *Apologia Pro Vita Sua*." *Victorian Studies* 35 (1992): 359–82.
Butler, Marilyn. *Romantics, Rebels and Reactionaries: English Literature and Its Background 1760–1830*. New York: Oxford University Press, 1981.
Calabria, Michael D., and Janet A. Macrae, eds. "Introduction" to *"Suggestions for Thought" by Florence Nightingale: Selections and Commentaries*. Philadelphia: University of Pennsylvania Press, 1994.
Canton, William. *A History of the British and Foreign Bible Society*. 2 vols. London: John Murray, 1904.
Carlile, Eliza Sharples. Editorial. *Isis* 1.27 (1832): 444–45.
Carlile, Richard. Editorial. *Isis* 1.27 (1832): 430–34.
Carlyle, Thomas. "Death of Edward Irving." In *Critical and Miscellaneous Essays*, vol. 3. London: Chapman and Hall, 1899.
———. *On Heroes, Hero-Worship and the Heroic in History* (1840). In *The Works of Thomas Carlyle*, 2nd ed., vol. 5. New York: AMS Press, 1980.
———. *Sartor Resartus* (1833–34). In *The Works of Thomas Carlyle*, 2nd ed., vol. 1. New York: AMS Press, 1980.
Cashdollar, Charles D. *The Transformation of Theology, 1830–1890: Positivism and Protestant Thought in Britain and America*. Princeton: Princeton University Press, 1989.
Chadwick, Owen. *The Victorian Church*, 2nd ed. 2 vols. London: Adam and Charles Black, 1970.
"Charles Dickens and *David Copperfield*." *Fraser's* 42 (Dec. 1850): 698–709.
"Childhood and its Reminscences." *Fraser's* 37 (Mar. 1848): 261–72.
Christ, Carol. "'The Hero as Man of Letters': Masculinity and Victorian Nonfiction Prose." In *Victorian Sages and Cultural Discourse: Renegotiating Gender and Power*, ed. Thaïs E. Morgan. New Brunswick, N.J.: Rutgers University Press, 1990.
Christensen, Jerome. *Coleridge's Blessed Machine of Language*. Ithaca: Cornell University Press, 1981.
Church Missionary Juvenile Instructor, vol. 4. London: Seeley, Jackson, and Halliday, 1855.
Clark, Robert. "Riddling the Family Firm: The Sexual Economy in Dombey and Son." *ELH* 51 (1984): 69–84.
Clifford, James. "On Ethnographic Allegory." In *Writing Culture*, ed. James Clifford and George E. Marcus, 98–121. Berkeley: University of California Press, 1968.
Coleridge, Samuel Taylor. *Biographia Literaria* (1817). 2 vols. Ed. James Engell and W. Jackson Bate. In *The Collected Works of Samuel Taylor*

Coleridge, vol. 7. Kathleen Coburn, General Editor. Princeton: Princeton University Press, 1965.

———. *Confessions of an Inquiring Spirit* (1840). Menston, England: Scolar Press, 1971.

———. *The Friend* (1809–10, 1818). 2 vols. Ed. B. I. Rooke. In *The Collected Works of Samuel Taylor Coleridge*, vol. 4. Kathleen Coburn, General Editor. Princeton: Princeton University Press, 1965.

———. *A Lay Sermon* (1817). In *Lay Sermons*, ed. R. J. White. *The Collected Works of Samuel Taylor Coleridge*, vol. 6. Kathleen Coburn, General Editor. Princeton: Princeton University Press, 1972.

———. *Letters of Samuel Taylor Coleridge*. 2 vols. Ed. Ernest Hartley Coleridge. London: William Heinemann, 1895.

———. *Marginalia*, vol. 1, ed. George Whalley. In The *Collected Works of Samuel Taylor Coleridge*, vol. 12. Kathleen Coburn, General Editor. Princeton: Princeton University Press, 1980.

———. *Marginalia*, vol. 3, ed. H. J. Jackson and George Whalley. In *The Collected Works of Samuel Taylor Coleridge*, vol. 12. Kathleen Coburn, General Editor. Princeton: Princeton University Press, 1992.

———. *On the Constitution of Church and State* (1830). Ed. John Colmer. In *The Collected Works of Samuel Taylor Coleridge*, vol. 10. Kathleen Coburn, General Editor. Princeton: Princeton University Press, 1976.

———. *The Statesman's Manual* (1816). In *Lay Sermons*, ed. R. J. White. *The Collected Works of Samuel Taylor Coleridge*, vol. 6. Kathleen Coburn, General Editor. Princeton: Princeton University Press, 1972.

Comaroff, Jean, and John Comaroff. *Of Revelation and Revolution: Christianity, Colonialism, and Consciousness in South Africa*. Vol. 1. Chicago: University of Chicago Press, 1991.

Comte, Auguste. *A General View of Positivism* (1875). Trans. J. H. Bridges. New York: Robert Speller and Sons, 1957.

[Conington, John.] "Sacred and profane." *Fraser's* 39 (Feb. 1849): 197–201.

Cook, Sir Edward. *The Life of Florence Nightingale*. 2 vols. London: Macmillan, 1914.

Davidson, Samuel. *Lectures on Biblical Criticism*. Edinburgh: Thomas Clark, 1839.

Dellamora, Richard. *Masculine Desire: The Sexual Politics of Victorian Aestheticism*. Chapel Hill: University of North Carolina Press, 1990.

de Man, Paul. "The Rhetoric of Temporality." In *Blindness and Insight: Essays in the Rhetoric of Contemporary Criticism*. Minneapolis: University of Minnesota Press, 1983.

De Quincey, Thomas. *Confessions of an English Opium-Eater* (1821). In

Confessions of an English Opium-Eater and Other Writings, ed. Grevel Lindop. Oxford: Oxford University Press, 1985.

———. "The Poetry of Pope" (1848). In *Collected Writings of Thomas De Quincey*, vol. 10. Ed. David Masson. 14 vols. Edinburgh: Adam and Charles Black, 1890.

———. *Suspiria De Profundis* (1845). In *Confessions of an English Opium-Eater and Other Writings*, ed. Grevel Lindop. Oxford: Oxford University Press, 1985.

Derrida, Jacques. *Of Grammatology*. Trans. Gayatri Chakravorty Spivak. Baltimore: Johns Hopkins University Press, 1976.

de S. Honey, J. R. *Tom Brown's Universe: The Development of the English Public School in the Nineteenth Century*. New York: Quadrangle/New York Times Book Co., 1977.

Dickens, Charles. *Dombey and Son* (1846–48). Harmondsworth, England: Penguin Books, 1970.

———. *The Life of Our Lord* (1848). New York: Simon and Schuster, 1934.

———. "Old Lamps for New Ones." *Household Words* 1 (1850): 258–69.

———. *Pilgrim Edition of the Letters of Charles Dickens*, vol. 5, *1847–49*. Ed. Graham and K. J. Fielding Storey. Oxford: Clarendon Press, 1981.

"Dr. Chalmers and Mr. Irving." *Liberal* 4 (1823): 299–313.

Drummond, Andrew Landale. *Edward Irving and His Circle*. London: James Clarke and Co., 1937.

[Edwards, Edward.] "British and Foreign Bible Society." *Quarterly Review* 36 (June 1827): 1–28.

Eilenberg, Susan. *Strange Power of Speech: Wordsworth, Coleridge, and Literary Possession*. Oxford: Oxford University Press, 1992.

Ellis, Sarah Stickney. *The Daughters of England: Their Position in Society, Character, and Responsibilities*. New York: D. Appleton, 1843.

[Empson, William.] "Review of the *Life and Correspondence of Thomas Arnold, M.A.*" *Edinburgh Review* 81 (Jan. 1845): 190–234.

Farrar, Frederic W. *Companions for the Devout Life*. London: John Murray, 1877.

———. *The Life of Christ*. Vol. 1. London: Cassell, Petter, and Galpin, 1880.

Fliegelman, Jay. *Declaring Independence: Jefferson, Natural Language, and the Culture of Performance*. Stanford, Calif.: Stanford University Press, 1993.

Forbes, Duncan. *The Liberal Anglican Idea of History*. Cambridge: Cambridge University Press, 1952.

Forster, John. *The Life of Charles Dickens (1872–74)*. Vol. 2. Boston: Estes and Lauriat, n.d.

Foxton, F. J. *Popular Christianity: Its Transition State, and Probable Development*. London: John Chapman, 1849.

Frei, Hans W. *The Eclipse of Biblical Narrative: A Study of Eighteenth and Nineteenth Century Hermeneutics*. New Haven: Yale University Press, 1974.

Froude, James Anthony. *The Nemesis of Faith*. London: James Chapman, 1849.

Gagnier, Regenia. *Subjectivities: A History of Self-Representation in Britain, 1832–1920*. Oxford: Oxford University Press, 1991.

Gates, Barbara T. "Not Choosing Not To Be: Victorian Literary Responses to Suicide." *Literature and Medicine* 6 (1987): 77–91.

Hair, John. *Regent Square*. London, 1899.

Haley, Bruce. *The Healthy Body and Victorian Culture*. Cambridge, Mass.: Harvard University Press, 1978.

Harding, Anthony John. *Coleridge and the Inspired Word*. Kingston and Montreal: McGill-Queen's University Press, 1985.

Hare, Julius, and Augustus [Hare]. *Guesses at Truth by Two Brothers*. 2nd series (1847–48). London: Taylor and Walton, 1847–48.

Hilliard, David. "UnEnglish and Unmanly: Anglo-Catholicism and Homosexuality." *Victorian Studies* 25 (1982): 181–210.

Hilton, Boyd. *The Age of Atonement: The Influence of Evangelicalism on Social and Economic Thought, 1785–1865*. Oxford: Clarendon Press, 1988.

Hinchliff, Peter. *Benjamin Jowett and the Christian Religion*. Oxford: Clarendon Press, 1987.

Hogg, T. J. "Niebuhr's *History of Rome*." *Edinburgh Review* 51 (Apr. 1830): 356–95.

Holcomb, Adele M. "Anna Jameson (1794–1860): Sacred Art and Social Vision." In *Women as Interpreters of the Visual Arts, 1820–1979*, ed. Clare Richter Sherman and Adele M. Holcomb. Westport, Conn.: Greenwood Press, 1981.

[Holinsworth, Charles B., ed.] "Introduction" to *Zion's Works: New Light on the Bible*. 10 vols. Birmingham, 1899.

———. *Memoir of John Ward*. Birmingham, 1881.

———. The *Shilohite's Bible, or the Literal 'Bible', as transformed into Spirit and Life by the revelation of God to Zion Ward*. [1928.]

Holloway, John. *The Victorian Sage*. New York: W. W. Norton, 1953.

Holton, Sandra. "Feminine Authority and Social Order: Florence Nightingale's Conception of Nursing." *Social Analysis* 15 (Aug. 1984): 59–72.

Homans, Margaret. *Bearing the Word: Language and Female Experience in*

Nineteenth-Century Women's Writing. Chicago: University of Chicago Press, 1986.

Hopkins, James K. *A Woman to Deliver Her People: Joanna Southcott and English Millenarianism in an Era of Revolution.* Austin: University of Texas Press, 1982.

Howsam, Leslie. *Cheap Bibles: Nineteenth-Century Publishing and the British and Foreign Bible Society.* Cambridge: Cambridge University Press, 1991.

Hughes, Thomas. *Tom Brown's Schooldays* (1857). New York: Grosset and Dunlap, 1930.

Hunt, William Holman. Pre-*Raphaelitism and the pre-Raphaelite brotherhood.* 2 vols. London: Macmillan, 1905-6.

Ingham, Patricia. *Dickens, Women, and Language.* Toronto: University of Toronto Press, 1992.

Irving, Edward. "Facts connected with recent manifestations of spiritual gifts." *Fraser's* 4 (Jan. 1832): 754-61.

———. *The Nature and Use of the Gift of Tongues.* London, 1829.

———. *The Orthodox and Catholic Doctrine of Our Lord's Human Nature.* London: Baldwin and Cradock, 1830.

———. *Sermons, Lectures, and Occasional Discourses.* 3 vols. London: R. B. Seeley and W. Burnside, 1828.

Jacobus, Mary. "The Art of Managing Books: Romantic Prose and the Writing of the Past." In *Romanticism and Language*, ed. Arden Reed. Ithaca: Cornell University Pres, 1984.

James, C. L. R. *Beyond a Boundary* (1963). New York: Pantheon Books, 1983.

James, Louis. *Fiction for the Working Man, 1830-1850.* London: Oxford University Press, 1963.

Jameson, Anna. *A Commonplace Book of Thoughts, Memories, and Fancies, Original and Selected.* London: Longman's, 1855.

———. *Legends of the Madonna, as Represented in the Fine Arts* (1852). Boston and New York: Houghton, Mifflin, 1885.

———. *Sacred and Legendary Art* (1848). 2 vols. Boston and New York: Houghton, Mifflin, 1885.

Jann, Rosemary. *The Art and Science of Victorian History.* Columbus: Ohio State University Press, 1985.

Jay, Elisabeth. *The Religion of the Heart: Anglican Evangelicalism and the Nineteenth-Century Novel.* Oxford: Clarendon Press, 1979.

Johnson, Edgar. *Charles Dickens: His Tragedy and Triumph.* Harmondsworth, England: Penguin Books, 1979.

Jordan, Thomas E. *Victorian Childhood.* Albany: State University of New York Press, 1987.

Jowett, Benjamin. *Dear Miss Nightingale: A Selection of Benjamin Jowett's Letters to Florence Nightingale, 1860–1893.* Ed. Vincent Quinn and John Prest. Oxford: Clarendon Press, 1987.

Kaplan, Fred. *Sacred Tears: Sentimentality in Victorian Literature.* Princeton: Princeton University Press, 1987.

Kincaid, James R. *Child-Loving: The Erotic Child and Victorian Culture.* New York and London: Routledge, 1992.

[Kingsley, Charles.] "The poetry of sacred and legendary art." *Fraser's* 39 (Mar. 1849): 283–98.

Klancher, Jon. *The Making of English Reading Audiences, 1790–1832.* Madison: University of Wisconsin Press, 1987.

Knapp, Steven. *Personification and the Sublime: Milton to Coleridge.* Cambridge, Mass.: Harvard University Press, 1985.

[Lake, W. C.] "Stanley's *Life of Dr. Arnold.*" *Quarterly Review* 74 (June–Oct. 1844): 467–509.

Landow, George P. "Aggressive (Re)interpretations of the Female Sage Florence Nightingale's *Cassandra.*" In *Victorian Sages and Cultural Discourse: Renegotiating Gender and Power*, ed. Thaïs E. Morgan. New Brunswick, N.J.: Rutgers University Press, 1990.

———. *Elegant Jeremiahs.* Ithaca: Cornell University Press, 1986.

Langbauer, Laurie. "Dickens's Streetwalkers: Women and the Form of Romance." *ELH* 53 (1986): 411–31.

Larson, Janet L. *Dickens and the Broken Scripture.* Athens: University of Georgia Press, 1985.

[Lewis, G. C.] "The Codification of English Laws." *Foreign Quarterly Review* 6 (Oct. 1830): 72–81.

"Life and Correspondence of Dr. Arnold." *Gentleman's Magazine* 23 (Apr. 1845): 339–60.

Livingstone, David. *Missionary Travels and Researches in South Africa* (1857). New York: New Amsterdam Book Co., n.d.

Maas, Jeremy. *Holman Hunt and 'The Light of the World'.* London: Scolar Press, 1984.

[Maitland, Edward.] "Life and Writings of Dr. Arnold." *North British Review* 2 (Feb. 1845): 403–44.

Marsh, Joss Lutz. "Good Mrs. Brown's Connections: Sexuality and Story-Telling in Dealings with the Firm of Dombey and Son." *ELH* 58 (1991): 405–26.

Marshman, John Clark. *Life and Times of Carey, Marshman, and Ward.* 2 vols. London: Longmans, Green, 1859.

Marx, Karl. *Early Writings.* Trans. Rodney Livingstone and Gregor Benton. New York: Vintage Books, 1975.

Massey, Marilyn Chapin. *Christ Unmasked: The Meaning of the 'Life of Jesus' in German Politics*. Chapel Hill: University of North Carolina Press, 1983.

[Masson, David.] "Pendennis and Copperfield." *North British Review* 15 (May 1851): 57–89.

Matthews, Ronald. *English Messiahs: Studies of Six English Religious Pretenders*. New York: Benjamin Blom, 1971.

Maynard, John. *Victorian Discourses on Sexuality and Religion*. Cambridge: Cambridge University Press, 1993.

McGann, Jerome. *The Romantic Ideology*. Chicago: University of Chicago Press, 1983.

Mileur, Jean-Pierre. *Vision and Revision: Coleridge's Art of Immanence*. Berkeley: University of California Press, 1982.

Miller, J. Hillis. *The Disappearance of God: Five Nineteenth-Century Writers*. Cambridge, Mass.: Harvard University Press, 1963.

Moffat, Robert. *A Life's Labours in South Africa*. London: John Snow, 1871.

———. *Missionary Labours and Scenes in South Africa*. London: John Snow, 1842.

Mozley, Rev. Thomas. *Reminiscences, chiefly of Oriel College and the Oxford Movement*. 2 vols. London: Longmans, Green, 1882.

Mulvihill, James. "The Revered Edward Irving and London Pulpit Popularity." *Nineteenth-Century Contexts* 14: 2 (1990): 175–92.

Newman, John Henry. *Apologia Pro Vita Sua* (1864). New York: Doubleday, 1956.

Nightingale, Florence. *"Cassandra" and Other Selections from "Suggestions for Thought"*. Ed. Mary Poovey. New York: New York University Press, 1992.

———. *Ever Yours, Florence Nightingale: Selected Letters*. Ed. Martha Vicinus and Bea Nergaard. London: Virago Press, 1989.

———. *"I Have Done My Duty": Florence Nightingale and the Crimean War, 1854–56*. Ed. Sue Goldie. Iowa City: University of Iowa Press, 1987.

———. "Introduction" to *Sketch of the History and Progress of District Nursing*, by William Rathbone. London: Macmillan, 1890.

———. *Letters From Egypt: A Journey on the Nile, 1848–1850*. Ed. Anthony Sattin. New York: Weidenfeld and Nicholson, 1987.

———. *Notes on Nursing: What It Is, and What It Is Not* (1859). New York: D. Appleton, 1912.

———. Papers. The Florence Nightingale Museum. London.

———. *Suggestions for Thought to Searchers After Religious Truth Among the*

Artizans of England. 3 vols. London: George E. Eyre and William Spottiswoode, 1860.

———. *"Suggestions for Thought" by Florence Nightingale: Selections and Commentaries*. Ed. Michael D. Calabria and Janet A. Macrae. Philadelphia: University of Pennsylvania Press, 1994.

"Ninth Annual Report of the British and Foreign Bible Society" (1813). Stanford, Calif.: University Microfiche.

Norton, Robert, M.D. *Memoirs of James and George M'Donald of Port Glasgow*. London: J. F. Shaw, 1840.

[Oliphant, Margaret.] "Charles Dickens." *Blackwood's Magazine* 77 (Apr. 1855): 451–66.

Oliver, W. H. *Prophets and Millennialists: The Uses of Biblical Prophecy in England from the 1790s to the 1840s*. Auckland: Auckland University Press, 1978.

Olmstead, John Charles, ed. *A Victorian Art of Fiction: Essays on the Novel in British Periodicals*, vol. 1, *1830–1850*. New York: Garland Press, 1979.

Ong, Walter. *Orality and Literacy*. New York: Methuen, 1982.

The Only and Unabridged Edition of the Life of Miss Nightingale. London: Coulson, [1855?].

Owen, Rev. John. *History of the Origin and First Ten Years of the British and Foreign Bible Society*. 2 vols. London: Tilling and Hughes, 1816.

Philpot, Charlotte. *Ann Sayle: A Simple Narrative of Her Illness, Conversion, and Death*. Leamington Spa: J. Dewe, Theological Library, 1835.

Pilkington, George. *The unknown Tongues Discovered to be English, Latin, and Spanish; and the Rev. Edw. Irving proved to be erroneous in attributing their utterance to the influence of the Holy Spirit*. London: Field and Bull, 1831.

Poovey, Mary. "Introduction" to *"Cassandra" and Other Selections from "Suggestions for Thought"*, by Florence Nightingale. New York: New York University Press, 1992.

———. *Uneven Developments: The Ideological Work of Gender in Mid-Victorian England*. Chicago: University of Chicago Press, 1988.

Pope, Hugh. *English Versions of the Bible*. St. Louis: Herder Publishing, 1952.

Pope, Norris. *Dickens and Charity*. London: Macmillan, 1978.

Preston, Thomas R. "Biblical Criticism, Literature, and the Eighteenth-Century Reader." In *Books and Their Readers in Eighteenth-Century England*, ed. Isabel Rivers. New York: St. Martin's Press, 1982.

Prickett, Stephen. *Words and 'The Word'*. Cambridge: Cambridge University Press, 1986.

Pugh, Evelyn L. "Florence Nightingale and J. S. Mill Debate Women's Rights." *Journal of British Studies* 22 (Spring 1982): 118–38.
Qualls, Barry V. *The Secular Pilgrims of Victorian Fiction*. Cambridge: Cambridge University Press, 1982.
Rajan, Tilottama. *The Supplement of Reading*. Ithaca: Cornell University Press, 1990.
"The Reverend Edward Irving and his adversaries." *Fraser's* 3 (May 1831): 423–28.
Riede, David G. *Oracles and Hierophants: Constructions of Romantic Authority*. Ithaca: Cornell University Press, 1991.
[Robinson, David.] "The Bible Societies." *Blackwood's Edinburgh Magazine* 18 (Nov. 1825): 621–35.
[Rogers, Henry.] "Reason and Faith." *Edinburgh Review* 90 (Oct. 1849): 309–23.
Rosenberg, Philip. *The Seventh Hero: Thomas Carlyle and the Theory of Radical Activism*. Cambridge, Mass.: Harvard University Press, 1974.
Ruskin, John. "Lectures on Architecture and Painting" (1854). In *The Works of John Ruskin*, vol. 12, ed. E. T. Cook and Alexander Wedderburn, 134–64. London: George Allen, 1903.
———. *Modern Painters II*. In *The Works of John Ruskin*, vol. 4, ed. E. T. Cook and Alexander Wedderburn. London: George Allen, 1903.
Said, Edward. *Culture and Imperialism* (1993). New York: Vintage, 1994.
———. *Orientalism*. New York: Random House, 1979.
Sanders, Charles Richard. *Coleridge and the Broad Church Movement*. Durham, N.C.: Duke University Press, 1942.
Sandilands, A. "The Historical Background of the Tswana 'Centenary' New Testament." *Botswana Notes and Records* 3 (1971): 1–5.
Sawyer, Paul L. *Ruskin's Poetic Argument: The Design of the Major Works*. Ithaca: Cornell University Press, 1985.
Seeley, J. R. *The Expansion of England* (1881). Ed. John Gross. Chicago: University of Chicago Press, 1971.
Shaffer, Elinor S. *'Kubla Khan' and 'The Fall of Jerusalem': The Mythological School in Biblical Criticism and Secular Literature, 1770–1880*. Cambridge: Cambridge University Press, 1975.
Shaw, P. E. *The Catholic Apostolic Church, Sometimes Called Irvingite: A Historical Study*. New York: King's Crown Press, 1946.
Shaw, William. *Memoirs of Mrs. Anne Hodgson*. London: J. Mason, 1836.
Showalter, Elaine. "Florence Nightingale's Feminist Complaint: Women, Religion, and *Suggestions for Thought*." *Signs: A Journal of Women and Society* 6 (Spring 1981): 395–412.

———. "Miranda and Cassandra: The Discourse of the Feminist Intellectual." In *Tradition and the Talents of Women*, ed. Florence House. Urbana: University of Illinois Press, 1991.

Simpson, David. *Irony and Authority in Romantic Poetry*. London: Macmillan, 1979.

———. *Romanticism, Nationalism, and the Revolt Against Theory*. Chicago: University of Chicago Press, 1993.

Siskin, Clifford. The *Historicity of Romantic Discourse*. New York: Oxford University Press, 1988.

Slater, Michael. *Dickens and Women*. London: Dent, 1983.

Smit, A. P. *God Made It Grow: History of the Bible Society Movement in South Africa*. Trans. W. P. DeVos. Cape Town: The Bible Society of South Africa, 1970.

A Soldier of the American Revolution. "Letter in Answer to the Speech of Dr. Mason at the Thirteenth Anniversary Meeting of the British and Foreign Bible Society" (1818). Stanford, Calif.: University Microfiche.

Stanley, Arthur Penrhyn. *Addresses and Sermons, delivered during a visit to the United States and Canada*. New York: Macmillan, 1879.

———. *Life and Correspondence of Thomas Arnold, D.D., Sometime Head-Master of Rugby School, and Regius Professor of Modern History in the University of Oxford* (1844). London: Ward, Lock and Co., 1890.

Steiner, George. *After Babel: Aspects of Language and Translation*. London: Oxford University Press, 1975.

Stokes, Eric. *The English Utilitarians and India*. Oxford: Clarendon Press, 1959.

Story, Rev. Robert. *Memoir of the Life of the Rev. Robert Story*. London: Macmillan, 1862.

———. *Peace in Believing: A Memoir of Isabella Campbell*. N.p., 1830.

Stott, George. "Charles Dickens." *Contemporary Review* 10 (Jan. 1869): 203–25.

Strauss, David Friedrich. *The Life of Jesus Critically Examined*, 2nd ed. Trans. George Eliot (1846). 4th ed. London: Swan Sonnenschein, 1892.

"Strauss—*Life of Christ*." *Foreign Quarterly Review* 22 (Oct. 1838): 135–42.

Strachey, Lytton. *Eminent Victorians* (1918). London: Chatto and Windus, 1920.

Strong, Roy. *'And when did you last see your father?': The Victorian painter and British history*. London: Thames and Hudson, 1978.

Sussman, Herbert. *Victorian Masculinities: Manhood and Masculine Poetics in Early Victorian Literature and Art*. Cambridge: Cambridge University Press, 1995.

Symonds, John Addington. *The Memoirs of John Addington Symonds.* Ed. Phyllis Grosskurth. New York: Random House, 1984.

Taylor, Barbara. *Eve and the New Jerusalem: Socialism and Feminism in the Nineteenth Century.* London: Virago, 1983.

Thompson, E. P. *The Making of the English Working-Class* (1963). New York: Vintage Books, 1966.

Tillotson, Kathleen. *Novels of the Eighteen-Forties.* Oxford: Clarendon Press, 1954.

Tonna, Charlotte. *The Bible the Best Book.* New York: American Tract Society, n.d.

Twining, Thomas. "A Letter to the Chairman of the East India Company, on the danger of interfering in the Religious Opinions of the Natives of India; and on the Views of the British and Foreign Bible Society, as directed to India." 2nd ed. London: Hazard and Carthew, 1807.

The Unknown Tongues!! &., or the Rev. Edward Irving and the Rev. Nicholas Armstrong arraigned at the bar of the scriptures of truth, and found 'guilty'. London: William Kidd, 1832.

Valenze, Deborah M. *Prophetic Sons and Daughters: Female Preaching and Popular Religion in Industrial England.* Princeton: Princeton University Press, 1985.

Vance, Norman. *Sinews of the Spirit: The Ideal of Christian Manliness in Victorian Literature and Religious Thought.* Cambridge: Cambridge University Press, 1985.

Vincent, David. *Literary and Popular Culture: England, 1750–1914.* Cambridge: Cambridge University Press, 1989.

Walder, Dennis. *Dickens and Religion.* London: Allen and Unwin, 1981.

Walkowitz, Judith R. *Prostitution and Victorian Society: Women, Class, and the State.* Cambridge: Cambridge University Press, 1980.

[Ward, John Zion.] *A Complete Refutation of the False Notions of the Messiah, printed in a pamphlet against the City of Zion, by John Collins, of Birmingham.* Birmingham: J. Bradbury, 1830.

———. *Letters, Epistles, and Revelations of Jesus Christ.* London: C. W. Twort, 1831.

———. *The Living Oracle; or, the Star of Bethlehem.* Nottingham: C. W. Twort, 1830.

———. *The True Explanation of the Day of Judgment, the burning up of the whole world, and of resurrection.* Birmingham: J. Bradberry, 1830.

———. *The Vision of Judgment; or, the return of Joanna from her trance.* London: C. W. Twort, 1829.

———. "Zion's preface to a work not published [1830]." BL, Add. MSS 43, 509.

———. *Zion's Works: New Light on the Bible*. Ed. C. B. Holinsworth. 10 vols. Birmingham, 1899.

Welsh, Alexander. *From Copyright to Copperfield*. Cambridge, Mass.: Harvard University Press, 1987.

Wihl, Gary. *Ruskin and the Rhetoric of Infallibility*. New Haven: Yale University Press, 1985.

Wilberforce, William. *A Practical View of the Prevailing Religious System of Professed Christians*. New York: Leavitt, Lord, and Co., 1835.

Wilson, Paul Scott. "Coherence in *Biographia Literaria*: God, Self, and Coleridge's 'Seminal Principle.'" *Philological Quarterly* 72 (Fall 1993): 451–69.

Woodward, Frances J. *The Doctor's Disciples: A Study of Four Pupils of Arnold of Rugby*. London: Oxford University Press, 1954.

Worboise, Emma Jane. *The Life of Thomas Arnold, D.D.* London: Hamilton, Adams, and Co., 1859.

Zwinger, Lynda. "The Fear of the Father: Dombey and Daughter." *Nineteenth-Century Fiction* 39 (1985): 432–59.

Index

In this index an "f" after a number indicates a separate reference on the next page, and an "ff" indicates separate references on the next two pages. A continuous discussion over two or more pages is indicated by a span of page numbers, e.g., "57–59." *Passim* is used for a cluster of references in close but not consecutive sequence.

Altick, Richard, 133
apRoberts, Ruth, 80, 236
Ariès, Philippe, 243–44
Arnold, Matthew, 95–96
Arnold, Thomas, 67–99, 101, 107, 120, 163–65, 183, 209; pedagogy and Rugby School, 68, 70, 80–85, 93–96

Barrell, John, 152–53
Barth, J. Robert, 37, 233
Baxter, Robert, Irvingite glossolalist, 46, 52, 56–57, 66
Benjamin, Walter, 210
Bentinck, William, govenor-general of India, 220–21
Bernal, Martin, 81
Bhaba, Homi, 195
Bible, 26–27, 71, 76–79, 86–87, 129–34; biblical interpretation, 4, 10, 130–32, 162–67; bible reading, 5, 23–25, 85, 88–89, 192–93, 198–202, 209; translations, 78–79, 191, 198–202, 207–13, 222–23, 236–37, 257. *See also* Coleridge, Samuel Taylor

Blake, William, 74, 215
British and Foreign Bible Society, 27, 188–223, 254, 258; and imperialism, 189–90, 194, 200–208, 214–15, 220–23, 259–60; and commodification of the Bible, 189–90, 194–95, 205, 218. *See also* Bible, translations; *and individual translators by name*
Broad Church, 10, 16, 69, 79, 92, 107, 127, 228
Browne, George, historian of the British and Foreign Bible Society, 208–9, 215, 221–22
Buchanan, Claudius, missionary and Bible translator, 220, 253

Campbell, Mary, Scottish glossolalist, 43–52 *passim*
Canning, George, 39
Carey, William, missionary and Bible translator, 191–92, 214
Carlile, Richard, radical atheist, 3, 9, 94, 130, 215, 227
Carlyle, Thomas, 39, 74, 99, 103, 105, 120, 166f, 182f, 240, 252

276 *Index*

Charles, Thomas, founder of the British and Foreign Bible Society, 190, 215–18
"Childhood and Its Reminiscences," 117–19
Children and childhood, 101–8 *passim*, 113, 117–28, 146–47, 193–94, 216–20, 243–44
Christ, 11, 63–72 *passim*, 91–98, 101–5, 109–47 *passim*, 120–38, 142–58 *passim*, 173–81 *passim*, 187, 240–41, 246. *See also* Incarnation
Christensen, Jerome, 36
Christian Socialism, 16, 228
Class, social: and religion, 2–3, 8–9, 28–30, 94, 158, 167–70, 174, 218–19, 190–91, 194, 213–14, 227, 237, 254
Clifford, James, 256
Clough, Arthur Hugh, 83–84, 156, 159
Coleridge, Samuel Taylor, 3–4, 10, 13–38, 53–67, 72f, 90, 114, 158, 163–67, 209; on inspiration, 13–18, 53–54, 57, 64–66, 79, 89–91; on Bible reading and biblical interpretation, 15, 18, 22–38, 66, 228–29. Works: *Biographia Literaria*, 34, 36, 54–56; *Confessions of an Inquiring Spirit*, 30–38, 72, 89; *Lay Sermons*, 27, 158; *Statesman's Manual*, 27–30, 35–37, 79, 89
Comaroff, Jean, and John Comaroff, 198f
Comte, Auguste, 110, 160, 242–23, 250
Conversion, 43, 48, 122, 134–37, 140–45, 202–3, 215–23 *passim*
Cook, Edward, 180, 250

Coutts, Angela Georgina Burdett, 121f, 130, 140ff
Crimean War, 148–49, 156–59

Darwinism, 78, 185–86
Davidson, Samuel, 73, 235
De Imitatione Christi, 151–52, 240
de Man, Paul, 61–62
De Quincey, Thomas, 21–25 *passim*, 229
de S. Honey, J. R., 83, 236–37
Derrida, Jacques, 34, 231–32, 256
Dickens, Charles, 3, 99–102 *passim*, 119–47, 150, 165, 174, 188, 247–48; and the Bible, 122, 124, 129–37 *passim*. Works: *Dombey and Son*, 120–42 *passim*, 148, 175, 245–48; *Life of Our Lord*, 120–29 *passim*, 135–37, 143–47
Disease theory, 184–86
Drummond, A. L., 39ff
Drummond, Henry, 41, 43, 47f, 52

East India Company, 191, 206, 220, 253, 257–59
Edwards, Edward, 212–14
Egypt, 150–57, 178–79, 186
Eilenberg, Susan, 36, 232
Ellis, Sarah Stickney, 102, 110

Farrar, Frederic W., 63, 101, 115, 240–41
Feuerbach, Ludwig, 64, 168, 252
Fliegelman, Jay, 41–42
Frei, Hans W., 231
Froude, James Anthony, 80

Gates, Barbara T., 182
German scholarship, 65–70, 73–84 *passim*, 234–35, 250–51

Glossolalia, 14f, 17, 19–20, 42–58, 238
Guilt, 6, 10–11, 19, 37–38, 56–57

Haley, Bruce, 80–82
Harding, Anthony J., 37, 228
Hare, Julius, 73, 75
Hegel, Georg Wilhelm Friedrich, 25, 160, 168, 179–80, 241, 252
Herbert, Sidney, 156f
Herder, Johann Gottfried, 76, 231, 236
Hilton, Boyd, 233
Hinduism, 160, 220–21, 257–58
History of the British and Foreign Bible Society (Browne), 189–223 *passim*, 255
History of the Origin and First Ten Years of the British and Foreign Bible Society (Owen), 189–95, 204–15, 220–23, 255
Holcomb, Adele M., 110
Holinsworth, Charles B., follower of John "Zion" Ward, 3–4, 227
Homans, Margaret, 5, 59
Hughes, Thomas, 94–95, 101, 105
Hunt, William Holman, 100, 103–4, 107, 242

Imperialism, *see* British and Foreign Bible Society
Incarnation, 4, 9–10, 20, 55, 57–62, 66, 112–13, 161–62, 168, 170–72, 179, 181–82, 233
Introductory Lectures on Modern History (Arnold), 88–90
Irving, Edward, 13–20, 38–67, 165, 167, 199; and oratory, 39–42, 46, 48; and glossalalia, 13–20, 43–57 *passim*, 65–66, 114

Jacobus, Mary, 22, 228–29
James, C. L. R., 83, 237–38
James, Louis, 219
Jameson, Anna, 105–11, 113, 242
Jane Eyre, 131–32
Jann, Rosemary, 90, 239
Johnson, Edgar, 129–30
Jordan, Thomas E., 118
Jowett, Benjamin, 159–60, 167, 176, 251

Kincaid, James R., 118, 243
Kingsley, Charles, 101, 105–9, 111, 113
Klancher, Jon, 231
Knapp, Steven, 29, 61

Landow, George, 170
Larson, Janet, 129
Life and Correspondence of Thomas Arnold (Stanley), 69ff, 96–99
Livingstone, David, 223
Lowth, Robert, 73, 236

Macaulay, Thomas, 74, 221
Macdonald family (Scottish glossolalists), 42–50 *passim*
Manliness of Christ, The (Hughes), 94–95
Marsh, Herbert, 73, 234, 259
Marsh, Joss Lutz, 142, 245
Marshman, Joshua, missionary and Bible translator, 214, 254
Martyn, Henry, missionary and Bible translator, 191–92, 207, 214
Marx, Karl, 168, 252
Mary or Madonna, 105, 108, 110–13 *passim*, 117–19, 203
Masculinity, 79, 83–85, 94–95, 101–5, 109–16 *passim*, 122–28, 137, 145–46, 238, 241–42, 247

Massey, Marilyn Chapin, 241
Masson, David, 133, 138, 248
Maurice, Frederick Denison, 228
Maynard, John, 105, 107
McGann, Jerome, 64, 229–30, 232, 234
Mileur, Jean-Pierre, 228–29, 232
Mill, John Stuart, 160, 182, 251–52
Millais, John, 100, 107, 115, 242, 246
Miller, J. Hillis, 234
Modern Painters (Ruskin), 112–15
Moffat, Robert, missionary and Bible translator, 191–92, 197, 200–201, 214, 223, 255
Morrison, Robert, missionary and Bible translator, 191–92, 201–2, 214
Mulvihill, James, 40, 42

Nationalism, 69–73 *passim*, 78–79, 82–85, 194, 206–8, 235
Newman, John Henry, 9f, 83f, 92, 98, 234, 238
Niebuhr, Barthold Georg, 74–76, 81, 86, 90, 236
Nightingale, Florence, 3, 67, 84, 99, 102, 110, 112, 148–88; and work, 149–50, 154–57 *passim*, 166–80 *passim*; and death, 149–50, 151–58, 173, 177–80, 242. Works: *Cassandra*, 112, 149, 160–61, 170–82 *passim*; *Notes on Nursing*, 186; *Suggestions for Thought to Searchers After Religious Truth*, 149f, 158–82 *passim*

Oliphant, Margaret, 138, 247
Ong, Walter J., 256–57
Oratory, 35, 39–42
Owen, John, historian of the British and Foreign Bible Society, 192, 208–9, 212, 215

Pasteur, Louis, 185
Paul, Saint, 23, 147
Philology and manuscript studies, 30, 68–70, 101, 160. *See also* German scholarship
Poovey, Mary, 149, 249, 252
Popular literature, 26–27, 132–39, 142, 219, 230
Pre-Raphaelites, 101–8 *passim*, 115, 242
"Principles of Church Reform" (Arnold), 85–86
Print culture, 3–4, 18–19, 20–28, 38, 80, 180–84, 191, 209–10, 228–29, 247–48
Prostitution, 104, 121–22, 130f, 136–46 *passim*, 248

Rajan, Tilottama, 24, 31, 34
Renan, Ernest, 63, 101, 115
Riede, David G., 228–29
Roman Catholicism, 105–8, 117–18, 203–7
Ruskin, 107–8, 112–16, 146, 243

Sacred and Legendary Art (Jameson), 105–9
Said, Edward, 189, 221
Sawyer, Paul, 113, 243
Schleiermacher, Friedrich, 75, 250
Seeley, John, 101, 257–58, 259
Sentimentality, 117–28 *passim*, 137, 144–46, 189, 193–94, 216–18, 244–46
Shaffer, Elinor S., 30–31, 63, 240
Shaw, Barnabas, missionary and Bible translator, 196–97, 201

Showalter, Elaine, 149, 170, 182, 249, 252–53
Simeon, Charles, 199, 214
Simpson, David, 228–29, 235
Siskin, Clifford, 25–26
Southcott, Joanna, 1–8 *passim*, 52, 111, 215, 232
Stallybrass, Edward, missionary and Bible translator, 202, 211
Stanley, Arthur Penrhyn, 69, 97
Steiner, George, 257
Story, Robert, 42f
Strachey, Lytton, 149
Strauss, David Friedrich, 63, 73, 100f, 115, 168, 235, 241, 251
Subjectivity, 17–18, 21–27, 34, 37–38, 65–66, 98–99, 104, 119
Sussman, Herbert, 101, 103
Swan, William, missionary and Bible translator, 202, 211
Symbolism, 61–62, 90–91, 234, 239

Taylor, Barbara, 51–52, 173, 232
Thackeray, William Makepeace, 130, 133, 247
Thirlwall, Connop, 73–75, 236
Thompson, E. P., 7

Tom Brown's Schooldays (Hughes), 94–95
Tongues, *see* Glossolalia
Tonna, Charlotte, 132
Twort, Charles William, follower of John "Zion" Ward, 8–9

Valenze, Deborah, 51–52, 232–33
Vance, Norman, 101, 104, 241–42
Venn, Henry, missionary and Bible translator, 200
Vico, Giambattista, 74, 236

Walder, Dennis, 144
Walkowitz, Judith, 141
Ward, John "Zion," religious leader and Messiah, 1–12, 67, 215
Wihl, Gary, 114
Wilberforce, William, 145
Women, and spiritual authority, 5–6, 50–52, 108, 110–12, 138–40, 146–47, 171–74 *passim*, 241–43, 247

Yuille, Robert, missionary and Bible translator, 202

Library of Congress Cataloging-in-Publication Data

Zemka, Sue
    Victorian testaments : the Bible, Christology, and literary authority in early-nineteenth-century British culture / Sue Zemka.
        p.   cm.
    Includes bibliographical references and index.
    ISBN 0-8047-2848-8 (cloth : alk. paper)
    1. English literature—19th century—History and criticism. 2. Christianity and literature—Great Britain—History—19th century. 3. Authority—Religious aspects—Christianity—History—19th century. 4. Christian literature, English—History and criticism. 5. Popular culture—Great Britain—19th century 6. Spirituality—Great Britain—19th century. 7. Great Britain—Civilization—19th century. 8. Bible—Criticism, interpretation, etc. 9. Jesus Christ—In literature. 10. Authority in literature. 11. Bible—In literature. I. Title.
PR468.B5Z45   1997
820.9'3823—dc21   97-26313
                                                              CIP

This book is printed on acid-free, recycled paper.

Original printing 1997
Last figure below indicates year of this printing:
06 05 04 03 02 01 00 99 98 97